*I*T is our intention each year to issue a publication which will prove enjoyable and of historical value to its readers, and we trust we have succeeded in doing so with this brochure. We hope the impression received will be so favorable that the reader will feel that our publications typify the institution which issues them and that the high standard maintained in their form and material is characteristic of the banking service we render.

We shall be very happy if the pleasure derived from our booklets induces our friends to think favorably of the State Street Trust Company when the occasion arises for opening a new bank account or renting a safe-deposit box at any of our three offices. We also have storage facilities for silverware and other bulky valuables at our Main and Massachusetts Avenue offices.

It may be that some of our readers are not aware of the fact that our Trust Department is qualified by experience to serve effectively as Agent in the handling of investments, as Trustee of living trusts, as Executor and Trustee under wills and in any other recognized trust capacity.

It will be a pleasure to us to furnish to those interested detailed information in regard to any of the various services which we render.

ALLAN FORBES,

President, State Street Trust Company

Boston, 1927.

FRANCE
AND NEW ENGLAND

Volume II

FIRST RECOGNITION OF THE "STARS AND STRIPES" BY A FOREIGN GOVERNMENT,

in Quiberon Bay, Brittany, France, on February 14, 1778. The French commanding officer was Admiral La Motte Picquet, and the American vessel was the "Ranger," commanded by Admiral John Paul Jones. The salute was the same as "authorized by the French court to be given an Admiral of Holland or any other republic." The original painting is in the National Museum in Washington.

Thus was American Independence first acknowledged in Europe.

FRANCE
AND NEW ENGLAND

Herein is AN ACCOUNT *of*
BITS *of* FRANCE IN BOSTON
INCIDENTS *of the* FRENCH STAY *at* NEWPORT
with a DESCRIPTION *of*
FRANKLIN *in* PASSY *and* PARIS
TOUCHING *also upon* HARTFORD *and* WETHERSFIELD
where WASHINGTON *and* ROCHAMBEAU MET *in* CONFERENCE
TOGETHER *with the* STORY *of*
the DISCOVERY *in* PARIS *of the* REMAINS *of* ADMIRAL JOHN PAUL JONES
and the FOUNDING *of the* SOCIETY *of the* CINCINNATI
with other INTERESTING FACTS
to which ARE ADDED
REPRODUCTIONS *of* MANY RARE VIEWS *and* OLD PRINTS

By ALLAN FORBES *and* PAUL F. CADMAN

Volume II

Issued by the
STATE STREET TRUST COMPANY
OF BOSTON
In its series of
HISTORIC MONOGRAPHS

1927

*The insert
at the top of
the cover is taken
from an old print
entitled "The Torch
of the World" in the collection of the State Street Trust
Company, and shows Franklin and
two of his French contemporaries,
Rousseau and Voltaire. These two great
Frenchmen both favored the cause of the
Americans. Voltaire surprised his friends by
suddenly journeying from Geneva to Paris in 1778, where
he had a dramatic meeting with Franklin. Rousseau spent
the last years of his life in obscurity, and it is probable
that he never actually met our American representative. The design on the left is from a picture
of John Paul Jones; that on the right is of
a monument to the Chevalier de Saint
Sauveur. In the left-hand lower
corner appears a reproduction
of the French fleet at Newport, and at the right is the
engagement between the
"Bonhomme Rich-
ard" and the
"Serapis."*

*Edited, designed and printed by direction of
Walton Advertising & Printing Co.
Boston, Mass.*

CONTENTS

Dessiné par Monsieur Vanloo de Roi.

Née Sculp. 1786.

L'INDÉPENDANCE DE L'AMÉRIQUE.

BAS-RELIEF OF THE OBELISK IN LOUIS XVI SQUARE AT PORT VENDRES, IN THE PROVINCE OF ROUSSILLON, FRANCE, on the Mediterranean, erected in the year 1786 to commemorate the establishment of American Independence and to honor King Louis. On the left of the picture are represented citizens of Boston assembled on the shore receiving the King's frigate, which is bringing to them the treaty assuring their independence. The monument itself was erected by the Province of Roussillon. King Louis XVI was to a large extent responsible for our independence. Many of our soldiers in the World War went to Port Vendres during their furloughs, including one of the officials of the Trust Company.

FOREWORD

TWO years ago, the State Street Trust Company issued a book in commemoration of the laying of the corner stone of Bunker Hill Monument by General Lafayette and the anniversary of the birth of another illustrious French officer, General Rochambeau. This volume told chiefly of the relations of Lafayette and Rochambeau with this country in its early days, when they rendered more effective service to our struggling colonies than is generally realized. In fact, the best authorities state that the French forces at Yorktown outnumbered the American. In our study of the events connecting France and New England there were found to be so many of such great historical interest that it was decided to publish on the same general subject another volume, which the Trust Company is now distributing. In this issue is a chapter descriptive of the different objects in Boston that are of interest both to New Englanders and to the French. Additional chapters which, by the way, are not chronologically arranged, treat of other events of our Revolutionary War that seem to call for particular comment. There are also two chapters compiled for the Trust Company by Mr. Paul F. Cadman while in France: one recalls many incidents of Benjamin Franklin's residence at Passy, and the other describes the search for and discovery in Paris of the remains of America's first Admiral, John Paul Jones.

Last year the Trust Company departed from its long-established custom of confining its publications to historical matters and issued a brochure describing the many objects of interest in the new Main Office—the State Street Counting House, as it is often called—to which the bank had recently moved. We have been pleased with the number of our friends who have come to visit our banking rooms during the year in which we have been in our new location, and we hope that any of our readers and friends who have not inspected our unique and homelike offices will feel free to do so.

The same careful regard for accuracy and authenticity which has characterized our other twenty-two brochures is observed in the present work. Our aim has been to make it worthy of preservation, also, from the standpoint of typography, illustration, arrangement, and design.

To Mr. Paul F. Cadman we are particularly indebted for the great amount of time he has given to the preparation of material for this book while in France, and in its final stages while serving as a professor at the University of California. As before, he was greatly helped by Mr. Bertram Winthrop, of New York, who has made Paris his business headquarters for some years.

As in Volume I, use has been made of the many diaries of French officers, with as many quotations as it was deemed advisable to include. These have been procured from Washington, Hartford, Providence, Newport, and Boston libraries and historical societies. The translations, as heretofore, have very kindly been made by Mrs. H. A. Crosby.

The Trust Company wishes likewise to thank Hon. Henry M. Hutchings for many valuable suggestions in regard to the material. As before, thanks are due also to Mr. Belden, Mr. Buckley, Mr. Blaisdell, and other officials and employees of the Boston Public Library, for help rendered in searching for material. Many pictures were procured by the late John R.

Hess of the *Providence Journal*, and from the excellent library of the late George L. Shepley of Providence, who was of great assistance. Mr. Howard W. Preston and Mr. Howard M. Chapin, the latter of the Rhode Island Historical Society, were also very helpful in furnishing material on the Providence chapters. To the aid of Colonel Louis R. Cheney of Hartford we are indebted for help on several chapters in connection with Connecticut, and to Mr. Lloyd M. Mayer and Mrs. R. Sherman Elliott of the Newport Historical Society for material for the chapters on Newport. Mr. Perry Walton and his staff have given much care to the preparation of this book. Of the Trust Company, Mr. Ashton L. Carr, Vice-President, Mr. Ralph M. Eastman, and Mr. Arthur L. Richmond, Assistant Vice-Presidents, have helped considerably. Miss Ruth C. Olson, Secretary to the President, has taken charge of the large volume of correspondence covering a period of over five years.

Those in France who have helped in the work are: Mr. Walter Gay; Docteur Jules Sottas; M. Louis Jaray, Secretary of the Comité France-Amérique; M. de La Roncière of the Bibliothèque Nationale; M. Henri Dehérain, Conservateur de la Bibliothèque de l'Institut; the late M. Babolon, Conservateur, Cabinet des Médailles, Bibliothèque Nationale; M. Marcel Poëte, Directeur de l'Institut d'Histoire et d'Économie Urbaine; M. de la Monnerai, Bibliothèque de la Ville de Paris; M. le Moine, Cabinet des Estampes, Bibliothèque Nationale; Madame la Comtesse de Rivoire de la Batie; M. Henri Cordier; Henri Batcave; M. T. Boucher, du Musée Carnavalet; M. G. Hartman; M. R. Cagnat, Secrétaire Perpétuel de l'Académie des Inscriptions et Belles-Lettres, Paris; M. Lyon-Caen, Doyen Honoraire de la Faculté de Droit; Baron d'Estournelles; M. Mozerelles, Conservateur, Musée de la Monnaie; M. Weiss, Bibliothécaire, Société de l'Histoire du Protestantisme Français; General Malleterre, Musée de l'Armée aux Invalides; M. Piccioni, Directeur des Archives au Ministère des Affaires Étrangères; M. Bayle; Mademoiselle Jeanne Rivard; Mademoiselle E. M. Rieder-Street.

There may be others whose names should be included, and to these persons we also extend our thanks.

Those who have helped us on the different chapters, and to whom we are greatly indebted, are:

Bits of France in Boston—Hon. A. Piatt Andrew, William Sumner Appleton, Frank C. Blaisdell, Dr. F. L. Bogan, Bostonian Society, Rev. Howard N. Brown, Miss Helen Capwell, Arthur H. Chase, Erskine Clement, Le Chanoine Leon Costecalde, Henry E. Dunnack, General Clarence R. Edwards, Mrs. Clarence R. Edwards, J. A. Favreau, J. C. J. Flamand, Otto Fleischner, George S. Godard, Miss M. P. Hamlen, the late E. M. Hartwell, Mrs. Florence C. Howes, Major John W. Hyatt, John W. Martyn, Professor Louis J. Mercier, John D. Parsons, Andrew F. Pope, F. H. Prince, Dr. Morton Prince, Public Library Commission, E. H. Redstone, William F. Seeger, General John H. Sherburne, Fitz-Henry Smith, Jr., Charles A. Stevens, Julius H. Tuttle, Vermont State Library, Horace G. Wadlin, Walter K. Watkins, Walter R. Whiting, Henry M. Williams.

With the French at Newport—F. Lauriston Bullard, Arthur Green, Mrs. C. F. Hoffman, Alfred G. Langley, Miss M. E. Powell, Miss Alice Preston, Miss Esther Morton Smith, Dr. Roderick Terry, Mrs. H. A. Wood.

The Death of a Great French Admiral—Herbert Putnam, Dr. Roderick Terry, Mrs. H. A. Wood.

Butts Hill, Chastellux and Conanicut Island Forts—John W. Martyn, H. W. H. Powel, Mrs. C. Lorillard Spencer, Mr. C. Lorillard Spencer, Dr. Roderick Terry, Mrs. H. A. Wood.

Memories of Franklin in Passy and Paris—William Sumner Appleton, John Hampton Barnes, Henri Batcave, Coffin & Burr, Detroit Publishing Co., Ralph L. Flanders, Otto Fleischner, James Hazen Hyde, Jesup Memorial Library, Charles E. Mills, Walter B. Russell, Julius H. Tuttle.

DE LAUZUN'S CAVALRY AT LEBANON, CONNECTICUT—Mrs. K. F. Bishop, F. C. Bissel, Miss Emma E. Lessey, Ernest E. Rogers, Julius H. Tuttle.

HARTFORD AND WETHERSFIELD, WHERE WASHINGTON AND ROCHAMBEAU MET IN HISTORIC CONFERENCES—Miss E. R. Case, Mrs. Mary E. Case, George S. Godard, Albert C. Bates, Emerson G. Taylor.

A STORY OF THE ILLUSTRIOUS FRENCH REGIMENTS OF OUR REVOLUTIONARY WAR—Marshall P. Thompson, Frederick S. Whitwell.

RODERIGUE HORTALEZ ET CIE—Randolph G. Adams, Hon. A. Piatt Andrew, F. Baldensperger, Frederic Contet, *The Dearborn Independent*, George R. Flamand, J. C. J. Flamand, John B. Whitton.

SOUVENIRS OF THE FRENCH IN PROVIDENCE AND BRISTOL, RHODE ISLAND—Miss Virginia Baker, Herbert O. Brigham, Mrs. H. H. Cabot, Miss Helen Capwell, John W. Church, John R. Gladding, R. F. Haffenreffer, Jr., Miss Julia Herreshoff, the late Louis Herreshoff, N. G. Herreshoff, Jr., M. A. DeWolfe Howe, Wallis E. Howe, Alfred G. Langley, Mrs. E. C. Larned, Willard B. Luther, Wilfred H. Munro, George S. Parker, the late John R. Rathom, Roger L. Scaife, Henry D. Sharpe, Granville S. Standish, Walter G. Tibbits, Colonel George Vernon, William B. Vernon.

THE "SALLY" OF WISCASSET—Mrs. J. W. Bartol, Hon. Percival P. Baxter, Mrs. Alexander Biddle, Jr., C. H. Butler, Mrs. Walter G. Chase, Miss C. Louise Corey, Mrs. Charlton Henry, W. D. Patterson, Mrs. Harold M. Sewall, the late Harold M. Sewall.

THE DISCOVERY IN PARIS OF THE REMAINS OF ADMIRAL JOHN PAUL JONES—Walter W. Beers, Miss Harriet K. Campbell, Mrs. A. H. Eastman, John W. Martyn, Mrs. Edwin Mende, Mrs. A. W. Ogden, Charles F. Read, Frederick S. Whitwell.

THE SOCIETY OF THE CINCINNATI—Charles A. Coolidge, the late Horatio A. Lamb, Hon. Winslow Warren, Frederick S. Whitwell.

There were three errors in Volume I which the compilers would like to correct: Page 40—the picture represents the Langdon House and not the Warner House. Page 52—"Warren" should read "Warner." Page 83—that part of the inscription under the Lafayette Statue at Puy, France, referring to Paul W. Bartlett as the sculptor and Thomas Hastings as the architect, should have been added to the inscription under the Lafayette Statue in the Place du Carrousel, opposite page 1.

ALLAN FORBES,
President, State Street Trust Company

BOSTON, 1927.

VUE DE LA PLACE LOUIS XVI. AU PORT VENDRES

Monument élevé à la gloire du Roi par la Province du Roussillon.

THE MONUMENT AT PORT VENDRES IN ROUSSILLON PROVINCE, FRANCE,

dedicated to Louis XVI and American Independence. On one side of the base of the obelisk is the sculpture depicting the Independence of America, which shows a French vessel bringing the treaty to Boston, Massachusetts. Many prints have been made of this view of the monument.

La Fayette Mall

FRANCE
AND NEW ENGLAND

VOLUME II

BITS OF FRANCE IN BOSTON

THERE are in Boston a number of connecting links with our twice ally, France, and we believe it will be of interest to describe in this chapter the different objects in our city that serve as continual reminders of the aid, of various kinds, rendered us by that country. Likewise, we have included the memorials and tablets that have been erected in Greater Boston for the purpose of commemorating those Frenchmen who have so well deserved our everlasting gratitude and thanks. To begin with, one of the most important links, and probably the least known, has to do with our Public Library; for it was a Frenchman, Alexandre Vattemare by name, who gave to this city the plan for starting one here. Vattemare, whose real name was Nicholas Marie Alexandre, also originated a system of international exchanges of books, works of art and documents between France and America, as well as with other European countries.

We believe that New Englanders will be interested in following the unique career of this versatile Frenchman, who distinguished himself as surgeon, actor, ventriloquist and student. He was born in Paris in 1797 of a Norman family, his father being an advocate of considerable importance in that city. The latter retired to a small estate at Lisieux in Normandy, and it was there that he discovered his son's extraordinary accomplishments of impersonation and ventriloquism. One day while playing hide and seek with a companion, young Alexandre wished to elude his friend, and so, in a feigned voice, made him believe he was hiding in a cellar nearby. His companion searched in vain for the origin of the voice, and then in despair complained to Alexandre's father, who assisted in the search, this time to hear the voice changed to that of an old woman groaning and crying for help. Another time, a dyer of Lisieux was hanging clothes to dry in the ruins of an old castle, whereupon this young impersonator, who was at that time only about ten years old, concealed himself among the ruins and used his voice in his extraordinary way so as to make it appear to come from the opposite direction and from some distance off. The dyer thought he was going to be robbed, and rushed upstairs with a long pole to attack the supposed intruder. In the meantime a fisherwoman happened to be passing by, whereupon the joker began to swear at her and challenged her to come up. She proceeded to attack the innocent dyer, who, she supposed, had been hurling vile epithets at her. Still another person he persuaded to enter the ruins, and a free fight ensued, the noise of which drew many of the inhabitants of the village to the spot. In the mix-up, young Nicholas eluded everyone and returned home. From then on, the castle was supposed to be haunted. It is related how he often fooled and aggravated his father on post days, when important letters were expected from Paris, by imitating the postman. Finally, he was found out by his parent. While crossing a bridge one day, this mischievous youngster uttered cries as if someone were drowning, and everyone, including the older Alexandre, who happened to be within hearing, rushed to the rescue of the supposed unfortunate. The voice grew weaker and weaker, until finally the onlookers departed believing that someone had actually lost his life. On the following morning at the breakfast table the family discussed this distressing event, whereupon the boy admitted he had been the cause of all the excitement. At first his elders would not believe him, but finally, being persuaded of the truth, made the lad promise he would be more careful in the future.

Nevertheless, soon afterwards he was almost caught in the act of imitating the Devil in a chimney of a farmhouse nearby, but succeeded in escaping by jumping a ditch and running away. The wife of the household was made ill by this prank, and the husband lodged a complaint with the Alexandre family. Nothing could persuade the youthful prodigy to give up his practical jokes, for we hear of him again causing trouble on the way to Honfleur with his father. While on shipboard he caused voices to come from all sorts of inconceivable places, until the sailors were almost on the point of turning back. His delight in deceiving people led him, while journeying through Moyaux, to carry out the most amusing, and at the same time the most reprehensible, prank of all. He learned that the steeple of the church was supposed to be weak and that it was feared it might some day fall. He determined to take advantage of this information, and when the congregation next assembled a shrill voice came apparently from the door of the building yelling, "Save your lives, save your lives, the steeple is falling!" Pandemonium, of course, reigned for a time, but the final result was that the steeple was promptly repaired by the village authorities. While still very young, he was asked to appear at Court; and on the way there, as he was passing through the town of Évreux, he imitated in such a realistic manner a voice coming from a drowning person at the bottom of a well that the chief police officer of the town, at considerable risk of his life, climbed down to search for the unfortunate person.

His success at the French court was very great. While performing at St. Cloud, a well-known Duchesse would not believe he was able to impersonate so many different parts in one evening, it being stated that he occasionally played as many as forty-four characters in the same play. On this special occasion he was impersonating a coachman, and appeared in a heavy cloak. He sat down at a table and fell asleep, whereupon the Duchesse crept up and caught hold of his coat. He managed, however, to crawl skilfully out of the garment and appeared at another door in the character of a nurse, with a baby in his arms, much to the

NICHOLAS MARIE ALEXANDRE (VATTEMARE) OF PARIS, FRANCE,

who gave to the citizens of Boston the idea for its Public Library. It was largely through his energy and foresight that he was able to persuade them to start a free library. He also encouraged a system of international exchange of books between other American States and many foreign countries, and was, besides, the donor of many literary works to the City of Boston. He later added Vattemare to his name. This picture shows him as an actor. He was also an impersonator and ventriloquist.

surprise of the lady, who was still holding the cloak when he appeared. Indeed, so versatile was he that it is said he could drink and sing at the same time.

His mother endeavored to make a minister of him, but to no purpose; for, instead, he decided to become a surgical pupil in the Hospital of St. Louis, where he made rapid progress. Even there he could not refrain from giving proof of his versatility as one of the most noted impersonators of all times. The bodies of the dead, in accordance with the custom at the hospital, were kept in the cellar several days before burial; and at midnight the weird idea occurred to him of imitating the voice of one of these corpses as if it had just come to life. It devolved, therefore, upon the surgeons to make an investigation, which was described as a most gruesome task.

Alexandre soon resigned his position to take up still more important duties at the Hôpital de la Pitié. While serving there, typhus broke out among the patients, most of whom were Prussian prisoners; but, without hesitation or fear, he undertook their care and succeeded in saving many lives. When they had recovered, they were ordered back to Germany, and Alexandre, still only about seventeen years of age, was assigned the duty of escorting them to Berlin. On his arrival he was detained as a prisoner of war owing to a political misunderstanding, and while in captivity he amused himself, much to the surprise of the officers, by using his power of ventriloquism. He was asked to become a surgeon in the Prussian army, but this he refused to do. After some time he was persuaded by the French Ambassador in Berlin to make a tour as a ventriloquist; and, as there happened to be at the German capital a family of French emigrants in straitened circumstances, he decided to begin his public career by giving a benefit performance for them. This he did, and curiously enough he finally married the daughter of this household.

In 1812 he visited England, after having given his performances in many countries on the continent, where he was received by kings and emperors. While in the British Isles he attracted the attention of Sir Walter Scott and his wife. The former was especially impressed with the extraordinary impersonations of this actor and related that crowds flocked to his entertainments. Lady Scott was so pleased with his skill that she presented him with a medal.

One day Sir Walter and Alexandre Vattemare decided to play a practical joke on a painter friend. There was in Edinburgh a peculiar-looking person called Dr. Taylor, whom Alexandre, while staying with Sir Walter, had been in the habit of impersonating, much to the latter's amusement. The Frenchman, in the guise of the doctor, called on the painter to have his portrait done, and when it was finished the artist exclaimed, "What a fine resemblance, isn't it?" At the same moment, much to the bewilderment of the painter, Alexandre threw off his impersonation and became himself. The joke was thoroughly enjoyed by the two conspirators.

Wherever Alexandre Vattemare went, though, his taste led him to the libraries, and soon he conceived the idea of effecting an exchange among the nations of books, documents relative to municipal administration, and agricultural and scientific works. For twelve years he devoted himself to European libraries and museums, and in May, 1839, he came to this country to prosecute his hobby. He had obtained Lafayette's approval of his undertaking just previous to the great General's death a few years before. In describing his arrival in New York, Vattemare said: "My first sentiments were those of despair, for I found no institutions like our own open to the public, and therefore no means of laying the treasures which I proposed to bring into the United States before the people." He had, therefore, not only to bring the books to America, but found it would devolve upon him also to secure the establishment by the people of free libraries in which the books might be placed. He first visited Montreal and Quebec, then parts of this country, arriving in Boston in the spring of 1841. Here he was received with attention, the first public meeting being held on April 24th in the rooms of the Mercantile Library Association, where Vattemare, as he now called himself, was given an opportunity to explain his ideas. It was resolved:

"That Mr. Vattemare's plan having received the encouragement, and been stamped with the approbation of the most eminent sovereigns, statesmen, and literary men of Europe, from the Sultan of Turkey to Lafayette and La Martine—of the President, Chief Justice, and both Houses of Congress of our own country—and moreover as it is a plan to carry out which all parties and religions, and sects, cheerfully unite . . . that the plan is practicable, is worthy the attention of every man who has a faculty to educate. . . .

Resolved, That a Committee of twelve be appointed from this meeting, to correspond with the influential men in the community, for the purpose of soliciting them to call a meeting of the citizens at Faneuil Hall, to consider the subject in all its bearings.

Resolved, That the thanks of this meeting be tendered to Mr. Vattemare for his attendance this evening. . . ."

In May, a second meeting was held, this time in Masonic Temple, over which Mayor Chapman presided. The following were appointed a special committee: Dr. Walter Channing, Josiah Quincy, Jr., Rev. Ezra S. Gannett, Rev. George W. Blagden and Charles F. Adams. The meeting thanked the visitor "for his interesting, instructive, and eloquent exposition of his noble project," and pledged to him its cordial co-operation.

These two meetings were the first which gave expression to a public library movement in Boston; but the scheme unfortunately was opposed by some persons who for various reasons were not carried away by Vattemare's enthusiasm, and therefore the agitation was not immediately fruitful. It was seven years later before his suggestion had a definite result. In the meantime, the need for public libraries was becoming apparent to scholars, and Vattemare's seed germinated. In 1843 he sent to Boston fifty volumes as a present from the City of Paris, returning again in 1847 to renew his appeal, which this time met with success. He told the authorities of this city that then was the time to act and that the "books received from France must be made the nucleus of a great public institution," as expressed by Josiah Quincy, then Mayor. He finally succeeded in persuading this official to make a conditional offer of $5,000 towards the purchase of books for a library, and also to urge a petition to the Legislature to authorize the levying of taxes for its support. In August, 1847, a joint special committee of the City Council, headed by Mayor Quincy, was directed to "consider and to report what acknowledgment and return should be made to the City of Paris for its gift of books and to provide a place for the same." In its report, submitted in October, the committee said: "The City of Paris has a library open to all, and in order to commence this system of exchanges has sent a valuable and interesting donation to the City of Boston." Mention also was made that some books had been given by citizens to the Mayor to be sent to Paris. The committee recommended setting apart a room on the third floor of City Hall for the temporary deposit of such books, and finally referred to the proposed library as follows:

"The Committee cannot close their report without recommending to the City Council a consideration of the propriety of commencing a public library. Many of the citizens would, they believe, be happy to contribute both in books and money to such an object and the Committee are informed that a citizen, who wishes that his name may be concealed, has offered the sum of $5,000 for the purpose of making the commencement, on condition only that $10,000 are raised at large for the same purpose and that the library should be as fully used by all, as may be consistent with the safe-keeping of the property."

The Council authorized the Mayor to acknowledge the gift from the City of Paris, and also

FRENCH VIEW OF BOSTON

gave him power to transmit any volumes received as a return present. A joint special committee was also appointed, its report reading as follows:

"The establishment of the public library is recommended by many considerations. It will tend to interest the people at large in literature and science. . . . In this connection the Committee are of the opinion that the plan of national exchanges as proposed by Mr. Vattemare is worthy the attention and patronage of the city. Its tendency to unite nations and disseminate knowledge is too obvious to need illustration. The books we have already received from the City of Paris have proved of value, both in public and private undertakings, by furnishing the knowledge which has been acquired by the experience of the old world for the guidance of the new."

In April of the following year the library was authorized; and so from this little room in City Hall, obtained by Vattemare, has grown Boston's Public Library, with its thirty-one branches, handling millions of books a year for its multitude of readers. This library is the first important municipal institution of this kind authorized by a Special Act, permitting taxation for its support. The first building was on Mason Street, the second home was on Boylston Street, and the present main library was opened to the public in 1895. The many visitors there are also reminded that they owe a debt of gratitude not only to Alexandre Vattemare, but also to another Frenchman, Puvis de Chavannes, who painted the frescoes that surround the main staircase, the only examples of this artist's talent in this country. It is also of interest to mention that Charles F. McKim, the architect of the building, was influenced by the design of the Library of Sainte Geneviève in Paris. It was, therefore, fitting that Viviani on his mission here in 1917 during the World War should meet within it representatives of the many Boston War Relief Committees who had been helping France.

In the year 1849, Vattemare was able to obtain another official present of books for Boston. His letter transmitting it read: "The cities of Boston and Paris are now connected by so many ties, not only of ancient friendship, but of constantly increasing social and business relations, that I am most happy in being, in the present instance, the honoured instrument of that mutual exchange of public acts of courtesy and beneficence by which France hopes to be able to cement more strongly the kind and happy relationship which has ever existed between her and the United States of America." Mayor Bigelow, in acknowledging the gift, replied: "They are treasured not only as the gift of an illustrious people, but as the basis and no insignificant portion of a free municipal library, which we are taking active measures to establish." In return, the City Council of Boston solicited from citizens donations of books, and many were voluntarily donated by such distinguished persons as Mayor J. P. Bigelow, Henry Wadsworth Longfellow, Nathan Hale, Dr. James Jackson, Edward Everett, Ralph Waldo Emerson, Nathaniel I. Bowditch, William H. Prescott, Francis Parkman, Jr., Josiah Quincy, Charles Sumner, Robert C. Winthrop and a host of others. This gift was sent as "a noble response from a community in favor of a Free Public Library." The committee that collected the books closed its report by speaking of Vattemare as "the sagacious, zealous, and philanthropic individual whose mind conceived the vast benefits which would result to mankind from an interchange of books and works of art among Christian and civilized nations." Vattemare in acknowledging their receipt spoke of the books as "pledges of friendship from Boston," and at the same time he alluded to the hospitalities he had received from this city during the many years he had been conferring with its officials, including the Governor, members of the Legislature and the City Council. As Mayor Quincy well said: "To him, more than to any other man, we owe the foundation of the great public library which is the pride of this city . . . we must recognize his contagious energy, which induced State after State to succumb to his representations, so that by 1853 he had brought one hundred and thirty libraries and institutions within his operations, and between 1847 and 1851 had brought from France for American libraries 30,655 volumes, besides maps, engravings, etc." "This," added Mayor Quincy, who, by the way, visited Vattemare in Paris, "is truly a record of brilliant achievement; one going far to justify the prophecy of our minister to France, Mr. Cass, that Alexandre Vattemare would be 'ranked among the benefactors of mankind, and like them be rewarded with universal esteem.' "

Among the donors of books for the Boston Library was King Louis Philippe; Vattemare himself gave ninety-six volumes. One of these books that came to the attention of the writer is particularly interesting because it was written by Vattemare himself in 1861, and bears his autograph. The title is "Collection de Monnaies et Médailles de L'Amérique du Nord— 1652 à 1858." It was offered to the Bibliothèque Impériale as much in the name of the French Government and the States of the Union as in his own name. Among his many honors he mentions belonging to the Historical Societies of Connecticut, New Jersey, Maine, Pennsylvania, Maryland, Florida, Wisconsin and Iowa. It is with regret we have learned that the books from Boston were placed in the Library of the City of Paris, which was burned during the Commune.

While Vattemare was devoting himself to the exchanges between the United States and France, some Americans residing in Paris concluded to hold a meeting to encourage his efforts. It was held at the Athénée Royale on March 27, 1845, and was presided over by L. Draper, our Consul at Paris, Benjamin Perley Poore acting as secretary. At the meeting Vattemare's efforts were described, and it was at the same time reported that, in return for the kindness shown to him while in this country, Vattemare had sent to this Government a large model of the French man-of-war "Ville de Paris" which had been dispatched by Louis XVI to help us in 1781. The vessel itself was lost later in the year by Admiral de Grasse in an encounter with Admiral Rodney. The model is now at Annapolis and a picture of it appeared in our Volume I.

Also taking an interest in Vattemare's plan for international exchanges were Connecticut, Delaware, Florida, Indiana, Kentucky, Louisiana, Maine, Maryland, Michigan, Missouri, New Hampshire, New Jersey, New York, North Carolina, Pennsylvania, Rhode Island, South Carolina, Texas, Vermont, Virginia, the City of Washington, D.C., and other States and places.

On his visit to Augusta, Maine, in 1847, he was likened to Lafayette, though bearing "not the helmet, the sword and the armor," but "testimonials of universal brotherhood from the wise, the virtuous, the learned of France." The Governor of the State referred to his presence there as "an intellectual boon from the Government of France for the Maine State Library." Many volumes were exchanged between Paris and Maine as a result of Vattemare's efforts. Finally twenty-eight of our States had responded to his appeal, and the gifts sent by each State were placed in the Library of the City of Paris in an alcove inscribed with the arms of that particular State. Lyons, Nantes and Rouen also received books from this country. In all, one hundred and seventy thousand volumes were exchanged between the two nations.

Vattemare also made an address at Montpelier, in Vermont, and referred to the fact that the name of the State was derived from the French words "Verts monts" and that it would, therefore, seem only logical for the people of the State to exchange presents with France. When told that Vermont had little to offer of interest, Vattemare tactfully replied that "the very stones in the streets would be gladly received," meaning, undoubtedly, that the State was so rich in minerals that even samples would prove of much interest.

FAITS D'ARMES
DE LA 26ᵉ DIVISION D'INFANTERIE AMERICAINE
EN FRANCE
1918

CHEMIN DES DAMES · 28 FÉVRIER

BOIS BRULE · 10-13 AVRIL

SEICHEPREY · 20-21 AVRIL

CAMP DU MOULIN · 30-31 MAI

XIVRAY · MARVOISIN · 16 JUIN

CHATEAU-THIERRY
TORCY · GIVRY · ETREPILLY · TRUGNY
EPIEDS · BOIS DE TRUGNY · BOIS LA FERE
18-25 JUILLET

St MIHIEL · VIGNEULLES
12-13 SEPTEMBRE
BOIS BELLEU · BOIS D'ORMONT · BOIS D'HAUMONT · COTE 360
23-27 OCTOBRE

VILLE DEVANT CHAUMONT · BOIS DE VILLE
CAP DE BONNE ESPÉRANCE
7-11 NOVEMBRE

LE MÉTAL DE CETTE INSCRIPTION PROVIENT DU
CHAMP DE BATAILLE
DE St MIHIEL

VEVER PARIS

Photographed for the State Street Trust Company by George B. Brayton

PLAQUE IN THE SENATE RECEPTION ROOM OF THE STATE HOUSE IN BOSTON RECOUNTING THE DEEDS OF THE 26TH (NEW ENGLAND) DIVISION OF VOLUNTEERS IN THE WORLD WAR

It was made from metal picked up on the battlefield of St. Mihiel.   This plaque is preserved in the same case with the first shell fired by the National Guard against Germany, presented by Mrs. John H. Sherburne as a gift from her husband, General Sherburne, to the State of Massachusetts.

We quote a paragraph from the 1900 report of the State Librarian of Connecticut which covers the transactions between that State and Alexandre Vattemare:

"The growth of our Library like those of sister States was greatly stimulated and increased by the volumes given and received through the International Exchange inaugurated in 1849, by Alexandre Vattemare, of France, and conducted by him until his death in 1864. Since his death this work of foreign exchanges has been carried on more efficiently and practically by the Smithsonian Institute at Washington, through its several agencies. Through these agencies, States, institutions and individuals of the civilized world are placed in easy communication. Moreover to Mr. Vattemare's international exchange do we owe the early collecting of our own public documents and binding them into substantial volumes. Begun in 1850, with one small volume, this practice, inaugurated solely for convenience of foreign exchange, has been continued to the present time until our public documents now make four handsome volumes for ready reference."

Vattemare also induced this country to be represented at the French Exhibition in 1856. Almost every nation was to take part, and he declared that the Stars and Stripes also should be displayed there. As Mayor Quincy expressed it, "he conjured into existence a small display which provoked a smile from his trans-Atlantic friends." "Ah, you may laugh at my exhibition," exclaimed Vattemare, with the exultant glee of a schoolboy; "but it has put your good flag up aloft, and you will see it will win for you some medals and honorable mentions!"

Vattemare died in Paris in 1864. His son, Hippolyte, endeavored to carry on the system of exchanges so successfully inaugurated by his father, but failed owing to an article he wrote about America, which did not meet with approval here. Referring to his father's visits to this country, the son describes them as a "long ovation."

J. A. Favreau, who has helped us in preparing part of this material, reminds us that a small library collected by Major Edmond Mallet was purchased by "L'Union St. Jean-Baptiste d'Amérique," an organization in this country composed of 50,000 members.

It may now be well to turn our attention to the State House, the corner stone of which was laid by the son of a French exile to this country, Apollos Rivoire, a name which he later changed into the simple Paul Revere in order that New Englanders might more easily spell and pronounce it. The most recent acquisitions to our Capitol are the World War flags of a number of Massachusetts regiments, which fill three niches in the famous Hall of Flags. One flag was given by the Senate, and now stands in a niche in that Chamber; another was presented by the Jordan Marsh Company, and on it are recorded the important engagements. The regimental colors of the 104th Infantry, 26th Division, were decorated with the Croix de Guerre, the first instance of an American unit ever being so honored by a foreign government. The ceremony took place at Boucq, while the Yankee Division was in the Toul Sector. Another relic of the war is a shell case now in the reception room of the Senate Chamber, presented by Mrs. John H. Sherburne as a gift from her husband to Governor McCall, who transferred it to the Commonwealth. The shell contained in this case was fired by Battery A, 101st Field Artillery, Colonel John H. Sherburne commanding, and was the first shot fired by our National Guard against Germany. The gun used was, of course, French, as almost all the artillery was supplied to us by France while America was a participant. On this shell case is inscribed, "To his Excellency Governor Samuel Walker McCall. The first shell fired by the National Guard against Germany. Fired 3.45 P.M. Tuesday, February 5, 1918, by 1st Section, Battery A, 101st Regiment Field Artillery, Col. John H. Sherburne, Commanding." With this shell case is a plaque which was made from metal found on the St. Mihiel battlefield, and which was "Offert par La Ctsse. Du Boisrouvray aux Officiers, Sous-Officiers et Soldats de la Glorieuse 26me Division d'Infanterie Du Corps Expéditionnaire Américain." On the plaque are shown the

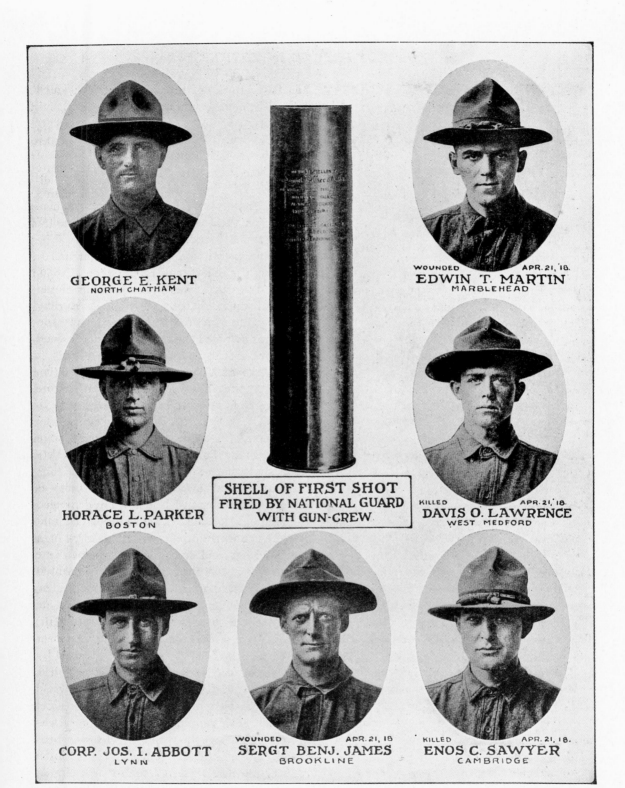

GEORGE E. KENT
NORTH CHATHAM

WOUNDED   APR. 21, '18.
EDWIN T. MARTIN
MARBLEHEAD

HORACE L. PARKER
BOSTON

SHELL OF FIRST SHOT
FIRED BY NATIONAL GUARD
WITH GUN-CREW

KILLED   APR. 21, '18.
DAVIS O. LAWRENCE
WEST MEDFORD

CORP. JOS. I. ABBOTT
LYNN

WOUNDED   APR. 21, 18
SERGT BENJ. JAMES
BROOKLINE

KILLED   APR. 21, '18.
ENOS C. SAWYER
CAMBRIDGE

Courtesy of Edwin H. Cooper and Ball Publishing Company

CASE OF THE FIRST SHELL FIRED BY AMERICAN NATIONAL GUARD

troops against Germany, and gun-crew of Battery A, 101st Field Artillery, 26th (New England) Division, which fired it. The shell case was sent home by General Sherburne, and was presented to Governor McCall, inscribed: "To his Excellency Governor Samuel Walker McCall. The first shell fired by the National Guard against Germany. Fired 3.45 P.M. Tuesday, February 5, 1918, by 1st Section, Battery A, 101st Regiment Field Artillery, Col. John H. Sherburne, Commanding."

Photograph by
Eug. Pirou Mascré, Paris

Kindness of Charles A. Stevens

COUNT AMAURY DE JACQUELOT DU
BOISROUVRAY,

*who was "Liaison" officer with the 26th Division until it
sailed for home in April, 1919. At Verdun, in
1914, his battalion occupied the same casements that the
Adjutant's office of the 26th Division occupied four
years later. He became very fond of the Americans, who
liked him equally well. The feats accomplished
by himself and his battalion at Verdun have been recounted
many times. He was awarded the D. S. C. by the
United States of America for heroism at Seicheprey, on
April 20 and 21, 1918. Among his eleven other
decorations he was given the Legion of Honor and the Croix
de Guerre. He has made a number of visits to
Mexico on business. It was his wife who gave to the Commonwealth of Massachusetts the bronze tablet now
in our State House, in memory of the officers and men of
the 26th Division.*

"Faits d'Armes" of the 26th Division; and it
recites the engagements, which include Chemin
des Dames, Château Thierry, St. Mihiel and
Bois Belleau. Both case and plaque are
illustrated. The husband of the Countess
du Boisrouvray was "Liaison" officer with
the 26th Division during the entire time it
was in France, and both still keep in close
touch with their many soldier friends on this
side of the Atlantic. At the time of writing
this chapter, the wife of General Clarence R.
Edwards, Commander of the Yankee Division
during the war, was visiting Count and
Countess du Boisrouvray, who have often
been urged to visit New England. This French
officer was awarded the D. S. C. by our Government for heroism at Seicheprey.

"While at Verdun, his battalion," writes
Charles A. Stevens of Boston, "was quartered
in the same casements in 1914 that the Adjutant's office of the 26th Division occupied four
years later." Du Boisrouvray is one of the
well-known de Polignac family. Of him Mr.
Stevens continues: "He loved the Americans,
I presume because their jollity and sense of
humor corresponded with his own and because
he could understand them. I know that he
thought the world of General Edwards, of the
26th Division, and of the individual men who
composed it. I am certain that his reports to
Marshal Foch in regard to the conduct of the
division were favorable, to say the least,
if they could be seen. No one loved the
Americans and appreciated them more than
du Boisrouvray."

One of the pleasant ways in which a
continuance of friendly relations has been
fostered between our Massachusetts soldiers
and the French people with whom they came
in contact during their war service was displayed, when, at a convention of the 104th
Infantry (26th Division) Veterans' Association
held in Cambridge in 1923, the following
testimonial was sent through the French Consul in Boston to the mayor and citizens of the
communities in which the various units of this

famous regiment—the first American regiment to have its colors decorated by the French Government in the World War— were quartered during their early days in France in 1917:

"To the Mayor and Citizens of Sartes, Pompierre, Harréville,—We, the Officers and Men of the 104th Infantry Veterans' Association, 26th Division, assembled in the City of Cambridge, in the Commonwealth of Massachusetts, United States of America, reunited for a brief day in memory of our service in the American Expeditionary Force, send you warm and cordial greetings to remind you that we do not forget the days we passed in your midst, days which are golden in our hearts and minds, gathering new strength with the passing of the years.

We do not forget. As you sit by your firesides; as you partake of your daily fare; as you bow in worship before your altars, thinking, perhaps, of your American friends, wondering if they think of you, be assured,— yes, be quite assured that our thoughts fly to you across the sea, and again in memory we walk your streets, sit by your hearth and share your hospitality.

Accept, then, this message which we send with full hearts. Our prayers and our affection go with it."

Photographed for the State Street Trust Company by George B. Brayton

TABLET NEAR THE HALL OF FLAGS IN THE STATE HOUSE, BOSTON, TO LIEUTENANT NORMAN PRINCE,

founder of the Lafayette Escadrille, who left for the battlefields of France four months after the outbreak of the war.
He waged 122 aërial conflicts, until he was killed while alighting near Luxeuil, France. A memorial to this Escadrille has been erected at Saint Cloud by William N. Cromwell of New York.

Another incident of the World War may prove of interest. When some of the members of the 101st Engineers of the Yankee Division attended the local church in Rolampont, the town in which they were first billeted after their arrival in France, much to their pleasure and surprise they found a curé who had once been pastor of the French Catholic Church on Isabella Street, Boston, just back of the Armory of the First Corps of Cadets, which unit formed the nucleus of the 101st Engineers.

A comparatively recent tablet (shown in an illustration) in the State House, near the Hall of Flags, commemorates the valiant services of "Lieutenant Norman Prince, Founder of the Lafayette Escadrille —a Pioneer in the World War—French Army—1914—who gave his life in humanity's cause 1916." Prince was a grandson of F. O. Prince, a former Mayor of Boston. He sailed for the front, four months after the war started, to serve as a volunteer in the French army "jusqu'au bout," as he expressed it. He organized the Escadrille

Photographed for the State Street Trust Company by George B. Brayton

TABLET AT THE HEAD OF STATE STREET, BOSTON,

to "Norman Prince, founder of Lafayette Escadrille in the World War."

Photographed for the State Street Trust Company by George B. Brayton

BUST OF LAFAYETTE IN THE SENATE ROOM
IN THE STATE HOUSE, BOSTON,

*presented in 1898 by Horatio S. Greenough to Governor
Wolcott. It was offered to the State by Augustus
P. Loring in behalf of the donor. Mr. Greenough's father
was the sculptor. There is a statue to Lafayette in
Lafayette Park, Fall River, erected by the French inhabitants
of the city.*

Américaine, which became the famous Lafayette Flying Squadron, the first soldiers to carry the American flag on the battlefield. This young and daring officer was awarded the Croix de Guerre, Médaille Militaire, and the Croix de la Légion d'Honneur. His aërial engagements reached a total of one hundred and twenty-two. While alighting in the dark, his machine struck a cable near Luxeuil and his injuries caused his death a few days later. His self-sacrifice is well described in an ode to the American volunteers by Alan Seeger, the American poet, who also gave his life for the cause of the Allies:

> Yet sought they neither recompense nor
>   praise,
> Nor to be mentioned in another breath
> Than their blue-coated comrades, whose
>   great days
> It was their pride to share—aye, share
>   even to the death!
> Nay, rather, France, to you they rendered
>   thanks
> (Seeing that they came for honor, not for
>   gain),
> Who opening to them your glorious ranks
> Gave them that grand occasion to excel—
> That chance to live the life most free from
>   stain
> And that rare privilege of dying well.

Prince's portrait was exhibited at the Allied Bazaar in Mechanics Building, which was the first opportunity the citizens of Boston had to come to the aid of the Allies. The net proceeds for the week were $500,000, the writer having the honor of serving as treasurer of the fund. The City of Boston, as all our citizens know, has also honored Norman Prince by naming the head of State Street for him, a quite proper, though curious, turn of events, in that he rarely saw State Street, as he did not share in the business life of the city. He was flying aëroplanes while his friends were attending to the more commonplace things of life.

The only other object of interest in the State House with a French connection is a rather good bust of Lafayette in the Senate, presented on January 26, 1898, by Horatio S. Greenough, whose father, Horatio Greenough, was the sculptor. It was offered to Governor Wolcott in a letter sent by Augustus P. Loring on behalf of the donor.

Another interesting memento in Boston is a tablet in memory of General Lafayette placed on the Mall named for him, running parallel to Tremont Street. The words on the tablet recite briefly his services to this country. It was erected by Mayor Curley to commemorate the one hundredth anniversary of Lafayette's visit to Boston to lay the corner stone of Bunker Hill. At one time, as late as the year 1917, ten streets, avenues, courts and parks in Boston were called either Fayette or Lafayette, but owing to the confusion five were changed to other names—leaving Fayette Court leading off Washington Street; Fayette Street, near Pleasant Street; La Fayette Avenue, from Prince to Endicott Streets; La Fayette Park, near Blue Hill Avenue in Roxbury; and the Mall already referred to. There is also a Lagrange Street in West Roxbury and a Lagrange Street between Washington and Tremont Streets, south of Boylston, named probably for Lafayette's Château in France.

There are in Boston three buildings that have a French connection. One is the school at 60 Gibson Street, Dorchester, named for Rochambeau about a month after this country declared itself against Germany, the record from the minutes of the School Committee under date of May 10, 1917, reading: *"Ordered,* That the new school-house on Gibson Street, Dorchester, in the Mary Hemenway district, be named the Rochambeau School, in honor of Jean Baptiste Donatien de Vimeur, Count de Rochambeau; a Marshal of France; Commander of the French forces in America in the Revolutionary War; allied with Washington in the siege and capture of Yorktown; a representative of the *first* alliance of France and America for the establishment of democracy and the right of self-government among nations." The vote was passed unanimously a week later. It will be noticed that the record mentions the "first" alliance of France, intimating that we formed a "second" alliance in the World War, but we were never officially an ally. The second building that concerns us is the Lafayette School at 31 Ruggles Street, Roxbury. The school report for the year 1913 states that it was "named in honor of Lafayette, a French General who rendered valuable service to the colonists during the Revolutionary War." The third structure of interest to us is made of brick painted yellow, is old and inconspicuous, and for many years has stood on the corner of Marshall Street and Creek Square, only a few yards from Hanover Street, and near the Boston Stone. A former proprietor put up a sign at the head of the stairway which reads as follows, though the upper line is now hidden by a large gaspipe: "This house

Photographed for the State Street Trust Company by George B. Brayton

THE LAFAYETTE TABLET ON LAFAYETTE MALL, RUNNING PARALLEL TO TREMONT STREET, BOSTON,

placed there by Mayor Curley to commemorate the one hundredth anniversary of the visit of the French General to our City and of his laying the corner stone of Bunker Hill Monument. This tablet was not placed in time to be included in Volume I of "France and New England."

LAFAYETTE MALL, RUNNING PARALLEL TO TREMONT STREET, BOSTON,
showing on the left the Lafayette tablet.   A closer view appears on the preceding page.

& property was bought & owned by Ebenezer Hancock in 1760. Genl. George Washington
and Lafayette were guests of this house frequently during the Revolutionary War, and all
the signers of the Declaration of Independence were in and stopped here from time to time
and also the Continental Army was paid off here by Deputy Paymaster-General Hancock.
J. A. Kierman, Prop." This Marshall House, as it is called, served as an inn, and here undoubtedly many famous men gathered during our Revolution, including General Washington,
Lafayette, Paul Revere, and probably most of the signers of the Declaration of Independence.
It has been said that when either Admiral d'Estaing's fleet or perhaps other vessels arrived in
our harbour, funds were brought over as loans to us by France. The house at that time was
the property of Ebenezer Hancock, a mason, and cousin of Governor Hancock. Another
Ebenezer Hancock, a brother of the Governor, held the position of Deputy Paymaster-General
during the Revolution, and here, it is said, he stored the coins before paying off the American
troops. One account describes this event: "How the poor fellows' eyes must have sparkled
when they received their long arrears in King Louis's bright silver crowns! The order of Gates
or Heath was now a talisman to unlock the strong-box of the paymaster, and for once it was not
empty. Two and a half million livres, in silver, were brought to Boston at one time." Later
owners of this building were Ebenezer Frothingham, Benjamin Fuller and William H. Learned.

The Massachusetts Historical Society has many objects of Franco-American interest,
chief of which is the suit of clothes, probably of French manufacture, that was worn by Benjamin Franklin the year of the signing of the Treaty of Alliance between America and France
in 1778. This suit was presented in 1803 to the Society by Elkanah Watson of New York,
and to it was attached a parchment certifying that "in the year 1781, being at Paris, in France,
the celebrated Mrs. Wright executed for me an excellent likeness in wax of the immortal
Doct^r Benjamin Franklin. Dining with her at the Doct^r F., in Passy, and on comparing the
heads, I suggested that such a head deserved a suit of his own clothes, on wch he rang for
his servant, directing him to bring the suit (hereunto annexed) he wore in the year of signing
the famous Treaty of Alliance between France and America in Feby., 1778." This historical

SUIT OF CLOTHES NOW IN THE MASSACHUSETTS HISTORICAL SOCIETY, SAID TO
HAVE BEEN WORN BY BENJAMIN FRANKLIN IN PARIS IN 1778, THE
YEAR OF THE SIGNING OF THE TREATY OF ALLIANCE
BETWEEN AMERICA AND FRANCE

*It is believed the cloth is of French manufacture. The suit was given to the society by Elkanah Watson
of Albany, New York, with a certificate described in the text. There are many Franklin and
Lafayette medals in the Society as well as other objects of Franco-American interest.*

society also possesses two portraits of Lafayette—one painted in Paris for Thomas Jefferson, and the other done by H. C. Pratt at the time the French officer came here to lay the corner stone of Bunker Hill. In one of the show cases are a number of objects loaned by Miss Clara G. Perry, who has been a great friend of France. These articles consist of a night lamp, candle snuffers, horse's bit, duelling pistols and writing desk, all from Chavaniac. There is also among the collection a flintlock gun with the initials of George Washington Lafayette on it.

In the Bostonian Society collection is an atlas published in Paris in 1766 which was presented by Lorenzo S. Russell. In it is a memorandum signed by Benjamin Russell in 1841 to the effect that it was purchased by him in 1797, describing that the *Centinel*, of which he was Manager, announced the arrival in Boston of the Duke of Orleans, later King of France, and two of his friends, exiles from France. Russell thereupon paid them a visit. Some time later a merchant tailor called Amblard, who kept a boarding house on the corner of State Street and Wilson's Lane (now part of Devonshire Street), and who was then boarding the

*Photographed for the State Street Trust   Photographed at the suggestion
Company by George B. Brayton   of Judge Henry M. Hutchings*

MARSHALL HOUSE, ONCE AN INN, ON THE
CORNER OF CREEK SQUARE AND MARSHALL
STREET, BOSTON, NEAR HANOVER STREET
AND THE BOSTON STONE

*It was owned in 1760 by Ebenezer Hancock, a cousin of Governor
Hancock. Another of the family with the same name
was a brother of the Governor. In this house were probably
stored coins brought from France with which to pay off
the American troops. It is said that Washington, Lafayette,
Paul Revere, and most of the signers of the Declaration
of Independence visited here.*

Duke, informed Russell that the French-men were desirous of selling some books they had with them in order to pay their expenses, as their remittances from France had not arrived on schedule time. Russell bought several, including this atlas, which was used in his newspaper office for many years afterwards. The editor of the *Centinel* alludes to the lack of a title-page— "as it has been purloined by some one," to use his language. The Bostonian Society has in its exhibit a Lafayette snuff box owned by Samuel Gore, also a pair of gloves and a sash similar to those worn by the people of Boston at the time of Lafayette's visits to Boston in 1824 and at the laying of the corner stone of Bunker Hill the following year. There is also a book given by the French General to Jefferson and presented to the Society by Dr. Charles T. Jackson.

Although it is situated outside of the city, we feel that we should include here the Star Fort, on Telegraph Hill, at Hull, for the reason that it was manned during the war by French troops under a French officer, after having been re-enforced and inspected by two French engineers. Furthermore, it is one of the few of the older visible relics now in existence that was actually used by our allies. Several French accounts declare that these fortifications were erected or at least were designed by Admiral d'Estaing, but it has been pointed out that a committee headed by J. Palmer made an investigation of the battery there in August, 1777, which shows that it was practically completed before the arrival of the French fleet. It is certain, however, that the French troops under d'Estaing did actually strengthen and man these defences, in 1778; for in d'Estaing's report, as explained by Fitz-Henry Smith, Jr., "detachments of Hainaut and of Foix became the garrison of the peninsula of Hull" commanded by de Bougainville, Count de Broves of the "César" having charge of Gallup's Island, the Marquis de Chabert of the "Vaillant" taking command at Peddock's Island. The largest number of troops, however, was at Hull.

It is an interesting fact, also, that

Photographed for the State Street Trust Company by George B. Brayton

ROCHAMBEAU SCHOOL, DORCHESTER, MASSA-
CHUSETTS,

*named for the French General a month after America entered the
World War, the school record stating that Rochambeau
was "a representative of the 'first' alliance of France and America
for the establishment of democracy."*

General Washington on September 29, 1778, sent Brigadier General du Portail, a French engineer who served with the American forces, to Hull "to form a plan from a view of the whole local situation of the place which shall appear to give it the most effectual security that circumstances will permit." He made a report to General Heath, which unfortunately has been lost. The latter General in October visited Hull, inspected the fort, and reviewed the battalion of French marines stationed there to assist our troops to man these important defences. According to one authority, this American General was well pleased with his visit there, for he is reported to have said that the "French manœuvred well and in every particular were well disciplined." D'Estaing not only had to strengthen and man this fortress, but was also obliged to land cannon from his vessels then at Nantasket Roads, as he was unable to procure

Photographed by the Alves Photo-Finishing Service   *Kindness of Clarence V. Nickerson and Walter R. Whiting*

PART OF FRENCH STAR FORT ON TELEGRAPH HILL, HULL, MASSACHUSETTS,

often so called for the reason that it was partially manned during the war by some French troops under a French officer called de Bougainville, was re-enforced by Louis de Maresquelle, an important French engineer serving the State of Massachusetts, and was inspected by du Portail, another well-known engineer under General Washington. This fort is in an excellent state of preservation and is now within the larger Fort Revere. Some of the French were buried nearby, and there should be a marker to designate the location.

any from us. Massachusetts did, however, send Louis de Maresquelle, a Colonel of Artillery serving as Inspector-General of the Foundries of this State, to direct the work.

The writer visited the fort with Andrew F. Pope of Hull (for whose family one of the batteries is named), and was surprised to find it in such a good state of preservation. The moat and earthworks are much the same as ever, but one of the five corners has been removed

Photographed for the State Street Trust Company by George B. Brayton

LAFAYETTE SCHOOL, ROXBURY, MASSACHUSETTS,

named in the year 1913, the school report stating that it was so called "in honor of Lafayette, a French General who rendered valuable service to the colonists during the Revolutionary War."

to make room for a signal tower. This latter was used to notify Boston of the approach of vessels, but was given up when the telegraph came into use. Within the fort there was once a deep well, which long since has been filled in. This ancient fortification, a part of which served at one time as a tee for the Hull Golf Links, is now included in Fort Revere (named, of course, for Paul Revere, the son of a French refugee), and is protected by several batteries of guns. During the Spanish War the Cadets were stationed there on account of its strategic position at the entrance to Boston Harbour. While serving at Hull, an epidemic of smallpox broke out, and several hundred of the French succumbed to this disease and were

From a picture given by Fitz-Henry Smith, Jr., to the Hull Public Library,
copied from the original in the Library of Dracut, Massachusetts

COLONEL LOUIS (LEWIS) ANSART DE
MARESQUELLE,

an important French engineer employed by the State of
Massachusetts and sent to Hull in August, 1778,
to oversee the erection of the fort there which was manned by
General de Bougainville and some French soldiers
under d'Estaing. He served this State as Colonel of Artillery
and Inspector-General of Foundries. He married
Catharine Wimble at Boston and lived in Dracut, Massa-
chusetts. Another French officer, General du
Portail, an important engineer serving with the American
forces, was sent by General Washington a short
time later to inspect this Hull fort.

buried in a field which tradition tells us was directly between the fort and Boston Light, near the old road running along the shore. Nearby are growing some small thorn-apple trees said to be offshoots of some similar ones, the seeds of which were brought over from France. Here the Town of Hull should erect some fitting tablet to mark this early French military cemetery. Across the road there existed at one time a small body of water, now filled in, which for many years was called French Lily Pond, and even to this day some of these flowers can still be seen growing in a small ditch. There is a plan of the fort made by J. Palmer in the Massachusetts State Archives which has been reproduced by Fitz-Henry Smith, Jr., in his admirable article entitled "The French at Boston during the Revolution."

There are four statuettes in Boston which were captured during the French and Indian War by Captain Thomas James Gruchy, a junior warden of the Old North Church, who, as recorded on a tablet there, was a "merchant adventurer from Jersey who in parlous times as captain of the Privateer 'Queen of Hungary' took from a French ship in the year 1746 the four figures of cherubim now in front of the organ." They were destined for a town on the St. Lawrence River. Lafayette visited this church in 1824 and was much impressed with the excellent bust of General Washington, declaring, "That is the man I knew, and more like him than any other portrait."

One of the most interesting links between the two Republics is the Saint Sauveur monument at King's Chapel, which has been so carefully described by Fitz-Henry Smith, Jr. The details in connection with this memorial to this distinguished French naval officer, who was killed together with a brother officer while endeavoring to quell a riot in a fleet bakery in Boston, are unique; for, between the passing of the vote by the Massachusetts House of Representatives, authorizing the erection of a monument, and the actual placing of it near the entrance to King's Chapel, one hundred and thirty-nine years elapsed. An extract from the records of the House, dated September 16, 1778, reads that

"WHEREAS on the Evening of the 8th Instant in an Affray which happened in the Town of Boston, by high insults offer'd to some French Bakers by certain riotous Persons unknown, the Chevalier de Saint Sauveur, in endeavoring to make Peace, received a wound in the Head which ended his life on the 15th, And as this Court hold in the highest detestation the Perpetrators and Abettors of this horrid Deed, and out of respect to the Memory of the deceased

Resolved, That this Government will provide a monumental Stone to be placed in the burial Ground where his Remains shall be deposited with such inscription as his Excellency the Count D'Estaing shall order.

And this Court will attend in Procession the Corps of the deceased to the Place of Interment.

Resolved, that Col. Thomas Dawes be a Committee to see the Monument Stone erected accordingly. Sent up for Concurrence.

JOHN PICKERING, SPKR."

A week previous, the following vote appeared in the council records:

"On motion ordered that Benjamin Austin & Daniel Hopkins Esq^{rs} be a Committee to examine one Mr. Sage respecting the Riot committed the last Evening in this town or to inquire of him what he knows respecting the affair & report.

On motion ordered that Francis Dana & Daniel Hopkins Esq^{rs} be a Committee to draft a Proclamation calling upon all Justices &c to apprehend all persons concerned in the Riot Committed in this Town the last evening & report."

On May 24, 1917, Massachusetts, somewhat tardily to be sure, kept her promise, carrying out the same program as arranged in 1778. A procession formed in front of the State House, headed by Governor McCall, Lieutenant-Governor Coolidge, now President of the United States, Mayor Curley, J. C. J. Flamand, the French Consul in Boston, Hon. Channing H. Cox, then Speaker of the House

Kindness of Rev. Howard N. Brown

DEDICATION OF THE SAINT SAUVEUR MEMORIAL SHAFT NEAR THE ENTRANCE OF KING'S CHAPEL, BOSTON, ON MAY 24, 1917

Massachusetts carried out her promise of 139 years before. In the centre of the picture is Governor McCall; on his right is Lt.-Col. Paul Azan, the head of the detachment of six French officers sent here to train the R. O. T. C. of Harvard University; and on his right is Calvin Coolidge, President of the United States of America, then Lieutenant-Governor. Fitz-Henry Smith, Jr., who has made a study of this subject, is at the other side of the picture.

of Representatives, Lt.-Col. Paul Azan, head of the French mission instructing the Harvard Regiment, and Fitz-Henry Smith, Jr., who delivered an address. Escorted by a detachment of bluejackets from the U. S. Battleship "Virginia," with militiamen of the 5th and 8th Regiments carrying the flags of the United States and France, the Commonwealth, the Society of the Colonial Wars, and the Sons of the American Revolution, and preceded by buglers, the procession marched down Park to Tremont Street and thence to King's Chapel. A large crowd was present to see the dedication of the monument, which was draped with the flags of the two nations Chevalier de Saint Sauveur had sought to serve. The company then entered the church, where prayer was offered by Rev. Howard N. Brown, D.D., minister of the church. Courtenay Guild, for the building commission, then formally reported to the Governor that the commission had completed its work and had erected the monument, which he said "not only represents a memorial to a gallant officer, but in the hearts and minds of the people typifies their admiration for what France is doing for the cause of civilization." Then came a blare of bugles, the bluejackets presented arms, and the Governor unveiled the memorial, placing upon its base a wreath with the tricolor of France. Governor McCall in his address pointed out the curious coincidence that the memorial perpetuated an event that happened when France was the ally of the United States, and that, when the order of the General Court was finally carried out, we found ourselves her ally once more.   Mayor Curley on this unique occasion said: "Were it not for the chivalry of France, the colonies would not have achieved their independence.   And in this hour of France's peril, when she is bereft of so many of her men and women, we try to repay a debt of one hundred and forty years ago, not as an obligation, not through compulsion, nor through necessity, but through a sense of love.   France is calling aloud, and we offer of our best to the end that liberty may be possible."   Fitz-Henry Smith, Jr., in his excellent address, said in part: "This stone which the Commonwealth has raised is more than a monument to one man, or evidence of the good faith of the state—it is a memorial to a time long since past; yes,—it is more than that, it is a perpetual reminder of the friendship of America and France, which has endured these hundred years, just as de Saint Sauveur hoped that it might—and which, pray God, may endure forever."

Kindness of Rev. Howard N. Brown

MEMORIAL TO SAINT SAUVEUR AT THE ENTRANCE TO KING'S CHAPEL, BOSTON,

erected by the Commonwealth of Massachusetts in 1917, in honor of this French officer in Admiral d'Estaing's squadron, who was killed in a riot in Boston on the 8th of September, 1778.   Through some oversight the vote of the 16th of September of that year authorizing the placing of a tablet here was forgotten and it was not until 139 years later that the State carried out the original vote in exactly the same manner as was intended. The many passers-by fail to appreciate the existence of this interesting memorial commemorating such an important event of the Revolution.

"And so the monument has been placed in the heart of this great and historic city of Boston, where so much has been done for human liberty and where so much has been done to alleviate the sufferings of mankind; placed where the throngs passing daily upon the street may see and pause to consider, and where in future years the American father may come with his son, and when the son asks, 'Father, what is that monument for?' may reply, 'My son, that is a memorial to a young French officer who lost his life in Boston when France was helping us to gain our independence, erected by the STATE to show that we have not forgotten the sacrifice which he and other Frenchmen then made for us, and as a mark of our regard for France, liberty-loving like us and one with us in the cause of humanity and civilization, a union which with God's help we shall neither of us sever.'"

There is another interesting detail in connection with the inscription on the monument.   Admiral d'Estaing, who had his fleet in Boston Harbour undergoing repairs, a few days after the death of his fellow officer, wrote a suitable inscription and forwarded it to the General Court, which acknowledged the receipt of it; he also had copies delivered from his flagship—the "Languedoc"—to all the other French vessels in the harbour.   With good judgment it was decided to place this inscription, written by d'Estaing at the time of the important incident, on the front of the shaft; and though it is near the street and easy to read, few of the many people who pass by this spot realize the reason for the erection of the monument, or understand the unique story connected with it. Massachusetts had finally fulfilled her promise, though the vote passed in the year 1778 had been for some unknown reason forgotten all these many years.

Saint Sauveur was a Lieutenant on the "Tonnant," which flew the flag of his brother-in-law, Count de Breugnon. He also was the first Chamberlain to the brother of Louis XVI. No wonder his death caused much anxiety to our officials, who did all in their power to atone for the incident. Saint Sauveur's body was buried quietly at night in the crypt of King's Chapel, though it is possible that his remains were at some later time sent back to France. Fitz-Henry Smith, Jr., found this interesting account of the funeral:

"Eight sailors of the 'Tonnant' bore the coffin on their shoulders. I preceded them with the sexton and grave digger; the recollet M. M. de Borda, de Puységur and Piervères followed; the servant of the deceased and perhaps two or three Frenchmen closed the procession. We started in that order at ten o'clock and arriving at the church called King's Chapel, found the basement of the church illuminated with many candles, without ostentation. The door of the vault having been closed and padlocked, we returned to sign a certificate of interment which I had already drawn up. In fine, what we had been charged to do could not have been done with more precision and exactness."

To Colonel Chaillé Long and to Captain A. A. Folsom, father of Mrs. Augustus F. Goodwin, falls the credit for discovering that the vote of the State had never been carried out. The former found the logbook of the "Languedoc" and decided to inquire in what cemetery the monument had been erected—of course, no memorial could be found in Boston. A committee of the Legislature then investigated the question, reporting at the close:

"In war and in peace Massachusetts keeps her promises. Here is an event filled with uncertain and distressing possibilities at the time, which, in the more comprehensive view of the present, had the matter not been disposed of to the entire satisfaction of the French officers, might have ended the French alliance, and changed materially the subsequent history if not the results of the war of the revolution. Yorktown might never have been a lustrous, historic name. The State had failed in its primal duty to keep the public peace; the death of a French officer of distinction had been the result. All the reparation possible at the moment was made. The omitted or forgotten detail should be supplied, and to this end the committee recommend the passage of the accompanying resolve."

Very carelessly this Legislature failed to carry out the old resolve and it was the Bostonian Society that in 1916 filed a petition to the Legislature which this time resulted in a more definite vote, appointing a committee consisting of Courtenay Guild, Chairman, Grenville H. Norcross, J. Randolph Coolidge, and the late Robert S. Peabody. A. W. Longfellow was the architect of the shaft.

On the tablet facing Tremont Street appears d'Estaing's inscription slightly changed from the original. This is shown in an illustration. Translated into English, it reads: "In memory of the Chevalier de Saint Sauveur, First Chamberlain of His Royal Highness Count d'Artois, brother of His Majesty, the King of France. This officer, Aide-Major of the French Fleet and a Lieutenant on the 'Tonnant,' after having had the happiness of risking his life for the United States, was in the performance of his duty when he became the victim of a tumult caused by persons of evil intent; dying with the same attachment for America, the ties of duty and sympathy which bind his compatriots to the City of Boston have been thus drawn tighter. May all efforts to separate France and America be as unfruitful! Such is the prayer to Almighty God which in the centuries to come every Frenchman and American will offer whose eyes shall fall upon this monument to a young man taken from his friends, who can be consoled for his loss only by seeing such funeral flowers spread upon his tomb." Over the inscription are

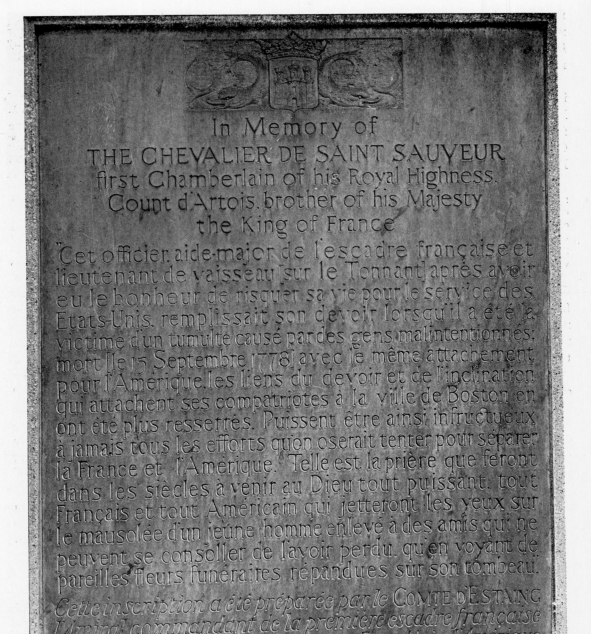

In Memory of
THE CHEVALIER DE SAINT SAUVEUR
first Chamberlain of his Royal Highness
Count d'Artois, brother of his Majesty
the King of France

"Cet officier, aide-major de l'escadre française et
lieutenant de vaisseau sur le Tonnant, après avoir
eu le bonheur de risquer sa vie pour le service des
Etats-Unis, remplissait son devoir lorsqu'il a été la
victime d'un tumulte causé par des gens malintentionnés,
mort le 15 Septembre 1778, avec le même attachement
pour l'Amérique, les liens du devoir et de l'inclination
qui attachent ses compatriotes à la ville de Boston en
ont été plus resserrés. Puissent être ainsi infructueux
à jamais tous les efforts qu'on oserait tenter pour séparer
la France et l'Amérique. Telle est la prière que feront
dans les siècles à venir au Dieu tout puissant, tout
Français et tout Américain qui jetteront les yeux sur
le mausolée d'un jeune homme enlevé à des amis qui ne
peuvent se consoler de l'avoir perdu, qu'en voyant de
pareilles fleurs funéraires répandues sur son tombeau."

Cette inscription a été préparée par le COMTE D'ESTAING
l'Amiral commandant de la première escadre française
envoyée par le Roy de France aux Etats-Unis d'Amérique

TABLET ON THE SAINT SAUVEUR MEMORIAL SHAFT AT KING'S CHAPEL, BOSTON,
*showing the inscription as written originally by Admiral d'Estaing, the superior officer of Saint Sauveur, 139 years before
the actual erection of this monument. It was necessary to make only a few changes from the original wording.*

the arms of the family of Saint Sauveur, while on the back of the monument are these words:

ERECTED IN CONSEQUENCE OF A RESOLVE OF THE STATE OF MASSACHUSETTS BAY 16 SEP- TEMBER 1778 AND OF A RESOLVE OF THE COM- MONWEALTH OF MASSACHUSETTS 1 JUNE 1916

There is a tablet in the New England Historic Genealogical Society of Boston in memory of Joseph Rochemont de Poyen de Saint Sauveur, who was a nephew of the Chevalier de Saint Sauveur. His father, de Poyen de Saint Sauveur, brother of the Chevalier, is interred in the "Old Hill" Cemetery at Newburyport, where he lived; and a picture of his gravestone appears in

Kindness of Miss Maria P. Hamlen

HOUSE FORMERLY OWNED BY GENERAL JOSHUA AND JULIA (DEARBORN) WINGATE

where Lafayette paid a visit when in Portland in 1825. General Wingate was a first cousin of the wife of Joseph Rochemont de Poyen de Saint Sauveur.

an illustration. He was a Royalist planter, and fled with three sons, a daughter and a nephew, Count de Vipart, to Newburyport from the island of Guadeloupe, West Indies, at the time of the Revolution in France. He died six months after his arrival here; but a number of his descendants still live in Portland, Maine, and other places in New England. The wife of Joseph Rochemont de Poyen de Saint Sauveur was a first cousin of General Joshua Wingate at whose house in Portland, shown on this page, Lafayette called in 1825, in order to pay his respects to the owner and his wife, as the latter was a daughter of his friend and commander, General Dearborn, during the war of the American Revolution.

The wife of the Count de Vipart (Mary Ingalls) was first cousin of Madame Joseph Roche- mont de Poyen. She is memorialized in Whittier's poem "The Countess." The country home at South Byfield, Massachusetts, of Miss Maria P. Hamlen, great-granddaughter of the immi- grant, who has assisted us in our investigations, is named in memory of her French ancestor, "St. Sauveur."

Notwithstanding the fact that a number of persons have interested themselves keenly in this Saint Sauveur story, strangely enough no one has hitherto ever taken the time, so far as we know, to study the interesting French family of which he was a member. Paul F. Cadman has now made such an investigation, which required a large amount of time and patience. He summarizes thus:

"When this task was undertaken, there were at hand, from all sources already consulted, the following general facts:

'That Saint Sauveur was a chevalier, that is to say, a knight; that he was the first chamberlain of the Count d'Artois who was the brother of Louis XVI and who later became King of France as Charles X. A chamberlain was supposed to be either the chief director of his Master's household or his treasurer. It is not probable that Saint Sauveur served in either capacity to the Count d'Artois but that the title was rather an honorary one. However, such a title would probably be reserved for a member of an old and well-known noble family.

It was found that the name Saint Sauveur was only a "nom de terre," that is to say, the name of an estate; that the family name of this officer was de Grégoire; that the coat of arms of the family bore a blue castle with crenelated towers on a silver background; and that Saint Sauveur was a brother-in-law of the Count de Breugnon who was the Commander of "Le Tonnant" and Chef d'Escadre in d'Estaing's fleet. Saint Sauveur was chief aide to the Count de Breugnon and was with him on this ship.'

Other than this, no data concerning this officer or his family had been presented.

ANCIENT CHÂTEAU DE SAINT SAUVEUR, NEAR ISPAGNAC, FRANCE,

showing the magnificent gorges of the Tarn. This site afforded superb protection during the Middle Ages. Here lived the ancestors of Saint Sauveur, who was killed in a riot in Boston during the Revolution. A memorial shaft, shown in another illustration, was placed near the entrance to King's Chapel, Boston, to mark the place of his burial. The old Abbé, who made the study of the Saint Sauveur history for the Trust Company, is seen in the picture, also the photographer's wife.

"Admirable as are the archives of the French Marine, it is unfortunately true that the records of hundreds of valiant naval officers were destroyed or lost during the Revolution and the long unsettled period that followed it. All the records of the Revolutionary period and those prior to that time are now kept in the Archives Nationales in Paris. Some days after the demand had been submitted to the officers of the Archives Nationales, notice was sent that the Saint Sauveur file had been brought down to the consulting room and was available for study. These documents contained only a brief account of the tragedy at Boston, a few papers which failed to disclose anything relative to the family, and a letter addressed to the Minister of the Marine asking that Saint Sauveur be returned from duty in Santo Domingo, which letter was signed by the Count de Nozières. The Count refers to Saint Sauveur as his nephew.

"Then followed a search lasting more than eighteen months, during which time every printed document of the French Marine of the epoch in question was consulted, the archivists of forty French Departments were enlisted, and an extensive correspondence was carried on with more than a score of persons directly interested in French Marine history. It is impossible to give all the details of this search, but a few of them are sufficiently romantic to deserve mention.

"The study of the printed sources confirmed the general facts about Saint Sauveur given above and also revealed that his mother was an assistant governess to the children of Louis XVI, which latter statement was confirmed by consulting the archives of the King's household, now carefully conserved in the Archives Nationales. 'La Dictionnaire de la Noblesse Française' recorded only one Grégoire de Saint Sauveur, Vitel Auguste de Grégoire de Saint Sauveur, Count de Nozières, but his arms were found to be the same as those of the young lieutenant. He was in all probability the uncle who signed the letter to the Minister of Marine mentioned above; but still there was no

Photographed for the State Street Trust Company   *Kindness of Paul F. Cadman*

ANOTHER VIEW OF SAINT SAUVEUR CHÂTEAU
showing the precipice and remaining vestige of the ancient wall dating back to the Middle Ages.

mention of the family seat, and Nozières is very vague, since there are a number of localities in France bearing that name.

"The next step was to write to every Department in France where a Saint Sauveur was recorded and to make inquiry as to the family of de Grégoire. The letters were answered with the utmost cordiality and promptness, showing a sympathetic desire to help in the chase, but none recorded any de Grégoires de Saint Sauveur either living or historical.

"In the meanwhile steps had also been taken to find out where the Count de Breugnon was married, with the hope that his marriage record would bear the name of his bride's parents, who would of course be the parents of the Lieutenant Saint Sauveur in question.

Kindness of Miss Maria P. Hamlen

ARMS OF THE CHEVALIER DE SAINT SAUVEUR

The Château of Saint Sauveur, the home of the de Grégoires from whom the Chevalier was descended, was situated in the Parish of Ispagnac, near the City of Mende, in the beautiful valley of the Tarn. It is now in ruins.

"Strangely enough, two private individuals, amateurs in Franco-American history, gave the most valuable help. A Monsieur Collière, in Alençon in the Department of the Orne, wrote that his archivist had referred our letter to him and that he was deeply interested. After a long correspondence with this excellent gentleman, he one day wrote of having discovered that a Bishop of Bazar in 1746 was a de Grégoire de Saint Sauveur and that he was probably born at Mende in the Department of the Lozère. He further aided in the search by suggesting the name of a historian in Mende, Monsieur l'Abbé Costecalde, who was an expert in searching genealogical history. In short, the services of this good Abbé were secured, and after many weeks of diligent search he submitted an excellent report, some of which is offered herewith; unhappily, he had not come upon our Lieutenant in any of his findings. He did, however, give an excellent history of the de Grégoires de Saint Sauveur, which family had for centuries made its home in the environs of Mende. [These de Grégoires were perhaps relatives of the de Grégoires who were identified with Hull's Cove, Bar Harbour, Maine.] Among others which he listed in chronological order was Jean Anne de Grégoire, who married Madeleine-Suzanne Goulet de Rugis, in 1746.

"Now about this time another amateur historian who had taken up the matter, a Monsieur Paul Beauchet-Filleau from Chef-Boutonne way over in Poitou, from an opposite corner in France, wrote this interesting statement:

'. . . I am sure that this family of de Grégoire does not belong in the Province of Poitou, and I am also very badly documented concerning it. I have nevertheless traced certain notes about it and I sincerely hope that they will put you on the track. Here they are: Hyacinthe Philémon de Grégoire de Saint Sauveur, Lieutenant General of the Armies of the King, Commander of the Order of Saint Louis, former lieutenant of the King's Body Guard, Luxembourg Company, died at Bagnières de Bigoire the eleventh of July 1784. Dame de Grégoire de Saint Sauveur was an Ursuline nun at Mende and was made the head Abbesse of Mercoire.'

The most precious, however, of all was the next entry, which was the first real light that was shed on the problem:

'. . . Louise-Jeanne Marguerite de Grégoire de Saint Sauveur, youngest daughter of the late Jean Anne de Grégoire, Marquis de Saint Sauveur, Squire to the King and to his Highness, the Dauphin, and of Madeleine-Suzanne Goulet de Rugis, made a contract of marriage before Regnault, notary, the 22nd of November 1767 with Pierre-Claude Haudeneau, Count de Breugnon, Chevalier of Saint Louis, ambassador of his very Christian Majesty to the Emperor of Morocco and Chief of Squadron in the Naval Armies. The marriage was celebrated the 25th of the same month in the parish of St. Pierre des Plaisirs in the diocese of Chartres. . . .'

Here then was the maiden name of the wife of the Count de Breugnon, the sister of Saint Sauveur, and, best of all, the names of both of her parents, which were identical with those found in the archives of Mende by our good Abbé historian. The purpose was not to make an extensive family tree of the de Grégoires, but rather to bring them out of the dark cupboards of history. It remains then only to mention a few of the high lights in the records of this noble house.

"The family seat of the de Grégoires was near the ancient see-city of Mende in that marvelous valley of the Tarn, famous for its beautiful gorges. This region is about a day's journey by rail south of the Château de Chavaniac, the birthplace of Lafayette; but let the gentle Abbé tell it in his own way:

GRAVES OF THE FRENCH REFUGEES FROM GUADELOUPE, WEST INDIES, IN "OLD HILL" BURIAL GROUND, NEWBURYPORT, MASSACHUSETTS

The second monument on the right in the foreground is the grave of de Poyen de Saint Sauveur, brother of the Chevalier de Saint Sauveur.

'The de Grégoires, Lords of Lambrandès, which was the name given to their castle at Ispagnac in the 14th century, played an important part in the history of their town, which is situated near the well-known Gorges of the Tarn.

The name de Grégoire indicates a Gallo-Roman origin. During the middle ages, from 1100 to 1793, Ispagnac had a monastery under the patronage of St. Peter and a well-known priory which the de Grégoires throughout the centuries have supported and endowed. Unfortunately the feudal deeds were burned in the Public Place during the Terror.

The first recorded de Grégoire was Odilon,

who is mentioned in a deed in 1247. Another, Raymond 1st de Grégoire is buried in the churchyard at Ispagnac, and his tombstone asserts that he died on October 7, 1357, being 120 years old, and having made a pious pilgrimage to the tombs of St. Peter and St. Paul.

The de Grégoires had a family chapel in the parish church at Ispagnac which is no longer in existence. One still sees their coat of arms: a castle with crenelated towers.

Tristan was one of the most famous.

The first de Grégoire to take the title of Saint Sauveur was Jean de Grégoire who in 1701 married Lucrèce de Chapelain. He kept the ancient title of Lord of Lambrandès. In 1702 he purchased the old Saint Sauveur Castle situated in the parish of Ispagnac. The notary's quaint entry states that he purchased this broken-down old ruin from Louis Grimard du Roure, baron and Governor of Florac, Marquis of Grisac, descendant of Pope Urban V.

This same John had served in the armies of Louis XIV and had reached the rank of Captain. From 1717 to 1720 he was Episcopal Bailiff of the Diocese of Mende and thus became an officer of the "Cloth" and the "Sword." It was his duty to be the "promoter and protector of all public interests." '

"This Jean, last mentioned, was the grandfather of our Lieutenant Saint Sauveur. This is certainly so, for the record of the births of all his children is now preserved in the archives of the Lozère and shows that his second son was Jean Anne de Grégoire, born 1709, married 1746, to Magdeleine Goelet de Rugis.

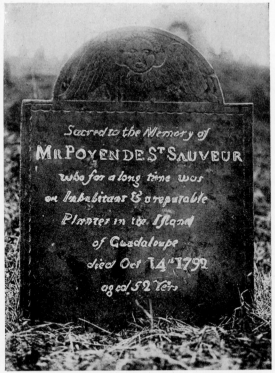

GRAVESTONE IN THE "OLD HILL" BURIAL GROUND, NEWBURYPORT, MASSACHUSETTS, OF DE POYEN DE SAINT SAUVEUR,

a brother of Chevalier de Saint Sauveur, who was killed in the riot and who was buried at King's Chapel, Boston. He was a French Royalist refugee from the island of Guadeloupe in the West Indies in 1792.

"Now what do we learn of this Château? Once more the Abbé speaks:

'. . . The Castle of Saint Sauveur was situated in the Parish of Ispagnac at the summit of a steep mountain on the south side of Montmirat Hill between the Villages of Nozières, Lonjagnes and Le Marazel. It was inaccessible on three sides and was built against a huge basaltic rock; its towers overlooked the mountain. It was a first-rate fortress and played an important part in the middle ages, during the 100 years' war and the religious wars. The Chapel was under the protection of Saint Sauveur and stood for some time after the castle had been destroyed. It has almost completely disappeared today except for one remaining wall.' "

The good Abbé was persuaded to take a photographer out to the ruins, and the result is the illustrations which show the famous ruins of the ancient house of Saint Sauveur and the magnificent Gorges of the Tarn with the Abbé historian and the wife of the photographer amid the ruins. A recent letter from the Director of the Archives in Paris informs us that from a register of the records of the Estate of Artois, a warrant dated December 17, 1777, gives this title to Hyacinthe Philémon Louis de Grégoire, thus making known his full name.

We have dwelt at length upon the history of this family owing to the high rank of the Saint Sauveur who was killed in Boston, and also on account of the serious effect his tragic death might have had on the history of not only our city, but of our country itself.

WITH THE FRENCH AT NEWPORT

THE arrival at Newport of the French officers with their brilliant costumes and their gay and courtly manners proved a great boon to the war-weary town; and the appearance of Thames Street, the "Parade" and the "Point," where most of the merchants of that day had their modest but attractive residences, presented a new aspect. Ships were again seen at the docks laden with wares, people again thronged the streets, and all the stores began to do a thriving business. It is a curious fact that just before the war, Newporters vied with one another in owning the tallest carriage—the taller the vehicle the more distinguished its occupant. The thoroughfares were bright with the white uniforms of the Deux-Ponts regiment, the green and white of the Saintonge, the black and red of the Bourbonnais, and the rose facings of the Soissonnais with their grenadier caps decorated with white and rose plumes. So pleased were the townspeople to see their foreign allies, that as much as possible was done for their comfort, and most of the finest houses were allotted to the French officers during their eleven months' or so sojourn in the town. These "mansions," as they were then called, are of course in the old colonial part of the town, near the waterfront, and those that are standing are much prized by the people of Newport, as they have a peculiar charm of their own in addition to their historical interest. Most of these dwellings date back to the eighteenth century, when commerce was flourishing, when the merchants were well-to-do, and when the foreign and domestic trade of Newport exceeded that of New York. The most interesting, undoubtedly, is the old Vernon house, on the corner of Mary and Clarke Streets, now owned by the Family Welfare Society, and shown free to the many visitors who visit the place where Rochambeau had his headquarters. There he received Washington,

Lafayette, and others of his staff—including Count de Fersen, Marquis de Damas, Baron de Closen, Count Mathieu Dumas, Rochambeau's nephew Dupont de Lauberdière, and his own son Vicomte de Rochambeau, then Colonel "en second" of the Bourbonnais regiment. Except for Rochambeau and his son, no one resided in this house, but lived across the way in New Lane or in Spring or Thames Streets. In this Vernon "Mansion" were held many councils of war and important meetings, and it is also said that the name of many a Newport belle was written on its window panes. To commemorate the occupancy of the house by this illustrious French General, a bronze tablet showing him at the age of fifty-eight and in the uniform of that day, was affixed in September, 1908, to a corner of the second story of the building—the words on it reading:

OLD VERNON "MANSION," IN NEWPORT, RHODE ISLAND, HEADQUARTERS OF ROCHAMBEAU AND HIS SON DURING THE WINTER OF 1780–81

Here he received Generals Washington and Lafayette, and held also many councils of war and meetings. On a corner of the building is a tablet shown on the following page. This ancient Newport landmark is now owned by the Family Welfare Society, and is shown to many hundreds of interested visitors each year. Within is, among other things, an etching of the statue of General Rochambeau at Vendôme, France.

1780 1781 | HEADQUARTERS | OF GENERAL | COUNT DE ROCHAMBEAU | COMMANDING | THE FRENCH ALLIED FORCES

This likeness of Rochambeau was obtained by the sculptor Pierre de Feitu, a Frenchman then living in New York. The plaque itself was presented by Professor B. L. A. Hénin, descendant of a French veteran of the Revolutionary War and president of the Alliance Française; it was unveiled in the presence of many important persons, including Count de Chambrun, then councillor of the French embassy at Washington and a descendant of Lafayette. Mrs. Julia Ward Howe pulled aside the tricolor that covered the tablet, while the Newport Artillery fired a salute and the Training Station band played the Marseillaise. The mayor of Newport in a graceful speech then accepted the donation. Count de Chambrun also made an address.

Within this attractively panelled domicile are pictures of the statues of Lafayette and Rochambeau in Lafayette Square, Washington, D.C., the latter being a reproduction of the one in the "Place" of Rochambeau's native city, Vendôme, France. Beneath this picture is the explanation that "this etching, presented to the Rochambeau headquarters of Newport

TABLET AND MEDALLION OF ROCHAMBEAU ON THE VERNON "MANSION" IN NEWPORT, RHODE ISLAND,

where this French General had his headquarters during the winter of 1780–81. This tablet was the gift of Professor B. L. A. Hénin, a descendant of Antoine Hénin, who fought in the French army during the Revolutionary War. It was unveiled in September, 1908, in the presence of Count de Chambrun, a descendant of Lafayette.

through Mrs. Manson Smith, is one of a collection sent to her by the artist, M. Albert Aviat of Vendôme, as a testimonial of gratitude for work done for the French wounded—October 1915." The Family Welfare Society is indeed to be congratulated for raising funds for the restoration of this relic of the days of French occupancy of Newport. The second floor is rented to boarders to help pay the upkeep.

The history of the Vernon property is an interesting one. It was first owned by Jeremy Clarke, for whom the street running past the house is named—the owner being one of the nine adventurers who founded Newport in 1639. In 1758 this piece of land was owned by a merchant of the town named Metcalf Bowler, and in the same year he built the present house. Bowler's father was an Englishman and lived in Boston on Beacon Hill, later moving to Newport, where he married the daughter of Major Fairchild. The house later became the property of William Vernon, an important Rhode Islander; but during the war he removed to Boston, serving on the Eastern Navy Board. A few days after the arrival of the French he sent his son, Samuel, with a letter to the French Admiral, de Ternay, saying that his son "will be happy in having it in his power of rendering Mr. de Ternay or any of his connection every service possible." Perhaps this may have led to the assignment of the house to Rochambeau. In November, 1780, a building known as "French Hall" was built by the Commander-in-Chief of the French troops, in which his officers could have dinners and dances, or receive their friends. This large hall, states Claude Blanchard, commissary of the French Auxiliary Army, in his diary (a valuable translation of which is in the Newport Historical Society), was "constructed for the purpose of assembling a large number of officers therein in the evening, to afford them recreation; it began to be used about this time" (early in January, 1781).

"We can imagine the scene"—writes Maud Lyman Stevens in her interesting pamphlet on the Vernon house—"the newly-built assembly room, lighted by candles in sconces, and, surely, in January, warmed by a blazing fire; the uniformed musicians, the discreet dowagers, and—observed of all observers—the brilliant band of young noblemen in their gala attire of white broadcloth, turned back with pink, blue or green according to their corps. In minuet or contradance, they lead out the gay young Newport beauties, whose charms they so admire." We hear that the names "Atlantic," "Bellevue," and others as appropriate, were given to the dances held in Newport at that time. Very likely an argument arose with the owner of the house over the building of this hall; for in December, 1780, William Vernon in a letter to his son, said: "I understand General Rochambeau had not your leave for building an assembly room in the garden. I can't think it polite of him." The matter was amicably adjusted, however, probably during Rochambeau's visit to Boston on the thirteenth of the same month, the only time he came to this city. There seems also to have been another slight rupture between landlord and tenant on account of injuries to the house; for in October, 1781, Samuel Vernon, the son, said: "I believe the General takes as much care of the house as the Frenchmen generally do, but it will sustain more damage than a family living in it seven years. The floors will be entirely spoiled!" The father in reply wrote: "I expect they will make a great waste in the house, if not ruin it." A bill, dated December 12, 1782, was sent to cover the cost of repairs, which amounted to one hundred and thirty-five pounds. This bill is still in existence and shows that no charge whatever was made for the year's use of the dwelling. The account was promptly paid just before Rochambeau's departure for France, thereby greatly relieving the mind of the owner; it was also fortunate that it was settled for in French livres, for at that time it took seven hundred Continental paper dollars to purchase one dollar's worth of property.

William Vernon returned to Newport in 1785 and lived in the old house until he died, in 1806. His son, Samuel, carried on a large foreign commerce until his death in 1834. A brother called William H. lived most of his life in France and was a prominent personage at the court of Louis XVI. He continued to reside there until the French Revolution. When he returned to Newport, so courtly were his manners that his friends called him "Count" Vernon. With him he brought many valuable paintings, one of which, a copy of the famous "Mona Lisa," was, according to the family tradition, presented to him by the Queen.

Near the foot of Church Street then stood the celebrated Assembly rooms of Mrs. Cowley, where, during that winter, Washington and the French danced with the Newport belles, of which there were many, if we believe the accounts of the officers themselves. The proprietor of this popular establishment catered to both sides; for when the British were in the town she hung out a sign on which was depicted a crown, which later she took down when the Americans arrived. The departure later on of the French army effected such a great contrast in the life of the town, that an old resident declared: "Newport, my dear friend, since the French army left it, has returned back again to its former situation. . . . Ladies, as many as you please, but few gentlemen. It makes me think, when I am walking the streets in an evening, of former times that we read of, when seven women got hold of the skirts of one man."

Continuing his rambles among the old houses associated with the French occupancy, the visitor should not fail to visit the Robinson house—so called from its first owner, Thomas

Kindness of Mrs. Henry A. Wood

ROBINSON HOUSE, NEWPORT, RHODE ISLAND,

in which was quartered Vicomte de Noailles, a brother-in-law of Lafayette, while the French army was in town. This French officer was most graciously received by the Robinson family and, after leaving Newport, carried on an intimate correspondence with Mary Robinson, one of the daughters of "Quaker Tom" Robinson, as he was called. Several paragraphs of these letters are printed in the text. This attractive old house, one of Newport's landmarks, is situated on the water side of Washington Street, near the foot of Poplar Street. It is the only one of the houses occupied by the French officers which has remained in the same family since the war, being the property today of Miss Esther Morton Smith, a cousin of the Hallowell family of Boston.

Robinson, or "Quaker Tom," as he was known—with its quaint fire buckets, old shutters and attractive panelling. It is situated on the water side of Washington Street near the foot of Poplar Street, and as far as we know is the only one now owned by the same family that occupied it when the French were there. Before the Revolution it was usually referred to as "The Old Tavern," and it was always said that between its kitchen and dining-room there was a hollow post in order to enable the masters of the house to hear the conversation of the servants, who in those days were probably slaves. There is also a tradition, according to Anna Wharton Wood—a great-great-granddaughter of Thomas Robinson—in her excellent history of the house, that for years the two negro cooks made use of opposite ends of the big fireplace without ever having spoken a word to each other. In this house lives Mrs. Wood's sister, the Quakeress Esther Morton Smith, a cousin of the Hallowell family of Boston. The two sisters cherish the history that connects the house with de Noailles, Lafayette's brother-in-law, who had his headquarters there.

The authorities ordered Robinson on September 28, 1780, to give his house for this purpose. When its new occupant arrived to take up his abode, he was surprised to find that the whole family were very proficient in the French language. The Vicomte left the Robinsons with much regret when the army left Newport in June of the following year, and as a parting gift presented to Mrs. Robinson a bronze tea-kettle that had served as part of his camp equipment—a relic that is still a prized possession of the family. The present owner, who lives in Philadelphia in the winter, also has among her possessions a valuable set of seven or eight pieces of Sèvres china which the Countess de Noailles, wife of this French officer and later a victim of the guillotine, sent, during the year 1781, to Sarah Robinson, wife of Thomas Robinson, and the great-great-grandmother of Miss Smith. With it came a letter in English dated October 10th, from Paris, which reads as follows:

"Madam, I do not know whether you will forgive my indiscretion, but your friendly kindness for my husband affects me so truly, that I cannot deny myself the pleasure of telling you how much, and with what sincerity I unite with him in his gratitude for all your favors. Since you know him, Madam, you will be able to judge of my uneasiness and of the continual alarms I am exposed to on his account! From what he has told me of your sensibility and tender feelings, I hope it will be pleasing to you to hear that in procuring him a happy life, you also give some consolation to a heart almost broken with such variety of affliction! I have a double obligation to you, Madam, for having admitted him into an intimate acquaintance in your family; he will see there each day, that real happiness is not to be found in the pursuit of military glory; to which nevertheless men make cruel sacrifices. May I hope, Madam, that you will permit me to present you some tea cups of a Manufactory we have here, and that in drinking your tea with your charming daughters, you will sometimes think of me. I should look upon it as a great happiness if circumstances should ever procure me an opportunity to offer you myself the homage of all those sentiments you have inspired in me, and with which I have the honor to be, etc."

Vicomte de Noailles carried on a long and intimate correspondence with one of the daughters, Mary Robinson (usually called by her family Molly), and we believe it may be of interest to quote a number of paragraphs exactly as they were written. The first is from Providence, sent in June shortly after leaving Newport:

"My friend: The hope of corresponding with you is a comfort very necessary to my heart; full of gratitude and friendship to your family it want to express all his own feelings. . . . Tho I may think I shall never feel myself so much attached to anybody in America; . . . thousand new society cannot cure the grief of a friend absence. . . . After a long navigation from Newport to Providence, I went on foot at nine o'clock through the night at Mr. Broun's house, two miles and a half far from our camp." (The reason that he walked to Mr. Broun's, at such inconvenience, was to say good-bye to Sarah Robinson, whom, however, he missed.)

His next letter (June 17th) reads in part as follows:

"I cannot cast any more my eyes upon Newport, but I have in it a tender interest, which never will be out of my heart. I thought I was safe in America of all those sentiments than expectations of glory; but now I fear for the inhabitants of the town you live in, as for the best city in France. . . . Since my last letter we are on the same situation our army lay in the camp of Providence. Tomorrow the Bourbonnais regiment will march; we expect to follow it two days after. Wherever I shall be, you will have a friend dearly attached to you. . . . I will ask you pardon, not because my letter is wrote in bad English, nor complain of the difficulty of expressing my sentiments, but because it is shorter than I had wished to wrait it, the officer who go to Newport is ready and I have only the pleasure to repeat to you once more that as long as I will breathe I shall be your most tender and most respected friend Noailles."

From Hartford towards the last of June he writes the following:

"I would be jealous if I think not that a line from you is better than a volume for any other body I am acquainted with in America. We are now as far as Hartford. We travelled with a fine weather, through a good country, very well improved. We were received everywhere with the signs of the greatest friendship; The officers and soldiers danced every day. . . . I am in my camp by a bade weather obliged to finish my letter because the hour of our departure is fixed two o'clock, and we are advanced in the night. Tell you father that a French army never was so well equipped as ours is, by the care of Mr. Wadsworth, everybody speak of him, as a man of the greatest character. . . ."

Mr. Wadsworth acted as commissary for the French army and many of his receipted vouchers may be examined in the Atheneum at Hartford. A careful perusal would doubtless disclose much interesting information.

The next letter is from Molly Robinson to de Noailles, dated Newport 31 of 6th Mo. 1781 ("6th Mo." stands for June). It was discovered by a friend of the Robinson family while prowling in a book store in New York, but how it happened to be left in this country will doubtless always be a mystery:

"Since I wrote last I have had the pleasure of receiving thine of the 17th; and the pain of perusing one of the 19th both from Providence—Pardon the latter expression, it is rough—the sensation which directs my pen, is not—I confess I was hurt at the idea of thy admitting a thought that it is in the power of absence to reduce our friendship to an acquaintance; or of time to banish him from our memory: indeed, we shall think it injurious, while our hearts speak a language so different, they say it will be impossible ever to forget what has made such pleasing impressions upon them—but if I proceed in this way, I shall be suspected of that inclination to quarrel which I have so often been accused of. I will therefore change the subject and thank thee most sincerely for the pleasure I received from the 17th and one of the 19th too. And so you have bid a long adieu to this part of the country, and are going far from us, but my letters shall pursue thee, they shall continually evince to thee the sincerity of that attachment. . . . How has thee contrived, Count de Noailles, to conceal from us the courtier, which might have dazzled our eyes, without touching our hearts; and appear to us only in the endearing light of a friend? . . . My mama . . . ever claims half thy letters; my father and sister demand their share of me, and if I was to submit quietly to all their requisitions, I should reserve none for myself. . . . Your departure from this place has furnished abundant employ-ment for the idle daughters of Parnassus; every murmuring rivulet and shady grove is called to witness their grief, and every weeping muse is invoked to describe their sorrows. This must doubtless be a very great consolation to you; and to add to thy private satisfaction I assure thee the red and white are distinguished. . . . Adieu, Count de Noailles, if thou wishes to make us happy, let us hear often from thee, and be assured that everything which concerns thee is very interesting to this family. May God Almighty preserve thee in every danger, prays M. R. 31st of ye 6th Mo. 1781."

Another letter from the Count to Mary Robinson reads in part as follows:

"1781, September 6th. My letters delivered the first time I read learn myself the death of my only child. This loss, the grief of her mother, this of my family increase my own feelings, and render them full of bitterness sentiments. What have I done to be bereft of my two children, dearly loved, in the age which is very scarce to know the tender sentiments of a father, indeed Miss Moley in such an instant your friendship had been of a great assistance in my sad disposition."

Again he wrote after the siege of Yorktown:

"My Lord Cornwallis supports his misfortune with a great fortitude, he is beloved by his whole army and deserves it. I found myself very often in company with him, and was charmed of the simplicity of the manners. It is allowed him to go to Europe. . . . My expectation is to see you at Rhode Island before we leave this country, and I hope it will be soon. What agreeable idea to find myself once more among your family. I wish you will be all at Rhode Island when I shall be there. Some business will oblige me to go to Boston before my departure, and I hope at the end of November I shall pass through Newport. You may recollect we spoke sometime of my family; in the number of them you mentioned a great curiosity to know my wife. In our correspondence I entertained her of the plaisir and happiness I had in your society; as she is a better wife than I am an husband, she desired to show her gratitude to Mrs. Robinson, wrote the incluse letter, and send me cups which she wish you will receive to preserve the remembrance of her. The cups are running in the country, if I can ever find them I shall be happy to see you in possession of it."

The next two letters are from Boston. The first is dated "4th 10bre, 1781" (4th of October):

"The French fleet is ready to sail tomorrow and my arrival will hast my departure of a few days. Dont forget Miss Molly, that I wish often to hear from you, and that I should look as an injury to friendship if you should not permit me to assure you of my most sincere and respectful attachment. My best compliments to all your family. I send you the cups of Mme. de Noailles. I cannot think that you will drink our health in but I will hope that great many people who make ardent wishes don't desire ourselves so happy as you do."

OLDEST ROOM IN THE ROBINSON HOUSE, NEW-
PORT, RHODE ISLAND,

*showing the same clock and the panelling as it was when Vicomte
de Noailles resided there while the French army was
quartered in the town.   De Noailles was a brother-in-law of
Lafayette and Colonel "en second" of the Soissonnais
regiment.*

The second one is dated

"Boston the 14th of 1obre, 1781. Mlle.—
I think indeed more easy to take a British
army than to have a frigate out of Boston
harbour. Since my arrival in this town I have
been running, speaking, disputing and I don't
believe we shall be able to go to sea before
these three days. You know my sentiments
well enough to suppose that I have been very
unhappy to spend so long while out of Newport. . . . The manner that General Cornwallis speaks of the treatment he received
from the French officers proof the goodness of
his heart."

A still later letter was sent from Paris,
the fifteenth of April, 1782:

"Think with pleasure that peace will soon
take place, and that you will be left free and
happy. The new ministry in England is as
much American as the congress itself. I expect
with very great impatience that I may go to
America, and see all your family again. . . .
My wife wants to be remembered to you. . . . She talks often of going to America. . . . I cannot
express how attached I am to that part of the world called America. When I say I think more of the
house built in Water Street where I was so long and so short a time in, than the whole continent."

Ten years later, on the 27th of December 1792, a pathetic letter was sent from London:

". . . I told you that I thought a revolution would take place in our country, that my love for
liberty wd. support it. Everything has happened as I foretold you, but what I never had thought, is
that the spirit of enmity, jealousy, and cruelty should take place of this mild, which was the character
of the French nation. As long as it was possible to serve the cause of liberty, I never deserted it, but
when it became criminal, I left my country, quitted the part of the world where crimes were committed, and fled to England, where I pity the errors of the French people, and cannot forget their
cruelty. . . ."

While the Vicomte de Noailles was in London at that time, he made arrangements for
the Vicomtesse to join him and then to go with him to America; but her devotion to her mother,
her children, and her sister, Madame de Lafayette, was so great that she could not at once
part from them. She delayed leaving until it was impossible for her to get away, and the
delay later cost her her life. After reaching America in 1793, de Noailles wrote from New York
as follows to Miss Robinson, who was now married to John Morton, a Philadelphia merchant:

". . . I have been in this town near ten days, and was not two hours in it without I visited your
eldest brother. . . . Since my arrival in this country I have made a purchase of five hundred thousand
acres of land in the state you have adopted. I have not purchased such an immense quantity of
uncultivated land to make a speculation upon it and resell with advantage. My intention has been
to prepare an exile to those of my countrymen, who disgusted of the horrid scene which took place in
France, will forever abandon the theatre which has produced it. My expectation has so well succeeded that now we are settling forty French families in easy circumstances. . . . Our manners will
be soft, our conversation animated, our labor active, we will be the French people you have known
at Newport and not the present nation. . . ."

De Noailles while in America founded this "Azilum" on the banks of the Susquehanna
as a retreat for French exiles, and a monument marks the site of the colony. It was visited
by Rochefoucauld in 1795. According to Samuel Breck, de Noailles was the best amateur

dancer in Paris before the Revolution, and at the court balls was often the partner of Marie Antoinette.

The following is an extract from a letter written by Mary Robinson Morton from Philadelphia in the spring of 1794 to a cousin in Boston:

"The Vicomte [de Noailles] often calls and dines with us, and seems to enjoy in our society one of the dearest privileges of the unhappy, that of freely imparting his feelings to friends who know to enter into and sympathize in them. He lately brought me a charming letter from his wife, in which she expresses the consolation she derives from the hope that he is now enjoying that satisfaction in our family in Newport. He bears his own private losses and depredation with great equanimity, tho he is evidently deeply affected by the calamitous condition of his country, and the precarious situation of parents, relations, wife and children. They still remain in France, and his father resides at his country seat, which I am astonished at, as his sentiments are known to be inimical to the present ruling powers and he has a large estate in possession, either of which circumstances, one would imagine, would render him a fit subject for the guillotine. . . ."

Mary Robinson's sister, Amy, also known as Emma, was so celebrated for her beauty that three men, it is said, came to Newport on the same vessel to beg for her hand. The story goes that she refused all three suitors, who departed dejectedly. The winds, however, proved adverse, which delayed their departure. One suitor, it is narrated, continued to stay in the town, and finally succeeded in winning his prize. Another suitor for the third daughter, Abby, is said to have jumped overboard from the ferry in order that he might have an excuse for returning to the house. The French were also much impressed with the manners, dignity and purity of the American women. They mentioned especially the Madeira, and our fondness for porcelain, which was a craze at that time. Some of the officers also were particularly surprised to see, in "the wilds of America," the headdresses of the women ornamented with French gauzes.

English as well as French officers were quartered in the Robinson house, and it is said that they too were completely captivated by the beauty of the Robinson girls, thereby causing their mother a great deal of worry. These foreigners claimed that the daughters and their mother would be an ornament to any court in Europe.

Kindness of the late John R. Hess of the "Providence Journal"

NICHOLLS, OR WANTON, OR HUNTER HOUSE, NEWPORT, RHODE ISLAND

Here died Admiral de Ternay, who brought Rochambeau and the French army to America in 1780. The corner room on the second floor is the one in which he is supposed to have succumbed. His headquarters were in this house, which is now used by the St. Joseph Convent. It is situated on the water side of Washington Street at the foot of Elm Street, near Long Wharf and the "Point," where many of the naval officers were quartered so as to be near their ships.

If the visitor wishes to continue his rambles among Newport's old houses with French associations, he should next take a short walk along Washington Street, which will bring him to St. Joseph's Convent, usually known as the Nicholls, or sometimes as the Wanton or Hunter house, where Admiral de Ternay had his headquarters until his death, which took place within its walls. This old building, which resembles others of its period, is situated on the water side of the street at the foot of Elm Street and was a favorite residence for the French, who while there would be near their ships. It was owned by Dr. Horatio Robinson Storer, who lived nearby,

Kindness of the late John R. Hess

LONG WHARF, NEWPORT, RHODE ISLAND,

over which Rochambeau and some of his army must have marched after landing in 1780. Its appearance is much different from that of Revolutionary times. Washington also landed there on his visit to Rochambeau.

and who took a deep interest in its history and in its connection with the great French Admiral, so unfortunate as to die of fever soon after arriving in Newport. To this dwelling, which is near Long Wharf, where most of the French army disembarked, there is attached a bit of romance associated with its secret staircase and the smuggling of rum. This house, to which Lafayette and other French officers often came, was built by Jonathan Nicholls, later becoming the property of Colonel Joseph Wanton and then of William Hunter. Not far away on Spring Street was the old "Bull" house where William Adancourt, a commissary under Rochambeau, kept a coffee house and taught French, preferring to remain in America after the departure of our allies. The notice of this French school read as follows:

"The subscriber informs the public that he continues to teach the French Language in Newport, in the house (commonly called the White Stone), nearly opposite John G. Wanton's, Esqrs., in Spring Street, which is opened five days in the week, for both sexes, and requests the encouragement of those desirous of learning that polite and beneficial language. Terms Two dollars entrance and one dollar per month for each scholar, who is to subscribe for no less than three months. He will also keep Boarding and Lodgings for young gentlemen and teach them the Rudiments of Latin.

Newport, Sept. 7, 1789.

WILLIAM ADANCOURT."

Near the head of Long Wharf, on the south side of the Mall on the corner of Touro Street and the Court of the same name, is an inconspicuous house (the second one in the illustration above), which, according to several authorities, was occupied by Quartermaster-General de Béville. The building was later owned by Commodore Oliver Hazard Perry, and is now used as the headquarters of the Salvation Army, with a small tailor shop on one side. Commodore Perry resided there only a short time, as he was ordered to sea soon afterwards. Its owners thereafter were numerous, and at one time it was used for banking rooms. The church that was nearby has gone the way of many buildings, having been remodelled for a theatre. The inspiration for the name of the Parisien Restaurant nearby may have originated from its proximity to this old house and to Long Wharf, where the French landed. Another authority places de Béville at 290 Congress Street, on the Mall (now called "the Parade") in the original old house now occupied by the Newport National Bank.

There is an amusing incident connected with the Mason house, which stood on the place where the Thames Street Methodist Church now is. When the town was being fired upon, a cannon ball struck this dwelling, tearing a hole in the wall. Presently one of the slaves of the household was noticed sitting with his back against the aperture; and, upon being questioned by Mr. Mason as to his peculiar attitude, he replied, "Massa, no two balls strike in de same place."

Other places with French associations include the so-called Garretson house, usually known as the Governor Gibbs house, now greatly enlarged, at No. 142 Mill Street, opposite the old historic stone mill. It was occupied by General Nathanael Greene for a short time, and while there he received Lafayette, Baron Steuben and Kosciusko. Former owners have been the Tillinghasts and Tuckermans. Mrs. Marie J. Gale, in her paper on old Newport houses read before the Historical Society of her city, also mentions the George Scott and the Nathaniel Mumford houses, both on Broad Street, now called Broadway, where lived the well-known Deux-Ponts brothers. Chastellux, whose "petits soupers" were eagerly welcomed by the Newporters, lived in the Maudsley house, at 91 Spring Street; Baron Vioménil and his son in the Wanton house, 274 Thames Street; Desandrouins at No. 28 of the same street; Blanchard at No. 78, in the house of Abraham Redwood; de Fersen at 299 New Lane; de Closen next door; Montesquieu in Lewis Street; Destouches at William Redwood's; de Choisy at the Rivera house; and de Charlus at Major Martin's. Many others were quartered in Newport's old houses, according to the list owned by Mr. Drowne of Fraunces' Tavern in New York.

The Old State House, now used as a Court House, overlooking the road leading down to Long Wharf, for a time was used as a hospital for the British wounded, and possibly for some of the French. The French who were incapacitated for service were taken care of in Dr. Hopkins' Congregational Church on Mill Street, now used by the Knights of Columbus, although much altered. During the World War, this old red building served as a Committee House. The State House was decorated when the French fleet arrived, and on the return of peace in 1783 a celebration was held there; at one time the French erected there an altar where Mass was held for the sick and dying. Another residence with a French connection, though not during the Revolution, was the Ayrault house—now torn down—part of the doorway of which is now in the Historical Society; while still another one is the dwelling on the corner of Farwell and Marlborough Streets, which was owned by Dr. Norbert Vigneron, a French Huguenot, about the year 1730.

Another interesting fact made clear by Mrs. Gale is that the white lilac tree on the Church Street property of Dr. David Oliphant, of Revolutionary times, was given to Mrs. Samuel Vernon, a relative and once owner of the premises, by a French officer during the war. An offshoot of this tree now grows in the dooryard of the Newport Historical Society; in fact, most of the lilac trees in Newport are supposed to have grown from slips brought over and presented by Frenchmen.

The French officers, from all accounts, were refined, attractive, considerate and gallant, and their many memoirs give interesting accounts of their life in New England—particularly while in Newport, Providence and Boston—of the many friends they made while in this country, of the manners and customs that made a particular impression upon them, and of the hospitalities received and reciprocated. This indulgence of the French officers in Newport society was evidently encouraged by Rochambeau to lessen the weariness of the long winter. Many of the friendships and romances that happened during these Newport days will never be known; but a few have come down to us, including the story of a French cavalryman who attempted to jump a fence at Castle Hill, then the property of John Collins, Governor of Rhode Island from 1786 to 1790, in order to show off his horsemanship to a young and attractive lady, a relative of the family. The French officer, Du Bourg, declared that the horses in Newport jumped well. Nevertheless, on this occasion the horse hit the jump, we are told, with such force that both mount and rider fell sprawling on the lawn, much to the amusement of the onlookers. A number of the French officers did a good deal of horseback riding over the island, a few being accompanied by "running footmen," an ancient custom of the old nobility.

Stone, in "Our French Allies," describes most attractively the life during this winter:

"The names and traditions of many of the 'Belles of Newport' (in 1780) are preserved with

Kindness of the late John R. Hess

PERRY'S HOUSE, ON THE SOUTH SIDE OF THE MALL, CORNER OF TOURO COURT, NEWPORT, RHODE ISLAND,

supposed by several authorities to have been the headquarters of Aide-de-Camp de Béville. It is near the head of Long Wharf and near the Old State House on the north side of the Mall and Washington Square, opposite Perry Monument. This building was later the property of Commodore Oliver Hazard Perry, a statue of whom is shown in this picture. It is now occupied by the Salvation Army. Another authority placed de Béville at 290 Congress Street.

almost the freshness of yesterday. Polly Lawton (or Leighton, as the name was then pronounced), 'the very pearl of Newport beauties,' and her sister Eliza; Polly Wanton, (Mollie, Amy and Abby Robinson) (Quakeresses) Isabel and Amey Ward, daughters of Governor Richard Ward; Eliza, Katherine and Nancy Hunter; Mehetabel Redwood, daughter of Abraham Redwood, founder of the 'Redwood Library,' Margaret and Mary Champlin, daughters of Christopher Champlin, an enterprising and a successful merchant; Betsey Ellery and her sisters, daughters of William Ellery, signer of the Declaration of Independence. These, with the many susceptible and attentive French officers, gave to social life in Newport a greatly increased brilliancy.''

Of Mrs. Hunter and her daughters, the very gay Duke de Lauzun, a "new Don Juan" (as one writer expressed it), known as the Duc de Biron de la Vendée, one of the most gallant of his time and once Ambassador to London, says:

"Madame Hunter, a widow of some thirty-six years of age, had two [three] charming daughters. . . . Chance introduced me to Madame, on my arrival in Rhode Island. She received me into her friendship, and I was presently regarded as one of the family. I really lived there, and when I was taken seriously ill, she brought me to her house, and lavished upon me the most touching attentions . . . had they been my sisters, I could not have liked them better, especially the eldest, who is one of the most amiable persons I have ever met.''

The impression made on his heart by Katherine Hunter was particularly strong, and on the night before he left Rhode Island for home, with characteristic gallantry, he rode from Providence to Newport in order to pass a final hour with her and to bid her good-bye. On a visit to France she married the Count de Cardigan, a French nobleman, and never returned to America.

Of Miss Champlin, the Prince de Broglie, who, we believe, was a brother-in-law of the Saint Sauveur killed in Boston in a fray, and who visited Newport just before returning to France, was especially enamoured; he wrote of her that,

"Having heard so much in favor of this place, my fellow-travellers and myself were naturally impatient to form the acquaintance of its inhabitants. M. de Vauban did not delay in duly introducing us. On the evening of our arrival he conducted us to the residence of a Mr. Champlin, a man of note on account of his great wealth, and still better known, at least in the army, on account of the beauty of his daughter. Miss Champlin was not in the drawing-room when we made our entrance, but she appeared a moment afterward. It is unnecessary to say that we examined her with great interest. She has fine eyes, a pretty mouth, the freshness of youth, a small waist, and pretty foot, and a figure that leaves nothing to be desired. To all these advantages she added that of being dressed and coiffed with much taste, that is to say, in the French style,—and of understanding and speaking our language.''

Of Christopher Champlin it is said that he used to stand at the stable door beside his saddled horse, while his groom kept watch in the street for the appearance of Martha Redwood Ellery. Occasionally he must have intercepted her, for later they were married. Champlin heard Mirabeau pronounce in Paris the eulogy of Benjamin Franklin. A daughter, Margaret, married a well-known merchant of Newport, Dr. Benjamin Mason.

Of the Misses Hunter, de Broglie said:

"Having paid to all these charms the tribute of admiration and gallantry that was their just due, we hastened to do the same to those of her rivals in beauty and reputation, the Misses Hunter. The elder of the two Misses Hunter, without being regularly beautiful, has what we call 'un ensemble noble et de bonne compagnie,' her face is animated and intelligent, she is graceful in all her movements, and she dresses quite as well as Miss Champlin, but she is not quite so fresh-looking. Her sister, Miss Nancy Hunter, is the very personification of a rose; she is gay, is always smiling, and has, what is very rare in America, beautiful teeth. We returned to our lodgings enchanted with these first samples of the belles of Newport. . . ."

Polly Lawton evidently made a deep impression on him, too, for of her he wrote:

". . . we easily guessed that we were in the house of a Quaker. All of a sudden the door opened, and there entered a very goddess of grace and beauty—Minerva herself, but with her warlike attributes exchanged for the simple garb of a shepherdess. It was the daughter of the Quaker, Polly Lawton. In conformity with the custom of her sect, she addressed us 'en nous tutoyant,' but with a simplicity and grace that was only equalled by the simplicity and grace of her dress: . . . she seemed entirely unsuspicious of her own charms. She addressed us simply and politely, but with all the freedom of her sect. I need not add that we were all enchanted, and I frankly confess that to me this seductive Quakeress seemed to be Nature's masterpiece. Every time that her image presents itself to me I am tempted to write a big book against the follies of dress and against the artificial graces and the coquetry of those ladies whom the world of fashion so highly admires. Polly had a sister, dressed exactly like herself, and who is also very pretty; but we had not time to look at her when her older sister was present."

The Prince then goes on to declare:

"After leaving our pretty Quakeress, I made the acquaintance of Miss Brinley, of Miss Sylven, and of some others, and I was soon fully convinced that Newport fully merited the reputation for beautiful women that it enjoyed in our army. All these young ladies lamented to us that there had been no amusements or conversation parties of any kind since our army had left; and this little complaint induced my companions and myself to get up a ball for their consolation. We experienced no difficulties nor refusals. Some twenty charming ladies and young misses assembled at our invitation. They were all dressed in good taste, and seemed to amuse themselves immensely; at supper we drank 'toasts' with much gayety, and everything passed off very agreeably. The day after this little festival we left Newport to rejoin the army at Providence."

Of Prince de Broglie's entrance into Newport he gives this description:

"We made a day's journey of fifty miles in order to reach New London; but our way was through such a beautiful country and we had such agreeable weather that we had no time to notice the fatigue. There are on this route three villages, about a league's distance from each other, which are remarkable for their charming situation on the banks of a river called the Thames, for their cleanliness, for the regularity of their houses, and for their numerous populations. These three villages

Kindness of the late John R. Hess

GOVERNOR GIBBS HOUSE, 142 MILL STREET, NEWPORT, RHODE ISLAND,

which General Nathanael Greene occupied during part of the war, receiving there visits from Lafayette and other important officers in the army of our allies. This "Mansion" is almost opposite Newport's old historic mill and is now greatly enlarged from the old days. Other owners have been the Tillinghasts and the Tuckermans.

have all the same name: they are called the three Norwiches. New London, on the Thames, about a mile above its mouth, was very rich and prosperous before its destruction by Arnold. . . . It was another long day's journey from New London to Newport over fifty-five miles of very bad roads. There were also two ferries to be crossed. The first one presented no great difficulties; but the second, called 'Canonicut Ferry,' which separates the island of Newport from the mainland, was at least a league in width, and is not always safe; besides, it was after dark when we reached it. The getting of our horses on board of the ferry-boat, and the anxiety of some among us at the frequent rolling of the boat, were not at all amusing, especially in the midst of the darkness which surrounded us. We passed about an hour in this uncomfortable situation, and the boatman finished by running us aground about two hundred yards from the landing-place. As the water was only two feet deep, we all walked ashore, and it was in this way that we made our entrance into the charming town of Newport, whose praises are the constant theme of the soldiers of the French army."

None the less interesting are the recollections of Count de Ségur, who seemed also to have been captivated by some of the same belles of the town, for he wrote:

"We afterwards set off for Newport and journeyed fifty miles upon a road in a shocking condition. This was the first bad road I had met with in the United States. After having passed two ferries, of which the second separates Rhode Island from the continent, we arrived in that island. I was destined, on every occasion, to meet with perils by water whilst I vainly sought to encounter them by land; our boat struck violently and was on the point of being upset; prompt assistance, however, soon extricated us from our perilous situation.

On seeing Newport it was easy to understand the regret felt by the French army on quitting that pretty town where it had so long sojourned. Other parts of America were only beautiful by anticipation, but the prosperity of Rhode Island was already complete; industry, cultivation, activity of trade were all carried to great perfection.

Newport, well and regularly built, contained a numerous population whose happiness was indicated by its prosperity. It offered delightful circles composed of enlightened and modest men and of handsome women, whose talents heightened their personal attractions. All the French officers, who knew them, recollect the names and beauty of Miss Champlin, the two Misses Hunter and of several others.

Like the remainder of my companions, I rendered them the homage to which they were justly entitled; but my longest visits were paid to an old man very silent, who very seldom bared his thoughts and never bared his head. His gravity and monosyllabic conversation announced, at first sight, that he was a Quaker. It must however be confessed that, in spite of all the veneration I felt for his virtue, our first interview would probably have been our last, had I not seen the door of the drawing-room suddenly opened, and a being, which resembled a nymph rather than a woman, enter the apartment. So much beauty, so much simplicity, so much elegance and so much modesty were perhaps never before combined in the same person. It was Polly Leiton (Lawton) the daughter of my grave Quaker. Her gown was white, like herself, whilst her ample muslin neckerchief and the envious cambric of her cap, which scarcely allowed me to see her light-colored hair, and the modest attire in short, of a pious virgin, seemed vainly to endeavor to conceal the most graceful figure and the most beautiful form imaginable.

Her eyes seemed to reflect, as in a mirror, the meekness and purity of her mind and the goodness of her heart; she received us with an open ingenuity which delighted me, and the use of the familiar word 'thou,' which the rules of her sect prescribed, gave to our new acquaintance the appearance of an old friendship.

In our conversations she excited my surprise by the candor full of originality of her questions: 'Thou hast then,' she said, 'neither wife nor children in Europe, since thou leavest thy country and comest so far to engage in that cruel occupation war.' Certain it is that, if I had not then been married and happy, I should, whilst coming to defend the liberty of the Americans, have lost my own at the feet of Polly Lawton."

Of the ball, he said:

"However, as the ladies of Newport had acquired strong claims upon our gratitude by the kind reception they had honored us with, and by the favorable opinion they expressed of our companions in arms, whose absence they deeply regretted, we resolved to give them a magnificent ball and supper.

I quickly sent for some musicians belonging to the regiment of Soissonnais. Desoteux, who since acquired some celebrity during our revolution, as a leader of Chouans, under the name of

Comartin, took upon himself, assisted by Vauban, to make the necessary preparations for the ball and supper, whilst we went about the town distributing our invitations.

This little fête was one of the prettiest I have ever witnessed; it was adorned by beauty, and cordiality presided over the reception and entertainment of the guests; but Polly Leiton (Lawton) could not be present, and I cannot deny that this circumstance occasionally 'cast a gloom over my spirits.' "

The Count de Ségur also referred to another girl, who was very beautiful "malgré les dents."

Some years later, when other distinguished Frenchmen visited this summer resort, the beautiful women, then a good deal older, retold tales of their days,

Kindness of the late John R. Hess

OLD STATE HOUSE, NEWPORT, RHODE ISLAND, *which was decorated when the French fleet arrived. Here on the return of peace in 1783, a celebration was held; also at one time the French erected an altar in the building, where Mass was held for the sick and dying. It was used as a hospital by the English and possibly for a short time by a few French soldiers. It now looks down Washington Square toward Long Wharf, and is at the present time used as a Court House.*

referring jokingly to their French "campaign." Stone, in "Our French Allies," well expresses the Newport of that day: "The youth of today whose highest praise for his fair partner of the Cotillion is often that she is 'an awfully good fellow' has little kinship with his ancestor, who used to wait at the street corner to see the object of his devotion go by under the convoy of her father and mother and a couple of faithful colored footmen, thinking himself happy, meanwhile, if his divinity gave him a shy glance. The gay girl of the period, who scampers in her pony chaise down the avenue, from one engagement to the other, . . . is with all her charms, quite different from the blushing little beauty of 1780, who, in powdered hair, quilted petticoat, and high red-heeled shoes, gave her lover a modest little glance at the street corner, thinking it a most delicious and unforeseen bit of romance to have a lover at all."

Louis, Baron de Closen, one of Rochambeau's aides and a Captain in the Royal Deux-Ponts regiment, in his journal declared Rhode Island "perhaps one of the prettiest islands on the globe" and further tells us that "nature has endowed the ladies of Rhode Island with the handsomest, finest features one can imagine; their complexion is clear and white; their feet and hands usually small." He was also especially surprised at the custom of shaking the hand of everyone on entering a room full of people. About twenty years ago de Closen's memoirs were discovered in Europe and were sent over for President Roosevelt to read, after which they were copied for the Library of Congress in Washington by Worthington C. Ford of the Massachusetts Historical Society. As Rochambeau's aide he travelled a great deal throughout this country, meeting such important men as John Langdon of New Hampshire, Jonathan Trumbull of Connecticut, and John Hancock of Massachusetts, as well as Washington, Lafayette, de Grasse and others. Among these papers was found a portrait of General Washington presented to him by Governor Hancock, and on the back was discovered this inscription written by de Closen himself: "I received this copy from Mister Hancock, and I'll never give it out of my hands. Boston, December, 1781." With these effects was discovered another interesting picture sketched by him and referred to as the "Hat Scene," depicting an incident that took place near Manhattan Island; it is described by him in these words:

"On this occasion my hat had caught itself in the branches of a tree and had fallen to the ground. A false vanity at that moment made me think more of the military derisive proverb, 'Ah, il a perdu son chapeau,' than of danger. I therefore alighted in the midst of a shower of balls for the sake of my hat, and returned some time after to the generals, who had believed me killed. On relating my story, I was laughed at by my comrades for my foolhardiness. The generals even reproached me for my temerity, but General Washington, tapping me on the shoulder, added in his good-natured manner: 'Dear Baron, this French proverb is not yet known among our army, but your cool behaviour during the danger will be.' "

Still another sketch by this French officer shows a page of silhouettes of different beautiful women whom he met in this country, which includes Miss Bowen of Providence and Miss Nancy Hardy of Newport; and on the opposite page appears this description:

"It is solely for the purpose of preserving, 'ad oculos,' the memory of a few pretty persons, more or less kind-hearted and interesting, either because of their good-breeding, education, or talents, and oddity of their coiffures (at that period almost uniform throughout the United States) that I have placed their profiles on the opposite sheet. I venture to claim the indulgence of my friends (in the matter of accuracy and resemblance) for these poor 'ipse feci,' which often amused me while sketching them beside the living originals at our winter headquarters in New England and Virginia."

De Closen then goes on to tell about Newport itself and of the manners of its inhabitants, all of which we cannot believe true even in those days:

"All the estates are enclosed by walls of stones piled one on top of the other or wooden barriers called fences, which produce an attractive effect. Before the war the population numbered 4,000 inhabitants, but on our arrival there remained at the most but 2,600 of which number ¾ were women. . . . There are but two principal streets in Newport. To one unfamiliar with the sight, it seems extraordinary that wooden houses built on stone foundations when entirely finished are often moved from one quarter to another and even moved into the country. The frame as it is, is placed on little carts attached to one another. I have seen them drawn by 30 or 40 oxen or horses. . . . As we begin to understand English better we mingle in the social life of America. I have made the following observations relative to the customs and manners of the leisure class in Newport. Their mode of living has little in common with ours but I can't avoid referring to the good as well as the bad, for the amusement of those who will read this diary. They are absolutely polite and as often as one meets an acquaintance he approaches you and you shake hands in the English manner. A private officer never offers to shake hands with his General, the latter offers his first. Their manners are nevertheless very simple. During a meal one leans against one's neighbor and one sits with one's elbows on the table while eating and what in France would be considered ill bred is here considered quite correct and universally accepted. The personal appearance of the American man in general is careless, almost indifferent, and one cannot but be astonished that with all this apparent indifference, when the occasion presents itself he fights with unquestioned courage and valour. . . . Who would think that the American who scarcely goes out when it rains, when he shoulders his musket unflinchingly faces great dangers and hardships? To return to their social and family life. I noticed that among the two better classes they serve for their breakfast tea or coffee with milk; when they take cream they ask 'how many drops'; slices of buttered and toasted bread, thin slices of ham, salt beef, smoked tongue or smoked fish, all of which quite suits my fancy. . . . One is invited at Christmas as in England to partake of mince pie. As to their drinks, they are multifarious; first of all punch is universally drunk in all well-to-do families and it never ceases to flow from morning till night. Sometimes it is supplemented by a drink called Grog which consists of rum and water, and when sugar or molasses are added it is called Toddy. . . . In many families, even those most highly respectable, the custom of toasting prevails and in spite of oneself one has to pretend to drink. The host always commences the ceremony. . . . Beer although inferior to Porter, is not bad, but as to the 'small beer' it is very poor. Another peculiarity of this country is the absence of napkins even in the homes of the wealthy. Napkins, as a rule, are never used and one has to wipe one's mouth on the tablecloth, which in consequence suffers in appearance. Also the people nearly all of them eat with their knives, like the English, which are round at the point and they do not use forks, which have but two prongs.

I will finish by saying that the fair sex is really quite extraordinary as to their charm and kindness. Nature has vouchsafed the greatest possible beauty of feature, their complexion is white and clear, their hands and feet are as a rule small, but their teeth are inferior, for which the great amount of tea which they drink may be responsible. One rarely sees a woman with a bad figure. Their style of dress and the way of arranging their hair is quite English. Nevertheless, French fashions are not unknown to them and one feels sure that the visit of the French army will have its good influence upon them in this respect. They are fond of dancing which they do most unpretentiously. . . .''

It was only quite natural that the French should amuse themselves, especially when one realizes that it was many months before the soldiers of France heard from home. Tea drinking, a novelty for these foreigners, was continually indulged in to a great extent; and at one of the first of these parties, at which many officers were present, an amusing incident took place. At that time it was customary to place the spoon in the cup when the drinker was satisfied. The servants, who passed the tea—which, by the way, the French claimed was nothing less than hot water—waited for this usual signal; but as it was not forthcoming, they continued to fill the cups until, as the story goes, everyone was thoroughly exhausted. To show how the French officers felt towards the tea-drinking habit, another story is told that an officer of the Hussars naïvely said to Mrs. Wanton, his hostess, on such an occasion, "I shall wish to send dat servant to hell for bringing me so much hot water to drink." Chaplain Robin calls it "an insipid drink" which gives "infinite pleasure" and writes that "the greatest hospitality one can extend is to offer one a cup of tea." According to Thomas Robinson Hazard in his amusing "Johnny-Cake Papers," which describe how a colored cook happened to be the remote cause of the French Revolution and the death of Louis XVI and Marie Antoinette, the negro cooks in Newport were very jealous of those who came over to serve the wants of the French army, declaring that they could provide far better dishes than could the chefs who were with "Old Chambo," "Go to Grass," "Admiral Stang," "Markis Fayette" and "them early Parleyvoos that came to Newport to fight." An abstainer of tea in New England previous to the war wrote these curious lines:

"Farewell the teaboard with its gaudy equipage   With Hyson, Congo and best double-fine.
  Of cups and saucers, cream bucket, sugar tongs, Full many a joyous moment have I sat by ye
  The pretty tea-chest, also lately stored   Hearing the girls tattle, the old maids talk scandal."

As to toasts, de Closen complains that he is "terribly" fatigued by the quantity of healths which are drunk. From one end of the table to the other, a "gentleman pledges you, sometimes with only a glance, which means that you should drink a glass of wine with him, a compliment which cannot be politely ignored." He also refers to fox hunting "through the woods, accompanied by some twenty horsemen. We have forced more than thirty foxes; the packs of hounds owned by these sportsmen are perfect." Rochambeau in his spare time availed himself of this sport. This aide also amusingly refers to the "hard-pressed twitchings of the hands" (in shaking hands) which, he declares, "are certainly on a par with European embracings."

From the pen of Claude Blanchard, Commissary of the French army, comes the following:

"On the 18th, I visited, in company with M. de Rochambeau, an Anabaptist temple, where we established a hospital [probably Dr. Hopkins' church].
On the 20th, I returned to Newport; I there learnt that the 'Isle de France' had put into port at Boston, which was very good news for me, as for everyone else.
On the 24th, the detachment of the regiment of Bourbonnais, which had landed at Boston, arrived at Newport. I saw my brother-in-law, to whom I gave a dinner the next day."

Blanchard was very complimentary of the climate of Rhode Island and of this country in general, making the statement that

"Notwithstanding this changeable weather which I have observed at Rhode Island during the whole winter, the country is healthy, the rest of my sojourn proved it to me.
I was invited to a great farewell dinner on board of the 'Duc de Bourgogne.' There were sixty persons present, several of whom were ladies, of Newport, and the vicinity. The quarter-deck had been arranged with sails, which made a very handsome hall."

Blanchard placed the population of the thirteen States at three million persons.

Chaplain Robin gives a rather curious description of Newport at the time of the landing of the French:

"The arrival of the army of M. le Comte de Rochambeau in Rhode Island spread terror; the Army found the country deserted, and those who came by curiosity to Newport (which is the capital of this province) found the streets empty. The richness of the soil and the mildness of the climate gave it the name of the paradise of New England; its commerce was very flourishing before the war.

All felt the necessity or the importance of dispelling these prejudices. . . . During the sojourn of a year not a single complaint was made. The French at Newport were no longer this frivolous nation, presumptuous, boisterous, ostentatious; at the entertainments they gave they were quiet, retiring, regulating their society to that of their hosts to whom they daily became more and more endeared. These young noblemen blessed with fortune, birth and the surroundings of the life at Court, who had been dissipated and accustomed to luxury, and to all the pomp of a great position, were the first to offer an example of the simplicity of a frugal life; they were affable and popular."

A tale is told of a French dentist in Newport, who some years after the war noticed a French vessel arriving in the harbour. Happening also to note that the newcomers spent very much money along Thames Street, he finally had the captain and crew locked up. They were found to be notorious pirates; and when this dentist returned to the town after a visit to his native country, it was noticed that he wore a red ribbon in his buttonhole. One of the saddest occurrences during the winter at Newport was the suicide of Laforest, a Captain in the Saintonge regiment, who insulted his superior officer, Count de Custine, and was so mortified that he killed himself in despair. It is not certain where this unfortunate officer was buried. Another officer committed suicide while in Newport, leaving a letter saying, "I defeat death as gayly and almost as eagerly as when our friend General Wayne sent me to attack Lord Cornwallis, and I hope that I may succeed better in outflanking life than I did in outflanking the English army." As to the resting place of other French soldiers, Stone, in "Our French Allies," mentions that the probable interment place was in the Burial-Ground Common; but there is no gravestone nor monument set up to their memory, as is the case in Providence. For Trinity Church and the French graves there, we reserve a special chapter.

Crèvecœur was another Frenchman who wrote later of Newport that "a man can farm with one hand and fish with the other. Here is the best blood in America, and the beauty of the women, the hospitality of the inhabitants, the sweet society, and the simplicity of their amusements have always prolonged my stay." He also describes it as the "healthiest country I know. Why might not this charming island be called the Montpelier of America?"

There was much rivalry between Newport and Providence, and, as the population of the latter place forged ahead, the Newporters are reported to have stated that they could still boast and console themselves in the fact that their ancestral chairs were more difficult to lift than the newer and lighter chairs used by the Providence people.

When the French left the town, it is said there was many a despondent female,—a fact that brought forth these lines:

"They say she died of a broken heart
  (I tell the tale as 'twas told to me);
But her spirit still lives, and her soul is part
  Of this sad old house by the sea.

Her lover was fickle and fine and French:
  It was nearly a hundred years ago
When he sailed away from her arms—poor wench—
  With the Admiral Rochambeau.

And ever since then, when the clock strikes two
  She walks unbidden from room to room,
And the air is filled that she passes through
  With a subtle, sad perfume."

INDIANS VISIT ROCHAMBEAU AT NEWPORT

ONE of the oddest and most interesting incidents that took place in Newport during the encampment there of the French army was the visit on the 29th of August, 1780, of some Iroquois Indian chiefs from Canada and the northern part of New York State, and other redskins from the Falls of St. Louis, not far from Albany. Many of the Iroquois had been very friendly to the French in former times, and when M. de Vaudreuil surrendered Canada he gave a golden crucifix and a watch to many of the redskins. Rochambeau deemed it wise to keep alive this amicable feeling by inviting them to visit the French army in Newport to witness the friendship that existed between the Americans and their foreign allies.

Their journey led them through Providence, where they were entertained at Aldrich's Hotel, James Deane acting as their interpreter during their trip from the north. Their visit in Newport is best described by Blanchard, the French Commissary:

"Among them was a mulatto, who had served with the Americans; he spoke French and they called him Captain Louis. . . . The only clothing which these savages had was a blanket in which they wrapped themselves; they had no breeches. Their complexion is olive, they have their ears gashed and their faces daubed with red. There were some handsome men among them and some tall old men of respectable appearance. . . . These savages, for a long time friendly to the French and who, in speaking of the King of France, called him 'our father,' complimented M. de Rochambeau, who received them very kindly and gave them some presents, among other things some red blankets which had been greatly recommended to us at our departure from Brest. . . . They dined that day with him at his quarters. I saw them at table for an instant, they behaved themselves well there and ate cleanly enough."

It must have been a curious sight, indeed, to see these rough and half-naked savages feasting with the courtly and gayly-dressed French officers. As a Newporter wrote: "Here were to be seen the extremes of the civilized and savage life. An Indian chief, in his savage habits, and the Count Rochambeau, in his splendid uniform, talked with each other as if they had been the subjects of the same government, generals in the same army, and partakers of the same blessings of civilized life." To the chiefs, medals were given on which the coronation of the French king was represented, and, in return, as de Closen writes in his diary, they "left their sandals, belts and other trifles."

"In the afternoon [continues Blanchard] the troops were shown to them, who manœuvred and went through the firing exercises; they showed no surprise, but seemed to be pleased with this exhibition. On the next day they dined on board the 'Duc de Bourgogne.' In the evening they were persuaded to dance; their singing is monotonous, they interrupted it with sharp and disagreeable cries. In singing, they beat time with two little bits of wood. In dancing, they content themselves with bending the hams without taking any steps; there is no jumping, no springing; they reminded me of those peasants in my province when they tread the grapes in the winepress; the movement which they then make resembles the dance of these savages."

Lieutenant Jean Baptiste Robertnier in his diary in the collection of the late George L. Shepley refers to this war dance. "These men," he wrote, "gave an exhibition of their games, of their dances and the way in which they scalp their enemies," which latter event made a deep impression upon the French.

On the fourth day the visitors, greatly pleased by the entertainment, departed, leaving with General Rochambeau the impression which he expressed in these words:

"The different deputations of savages who came to the camp showed no surprise at the sight of the cannons, troops and their exercises; but they did not recover from their astonishment at seeing the apple trees laden with fruit above the tents which the soldiers had occupied for three months. One of the chiefs of the savages, . . . made to me, in a public audience, a reflection that surprised me. 'My father,' said he, 'it is very astonishing that the King of France, our father, sends his troops to protect the Americans in an insurrection against the King of England, their father.' 'Your father, the King of France,' I replied, 'protects the natural liberty that God has given to man.'"

General Washington, hearing of this event, wrote: "The visit you have had from the Indians gives me great pleasure. I felicitate you on that [visit] which you must have had in the company of such agreeable and respectable guests. I dare say the reception they met with will have a good effect."

Chevalier Pontgibaud relates an incident in connection with an Indian who joined the army. While the French officers were dining at headquarters, a redskin entered the room, quite unconcerned, walked up to the table and proceeded to stretch out his tattooed arm, grabbing a large joint of hot roast beef, which he began to devour at the door of the tent.

The General Assembly at Providence entertained the chiefs on their return journey at Hacker's Hall, on South Main Street, where Rochambeau, General Sullivan, and other distinguished persons were from time to time received. Joshua Hacker, the owner of the building, sailed a packet between Providence and Newport for many years. This meeting at Newport had the desired result of keeping the Indians neutral during this entire campaign of the French in America.

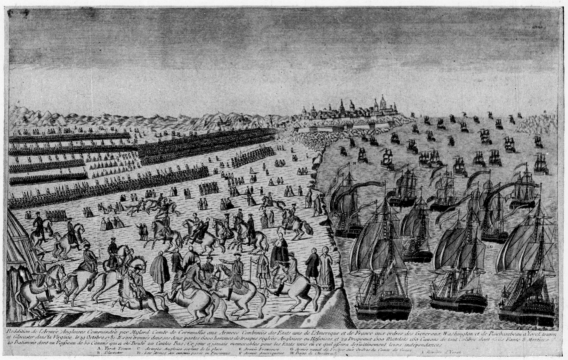

From an old print   *Kindness of E. F. Bonaventure and Gaston Liebert*

THE FRENCH FLEET AND THE ALLIED ARMIES RECEIVING THE SURRENDER OF YORKTOWN

THE DEATH OF A GREAT FRENCH ADMIRAL

ON the sixteenth of December, 1780, there was borne to his last resting place in Trinity Churchyard, in Newport, R.I., amid much pomp and ceremony, the well-known Charles Louis d'Arsac de Ternay, Admiral of the fleet that brought over Rochambeau and the French troops. We have several vivid accounts of this sad ceremony. Sidney Everett writes: " . . . the cortège—the most imposing ever witnessed in these streets, to the grave, where the priests, nine in number, chanted the funeral service, and the sailors who bore the corpse slowly resigned it to the earth. . . ." Stone, in "Our French Allies," quotes the words of Thomas Hornsby, an old chronicler: "From him I heard the story of the French Admiral de Ternay's death and funeral. . . . When quite a youth, he went, with those appointed for the purpose, into the chamber where the Admiral died and saw the body placed in the coffin. Every mark of honor was paid to the remains of the brave Admiral. The catafalque upon which he was placed was draped in black crêpe, but its distinctive decoration was the national flag, with the hat, the epaulettes and the sword of the deceased, together with the medals of honor he had received and the insignia of the Orders to which he belonged. . . . Dying in the Wanton house in Washington Street, the Admiral was carried from thence to Trinity church-yard by a select body of sailors from his own flag-ship. The funeral cortège was very imposing, as it took its way along Washington Street, up the long wharf, through Thames Street, and up Church Street. The bands of the army and navy played their mournful and melancholy strains as the brilliant procession passed along the streets. Every eligible place was used by the people to witness the scene; every window and housetop was crowded along the way. There, in the procession near the bier of their late commander, appeared the most distinguished Captains of the French navy, with badges of mourning. In the funeral train the forces of the navy were quite numerous. . . . All eyes were directed upon the more celebrated officers of the French army. The body of the French Admiral was carried into the church-yard by a select number of French sailors. . . . The coffin was sadly lowered into the grave, which was prepared for the Admiral in the north-east part of Trinity church-yard. The troops gave their last salute to their brave commander, and left him to sleep in the American soil, under the protecting care of the American flag. . . . The people were deeply impressed by this strange, fascinating and mournful scene."

Another contemporaneous account of his death appeared in the *Gazette Françoise*, a rare and interesting French newspaper printed on the press of the fleet at Newport in 1780 and 1781; under date of December 15 it records that "Charles Louis de Ternai, Knight of the Order of St. John of Jerusalem, commander of the squadron of naval forces, former Governor of the Isles of France and Bourbon, commandant of the French squadron on the coasts of North America, died today in this city. His talents, his enthusiasm and his distinguished services have given him the confidence and favor of the Government of his country, and his death fills the navy and army with sorrow. The command of the fleet now passes into the hands of M. Destouches, captain of a vessel, brigadier in the naval forces, an officer very highly esteemed by the entire personnel of the French navy and one who particularly distinguished himself in the battle of Ouessant." One of the few copies of this newspaper was recently discovered by Mr. Chapin of the Rhode Island Historical Society, which is now its possessor. The Royal Printing Office of the Squadron was at No. 641 Rue de la Point, at one time Water

Photographed by the late John R. Hess   *Kindness of the late John R. Hess*

TRINITY CHURCH, NEWPORT, RHODE ISLAND

Admiral de Ternay's tomb can be seen near the corner of the churchyard on the right near the fence. The tablet shown in another illustration is placed over the grave, and the large marble slab with a long inscription formerly was over his tomb, but now is in the western end of the church under the tower. Two other important French officers, de Fayolles and de Valernais, lie in the same burial ground, but their remains have never been found.

Street, and now called Washington Street. The pamphlet just issued by the Historical Society explains that this is probably the first service newspaper ever published by an expeditionary force; it was one of the few newspapers printed in America during the Revolutionary War, and was the only one printed in French.

This was probably the largest and most important funeral that had ever taken place in Newport up to that time—the procession, headed by chanting priests, reaching from the old house in Washington Street, where he died, to Trinity Church on Church Street. It is worthy of record to note that this church, though Protestant, welcomed to its churchyard the remains of the distinguished Frenchman, allowing the Roman Catholic service to be said over his grave.

Admiral de Ternay died in the house of Dr. William Hunter on Washington Street, also known as the Joseph Wanton house, the attractive dwelling now belonging to St. Joseph Convent and described more fully in the chapter "With the French at Newport." The same chronicler (Hornsby), quoted before, states that the Admiral died in the southeast chamber, and mentions also that the room directly underneath was used as the treasure room of the French army. A picture is shown in the chapter above referred to. The Admiral had been suffering from gout before leaving France, and while with Rochambeau en route to Hartford about three months before, to meet General Washington, he became seriously ill. In October he contracted a fever, and a few days before his death his physician, who visited him aboard his flag-ship, the "Duc de Bourgogne," ordered his removal to shore to his headquarters in the Hunter-Wanton house. It is an interesting fact to remember that General Rochambeau at that time was in Boston on his only visit to this city and that Baron Vioménil sent a courier to notify him of the death of his fellow officer, whereupon he promptly returned to Newport. Blanchard says little about his compatriot de Ternay, referring to his illness and death in these few words: "On the 14th I went to Newport by sea in an American vessel which was struck by a gale of wind and was nearly upset; we were laden with wood, even upon deck. The cold was very severe. M. the Chevalier de Ternay, the commander-in-chief of the squadron, had been sick for several days and had just been taken on shore; Mr. Corte, our chief physician, had been sent for, who told us that he found him very ill. On the 15th, M. de Ternay fell a victim to his disease; it was putrid fever. M. de Rochambeau was not then at Newport; he had gone to Boston. On the 16th,

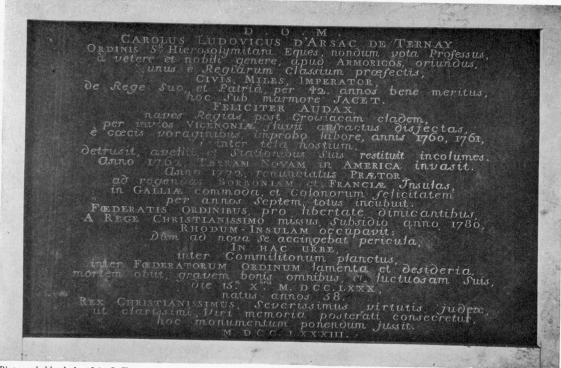

Photographed by the late John R. Hess

Kindness of the late John R. Hess

TABLET TO ADMIRAL DE TERNAY IN TRINITY CHURCH, NEWPORT, RHODE ISLAND

It is of black Egyptian marble, and was placed over the Admiral's grave by the King of France a few years after peace was declared. Some of the officers of the French frigate "Meduse," while in Newport Harbour in 1794, had it removed to the outer north wall of the church; in 1872, de Noailles had the present tablet placed over the grave and this memorial removed to the western vestibule of the church. A translation of part of the inscription, which is in gold letters, appears in the text.

fine weather, M. de Ternay was buried with great pomp; all the land forces were under arms."

Soon after peace was declared, the King of France placed, in the year 1785, a memorial in the shape of a small stone building over de Ternay's grave and over it a slab of black Egyptian marble, recounting in gold Latin letters his services for France, beginning with the words:

In the name of GOD | CHARLES LOUIS D'ARSAC DE TERNAY | Knight of the Order of St. John of Jerusalem, | Though the Vows of the Order he had never acknowledged, | descended from an ancient and noble Family of Bretagne | One of the Admirals of the King's Fleets, | a Citizen, a Soldier, a Chief, | serviceably faithful to his King and to his Country, | for 42 Years, | now rests beneath this marble.

and ending with this description of his part played in the Revolution:

Being ordered by His Most Christian Majesty in the | year 1780, with Assistance to the United States, engaged | in the Defence of Liberty—he arrived in Rhode Island | when, while he was prepared to encounter the Dangers of his | Command, | To the inconsolable Grief of his Fellow-Soldiers, | To the sincere Sorrow of the United States, | He expired in this City, | Regretted by all the Good; but particularly lamented by | those to whom he was related, | December 15th, M. DCC. LXXX, | Aged 58. | His Most Christian Majesty, strictly just to Merit, | In order that the Memory of this illustrious Man | might be consecrated to Posterity, | Hath ordered this Monument to be erected, | M. DCC. LXXXIII.

This slab became so broken that some officers from the French frigate "Meduse," which was riding at anchor in Newport Harbour in the year 1794, directed that the building be demolished and the monumental slab be placed against the outer north wall of the church, where it remained some years. The larger marble slab, with the long inscription, hitherto placed against the outer wall of the church, was at the same time renovated and removed to the western vestibule, where it is to be seen in an upright position with the marble insignia of the order of the Knights Hospitalers of St. John of Jerusalem, of which the dead Admiral was a member.

Stone again makes this statement in regard to the burial place: "In the course of years, subsequent to the removal of the monument from Admiral de Ternay's grave, the public had forgotten the spot where he was buried, and in 1850 but one citizen of Newport was living who could point it out. That was the late Dr. David King. In early youth, the location had been shown to him by an aged man who was present at the interment, and who saw the coffin lowered into the grave. Ever after having received this information, Dr. King kept the spot in view."

Dr. King received this information from the Newport antiquarian, Thomas Hornsby, and through him he was able to locate the grave. ". . . On the 29th of October, in 1850," said Dr. King, "finding a new grave made in that portion of the church-yard, I became apprehensive for the safety of the remains of the French Admiral, and instituted, immediately, some explorations by means of which I discovered the precise place of his burial. The gratifying result was, that the grave of the Admiral was easily found in the north-east part of the church-yard, about three feet below the surface of the ground, and to restore monuments which had been neglected, I obtained the consent of the committee to place over the grave of the French Admiral some large slabs, whose inscriptions had been effaced by time. The Admiral's grave remained in this state until the summer of 1872." During that year, the Marquis de Noailles, a relative of Lafayette, then French Minister at Washington, noticed that the masonry over the grave was crumbling, and ordered the present new granite stone, about six feet square, to be placed over it, bearing this inscription:

HOC SUB LAPIDE | ANNO MDCCCLXXIII POSITO | JACET | CAROLVS LVDOVICVS D'ARSAC | DE TERNAY | ANNO MDCCLXXX | DECESSVS | SUB PROXIMI TEMPLI PORTICVM | ANTIQVVM MONVMENTVM | RESTAVRATVM ET PROTECTVM | TRANSLATVM | EST

The translation is: "Beneath this Stone placed in the year 1873 lies Charles Louis d'Arsac de Ternay who died in the year 1780. Beneath the porch of the church nearby the ancient monument restored and sheltered lies removed."

In December, 1873, not many months after de Noailles had repaired his compatriot's burial place, Senator Henry S. Anthony introduced a bill in the United States Senate appropriating the sum of eight hundred dollars to "defray the expense of repairing and protecting from decay the monument erected at Newport, Rhode Island, to the memory of the Chevalier de Ternay, the commander of

Photographed by the late John R. Hess   *Kindness of the late John R. Hess*

GRAVE OF ADMIRAL DE TERNAY IN THE NORTH–EAST PART OF TRINITY CHURCHYARD, NEW-PORT, RHODE ISLAND

In 1873 the Marquis de Noailles placed this granite block over the grave and the larger slab inside the church.
A translation is in the text.

the French naval forces in aid of the American Revolution, in 1780, the money hereby appropriated to be expended under the direction of the Secretary of the Navy.

"The Chevalier de Ternay remained in command of the French naval forces in America till his death, which occurred on the 15th of the following December, very suddenly, at the house of Dr. William Hunter, the father of William Hunter, who was twice elected a member of this body, and afterwards was appointed minister to Brazil. The grandfather of William Hunter was for a long time connected with the Department of State.

"With the liberality in religious matters which, from the beginning, has distinguished the people of Rhode Island, a portion of a Protestant cemetery was set apart for his burial, and consecrated according to the rites of the Roman Catholic Church. . . ."

The bill also passed the House without a dissenting voice. In his speech, Senator Anthony said: ". . . And let the coming generations be taught that those who contribute to the defence, the advancement, the renown of the Great Republic, shall never be forgotten, but shall live in grateful remembrance, coeval with its immortal life." In the House, Hon. B. T. Eames said: "France, in aid of the colonies in their struggle for independence, expended upwards of fourteen hundred thousand francs, and laid upon the altar of liberty the sacrifice, not only of this treasure, but also the lives of many of her brave soldiers and sailors, and stood nobly and faithfully by her guarantee until the close of the contest. And it seems to me that this recognition is demanded on the part of the government of the United States in grateful remembrance of the aid of France, and as a means of keeping fresh in the memory of the American people her invaluable services, as well as of assuring the French people that, although the lapse of nearly a century may obliterate the inscription on the monument, erected by the French King in memory of this distinguished naval officer, yet it can never obliterate or efface from the hearts of the American people a grateful recollection of the generous support and sympathy of France in our struggle for national life." Soon after the passage of this bill, the Marquis de Noailles addressed this letter of appreciation to the sponsor of the bill:

"WASHINGTON, December 20th, 1873.

My dear Senator:

I have read with a deep feeling of gratitude, the bill passed on the 16th of December by the Senate, concerning the sepulchral monument of the Chevalier de Ternay. If anything could add to the value of such a manifestation of the most delicate sentiment, it would be the courteous manner in which this bill has been passed and adopted by unanimous consent. The French Government and the French people will certainly be extremely sensible of such a proof of the pious recollection which the present generation preserves of what has been done in former times, and it becomes my pleasant duty to remark that in American hearts, if I may use here a metaphor which does not seem foreign to the subject, the memory of the aid given by France to the young Republic has been more lasting than the Egyptian marble erected in the tomb of de Ternay. . . ."

The American Minister at Paris sent a copy of the bill to the French Minister of Foreign Affairs, the Duc de Cazas, which was answered by the latter under date of January 14, 1874.

"My dear Minister, [he said in part] I thank you for your note enclosing the speech of Mr. Anthony in support of the appropriation for the restoration of the tomb of the Admiral d'Arsac de Ternay, who died during the war of independence.

. . . I deem myself fortunate in the occasion to assure you how promptly the generous sentiments expressed on the other side of the Atlantic have found an echo in the hearts of the French people and of the government. The memories evoked in such felicitous terms by the Senator from Rhode Island, are equally precious to your country and to our own; and the eloquent voice which recalls to the attention of the living generation the achievements in which Admiral d'Arsac de Ternay bore a part, is heard with the same pleasure in Paris as in Washington. . . .

DUC DE CAZAS."

Photographed by the late John R. Hess   *Kindness of the late John R. Hess*

TRINITY CHURCH, NEWPORT, RHODE ISLAND

In the northeast corner of the burial ground is the grave of Admiral de Ternay. Two other French officers, de Fayolles and de Valernais, are buried somewhere in the same churchyard. Newporters in the old days used to say that their city compared favorably with London and Paris, and one writer declared that he had seen the dome of St. Peter's in Rome, and the top of Mont Blanc, neither of which he thought half as high as Trinity Church steeple at that time.

Rochambeau wrote of the distinguished Admiral who brought him and his troops to this country: "His greatest enemies can never deny that he had great probity, and that he was a very skillful navigator. The French Corps rendered him the justice to say that it was impossible to conduct a convoy with greater vigilance and skill than he displayed in bringing it to its destination." Count de Ségur declares him as a "man of information, brave, animated and pleasing; one who discharged his duties with as much intelligence as honor." The Newport *Mercury*, of December 22, 1780, says: "His talents, zeal, and distinguished services had merited the confidence and favor of his government and country."

Lafayette's opinion of de Ternay was not quite so complimentary, for he states in a letter to his wife: "The French squadron has remained blockaded in Rhode Island, and I imagine the Chevalier Ternay died of grief in consequence of this event. However this may be, he is positively dead. He was a very rough and obstinate man, but firm and clear in all his views, and, taking all things into consideration, we have sustained a great loss."

An interesting delegation, consisting of René, Comte de Rochambeau and Comte Salume de Lafayette and eighteen others, after witnessing the unveiling of the Rochambeau statue in Washington in the spring of 1902, visited Newport on their way to Boston and laid a wreath on de Ternay's grave. On its way to Trinity Church, the parade in which they were escorted passed by the Vernon house, and before leaving town the French insisted upon visiting the inside of the "Old Mansion," where the ancestor of one of the delegation had resided.

Miss M. E. Powel, who has made an extensive study of the French while in Newport, recalls that in the spring of 1920, the Saturday Club of the town placed upon de Ternay's grave a triple offering of white lilac blossoms. One spray was in memory of the French Admiral, the two others being placed there in honor of two other important Frenchmen whose remains lie somewhere in the same churchyard—de Fayolles and de Valernais. An account of this event was printed in a French newspaper, and one of the descendants of the Admiral sent a letter of thanks. De Fayolles, who by the way is doubtless an ancestor of General Fayolles of the World War, commander of the Americans on the Aisne-Marne and a visitor to New England soon after the War, was commissioned by Deane as a Lieutenant-Colonel in our army and served as an aide to Lafayette. He died on the eve of sailing, in the year 1777. De Valernais was wounded on the "Hermione" in a battle off the end of Long Island in June, 1780, and was brought to Newport, where he died a month later, Trinity Church recording that he "was buried in the churchyard on the 22d of July, 1780, with military honors." The only grave that can now be discerned, that of de Ternay, is consecrated by the Roman Catholics, and usually a joint service of Catholics and Protestants is held on Bastille Day and on Decoration Day, at which times, flowers, bound with the French colors, are laid on the final resting place of the French Admiral who gave his life for our cause.

Another French name associated with Trinity is the Huguenot Ayrault, who is buried near the gate of the churchyard of this old church—one of the most beautiful in all New England.

GENERAL WASHINGTON VISITS ROCHAMBEAU AT NEWPORT

O N the sixth of March, 1781, three months before the French army left Newport, Washington visited General Rochambeau to consult with him and to hasten the sailing of the expedition under M. Destouches, who temporarily had replaced de Ternay. The two generals had met in September of the year previous at Hartford. Of the arrival of the chief of our forces the French Commissary, Blanchard, makes this record in his diary:

"This day (5th) General Washington, who was expected, arrived about two o'clock. He first went to the 'Duc de Bourgogne,' where all our generals were. He then landed; all the troops were under arms; I was presented to him. His face is handsome, noble and mild. He is tall (at least five feet, eight inches). In the evening, I was at supper with him. I mark, as a fortunate day, that in which I have been able to behold a man so truly great. . . ."

As Washington landed at Long Wharf by way of Conanicut ferry, he was saluted by the French fleet and was received by the army of the allies drawn up in double lines all the way from the landing past the State House to Rochambeau's headquarters in the Vernon house. Here he was the Frenchman's guest. This notable occasion is best described by Hon. Daniel Updike:

"I never felt the solid earth tremble under me before. The firing from the French ships that lined the harbor was tremendous; it was one continued roar, and looked as though the very bay was on fire. Washington, as you know, was a Marshal of France; he could not command the French army without being invested with that title. He wore on this day the insignia of his office, and was received with all the honors due to one in that capacity. It is known that many of the flower of the French nobility were numbered in the army that acted in our defence. Never will that scene be erased from my memory. The attitudes of the nobles, their deep obeisance, the lifting of hats and caps, the waving of standards, the sea of plumes, the long line of French soldiers, and the general disposition of their arms, unique to us, separating to the right and left, the Chief, with Count Rochambeau on his left, unbonneted, walked through. The French nobles, commanders, and their under officers, followed in the rear. Count Rochambeau was a small, keen-looking man, not handsome as was his son, afterwards Governor of Martinique . . . the resplendent beauty of the two Viomésnils eclipsed all the rest. They were brothers, and one of them a General in the army, who bore the title of Count, too. Newport never saw anything so handsome as these two brothers. I thought, as the breeze lifted the shining curls from the fair forehead of the elder Viomésnil, and discovered the sparkling eyes, and blooming cheeks, and wonderfully fine mouth, that nothing could surpass him; but when I looked at his brother, I was puzzled to tell which was the handsomest.

But we, the populace, were the only ones that looked at them, for the eye of every Frenchman was directed to Washington. Calm and unmoved by all the honors that surrounded him, the voice of adulation or the din of battle had never disturbed the equanimity of his deportment. There were other officers of inferior grade too that followed, and I afterwards saw them on horseback, but they did not sit on a horse like Washington. The roofs and windows of every house in sight were filled with the fair part of creation; and oh! the fluttering of handkerchiefs, and showing of favors! It was a proud day for Newport."

De Closen also gives an excellent account of Washington's arrival in his unpublished diary, often referred to by us. He speaks of the American General as a man of simple manners, of affable character, and of great bravery.

A review of the troops by the two Generals was the next event on the program, the Newport *Mercury* giving this excellent account of it:

"In the evening of the day that Washington arrived, the town and fleet in the harbor were beautifully illuminated. At that time comparatively few were able to take part in the joyful ceremony; but that all should share in the honors paid to so distinguished a visitor, the Town Council ordered that candles should be purchased and given to all who were too much distressed through continued losses, to purchase for themselves, so that every house should show a light. The procession was led off by thirty boys, bearing candles fixed on staffs, followed by General Washington, Count Rochambeau, and the other officers, their aides, and the procession of citizens. The night was clear, and there was not a breath to fan the torches. The brilliant procession marched through the principal streets, and then returned to the headquarters.

An anecdote is related of Washington at this time. A little boy had heard so much of Washington that he conceived a strong desire to see him. His father, to gratify his wish, lifted him in his arms and approached an open window, near which Washington stood, whom he pointed out. The child was amazed, and exclaimed aloud, 'Why, father, General Washington is a man!' It reached the ear of the hero, who turned round and said, as he patted the boy on the head, 'Yes, my lad, and nothing but a man.' "

Photographed through the courtesy of the late John R. Hess

From a picture in the collection of the late George L. Shepley

HOUSE AT TIVERTON HEIGHTS OCCUPIED BY LAFAYETTE

as his headquarters either before or after the battle of Rhode Island. There is a Lafayette Road below Tiverton not far from here.

In response to an address of the Town Committee, Washington in part replied:

"My happiness," he said, "is complete in the moment that unites the expressions of their sentiments for me with their suffrages in favor of our allies. The conduct of the French army and fleet, of which the inhabitants testify so grateful and so affectionate a sense, at the same time that it evinces the wisdom of the commanders and the discipline of the troops, is a new proof of the magnanimity of the nation. It is a further demonstration of that generous zeal and concern for the happiness of America which brought them to our assistance, a happy presage of future harmony—a pleasing evidence that an intercourse between the two nations will more and more cement the union by the solid and lasting ties of mutual affection."

In the evening there was a gay ball at Mrs. Cowley's Assembly Room on Church Street, so frequently used for entertainments by the American and French officers during that winter. Washington opened the ball with Margaret Champlin, noted for her beauty and charm, who selected the popular dance, "A Successful Campaign." It is said that the French officers spontaneously grabbed the musical instruments from the musicians and played for the General and his beautiful partner. This was an event long remembered by the American and French who were fortunate enough to be present. An eye witness wrote:

"At the brilliant affair held at Mrs. Cowley's Assembly Rooms, the noble dames, 'though robbed of their wealth by war,' appeared in superb brocades with embroidered petticoats and were pleased to 'foot it' with such noblemen as de Ségur, M. Vauban, Baron de Viomésnil, and De Latouche for partners. The favorite dance of the moment was 'Stony Point' because of its recent successful storming by General Wayne. The soft light from silver candelabra was reflected in beautiful mirrors loaned from old mansions, as Washington opened the ball with beautiful Miss Champlin under festoons of bunting looped with rosettes of swords and pistols; Rochambeau, wearing the Grand Croix de l'Ordre Royal, and his suite took the instruments and played the dance selected by the partner of General Washington, 'A Successful Campaign' followed by 'Pea Straw' and 'I'll be Married in my Old Clothes' and 'Boston's Delight,' in honor of the guests from that city."

Another occasion of interest was a tea given by Christopher Ellery which was attended by a number of French officers. Metcalf Bowler, a prominent merchant of the town and probably the builder of the Vernon house, also gave a dinner party of eight to Washington, and among the guests were General Rochambeau and other Frenchmen. Stone, in "Our French Allies," gives an account of an amusing incident that took place during this occasion: "Mr. Bowler had caused to be prepared for the occasion a dozen bottles of cider made from the sunny-side half of mellow Rhode Island greenings, which he labeled 'Eden Champagne.' This, with two of the best brands of French Champagne, he placed before his guests, requesting their opinion of the merits of each. The Frenchmen, after a dozen bottles had been emptied, testified that never in France had they tasted anything as delicious as this 'Eden Champagne.' When the fact came to be revealed that this delicious beverage, which the French gentlemen declared 'could be no other than the fabled nectar of the gods,' was simply Rhode Island greening cider, Parson Hopkins, one of the guests, was heard to remark that 'he should always henceforth have more charity for Mother Eve's unfortunate slip!' "

Washington left Newport on the 13th for New Windsor, his departure being saluted by the French with thirteen guns from the artillery, while the French army was drawn up in line. Rochambeau escorted him some distance out of town, Count Dumas and other officers of the French army accompanying him as far as Providence. While at Warren, where the inhabitants turned out to give him an enthusiastic greeting, Washington turned to Count Dumas, who was by his side, and said, "We may be beaten by the English; it is the chance of war; but here is an army they can never conquer." His stay in Providence was the occasion for a brilliant military ball, probably held, as usual, in Hacker's Hall, at which Dumas was also present as representative of France. Our foreign allies to a man seemed to have been much impressed by the American Commander-in-Chief. Count Dumas, who met him first at Newport, said that "his dignified address, his simplicity of manners and mild gravity surpassed our expectation, and won every heart."

"His physiognomy," says Commissary Blanchard, "has something grave and serious, but it is never stern, and, on the contrary, becomes softened by the most gracious and amiable smiles. He is affable, and converses with his officers familiarly and gayly."

The Prince de Broglie was equally enthusiastic, writing that "in his private conduct he preserves that polite and attentive good breeding which satisfies everybody and offends no one. He is a foe to ostentation and to vain-glory."

Marquis de Chastellux declared: "The continent of North America, from Boston to Charleston, is a great volume, every page of which presents his eulogium. . . . It is not my intention to exaggerate. I wish only to express the impression General Washington has left on my mind. Brave without temerity, laborious without ambition, generous without prodigality, noble without pride, virtuous without severity, he seems always to have confined himself within those limits, where the virtues, by clothing themselves in more lively but more changeable and doubtful colors, may be mistaken for faults. . . . It will be said of him, at the end of a long civil war, he had nothing with which he could reproach himself."

Photographed through the courtesy of the late John R. Hess

DENNIS HOUSE, PORTSMOUTH, RHODE ISLAND, OCCUPIED BY LAFAYETTE AS HIS HEADQUARTERS
It is on the east road near Bristol ferry and Butts Hill Fort. It was recently presented to the Newport Historical Society.

Several summers ago, the people of Newport gave a representation of Washington's visit, with the minuet danced as of old.

The following verses, written by Governor Van Zandt and entitled "The Romance of a Rose," are well worthy of repetition:

It is nearly a hundred years ago,
Since the day that the Count de Rochambeau,
Our Ally against the foreign crown,
Met Washington in Newport town.

'Twas the month of March and the air was chill;
Yet, bareheaded, over Aquidneck hill,
Guest and host they took their way,
While on either side was a grand array

Of a gallant army, French and fine,
Ranged three deep in a glittering line;
And the French fleet sent a welcome roar
Of a hundred guns from Conanicut shore.

And the bells rang out from every steeple,
While from street to street the Newport people
Followed and cheered with a hearty zest
De Rochambeau and his honored guest.

And women out of the window leant,
And out of the window smiled and sent
Many a coy admiring glance
To the fine young officer of France.

And the story goes that the belle of the town
Kissed a rose, and flung it down
Straight at the feet of de Rochambeau;
And the gallant Marshal, bending low,

Lifted it up with a Frenchman's grace
And kissed it back, with a glance at the face
Of the daring maiden where she stood
Blushing out of her silken hood.

That night at the ball, still the story goes,
The Marshal of France wore a faded rose
In his gold-laced coat; but he looked in vain
For the giver's beautiful face again.

Night after night and day after day,
The Frenchman eagerly sought, they say,
At feast, or at church, or along the street
For the girl who flung her rose at his feet.

And she, night after night and day after day,
Was speeding farther and farther away
From the fatal window and fatal street
Where her passionate heart had suddenly beat

A throb too much for the cool control
A Puritan teaches from heart and soul;
A throb too much for the wrathful eyes
Of one who had watched in dismayed surprise

From the street below; and taking the gage
Of a woman's heart in a moment of rage,
He swore, this old colonial squire,
That before the daylight should expire,

This daughter of his with her wit and grace,
And her dangerous heart and her beautiful face,
Should be on her way to a sure retreat
Where no rose of hers should fall at the feet

Of a cursèd Frenchman, high or low;
And so while the Count de Rochambeau
In his gold-laced coat wore a faded flower
And awaited the giver, hour by hour,

She was sailing away in the wild March night,
On the little deck of the sloop "Delight,"
Guarded even in the darkness there,
By the watchful eyes of a jealous care.

.   .   .   .   .

Three weeks after, a brig bore down
Into the harbor of Newport town,
Towing a wreck.   'Twas the sloop "Delight."
Off Hampton Rocks, in the sight

Of the land she sought, she and her crew
And all on board of her, full in view
Of the storm-bound fishermen over the bay,
Went to their doom on that April day.

When de Rochambeau heard the terrible tale,
He muttered a prayer; for a moment grew pale;
Then, "Mon Dieu!" he exclaimed, "so my fine romance
From beginning to end is a rose and a glance."

So the sad old story comes to a close.
'Tis a century since; but the world still goes
On the same base round—still takes the gage
Of a woman's heart in a moment of rage.

BUTTS HILL, CHASTELLUX AND CONANICUT ISLAND FORTS

BUTTS HILL FORT, on the east road between Tiverton and Newport and in the township of Portsmouth, on the north end of the island of Rhode Island, has been permanently associated with Lafayette by placing at the southeast corner of the earthworks a native boulder, on the face of which is a bronze tablet, the inscription reading as follows:

TO MARK THE SITE OF
BUTTS HILL FORT IN THE FIELD OF
THE BATTLE OF RHODE ISLAND
AUGUST 29, 1778

THE MAJOR GENERALS
JOHN SULLIVAN AND NATHANAEL GREENE
COMMANDING THE CONTINENTAL TROOPS

PRONOUNCED BY THE MARQUIS DE LAFAYETTE
THE BEST FOUGHT ACTION OF
THE WAR OF THE REVOLUTION

ERECTED BY THE RHODE ISLAND
DAUGHTERS OF THE AMERICAN REVOLUTION
1922

The SIEGE OF RHODE ISLAND, taken from Mr Brindley's House, on the 25th of August, 1778.

Photographed through the courtesy of the late John R. Hess   *From a picture in the collection of the late George L. Shepley*

THE SIEGE OF RHODE ISLAND,

which ended with the battle of Butts Hill and the evacuation of Rhode Island. Lafayette arrived from Boston in time to take charge of the rear guard.

Photographed through the courtesy   *From a picture in the collection of*
of the late John R. Hess   *the late George L. Shepley*

TABLET ON BUTTS HILL, PORTSMOUTH,
RHODE ISLAND,

*dedicated on the 144th anniversary of the battle. The French
and Americans made an orderly retreat from the island,
and Lafayette arrived from Boston in time to assist the rear
guard. As the tablet records, Lafayette pronounced
this engagement "the best fought action of the War of the Revolution." The General himself arrived too late to take part
in the engagement, but in the retreat from the island he successfully
commanded the rear guard.*

This tablet was put there to commemorate one of the most historic places in the State, where part of the important battle of Rhode Island was fought. It was dedicated by the Society on the one hundred and forty-fourth anniversary of the battle. These interesting fortifications were erected by the British in 1777, were occupied by the Americans the following year, and in 1780 and 1781, after the evacuation of Newport and the island, it was for a time garrisoned by some of the French troops. Lafayette was unable to take part in this engagement, as he was in Boston the day before, urging d'Estaing to return to Newport with his fleet. It will be remembered that he arrived from his long ride from the Massachusetts capital to help in the well-executed retreat from the island to Tiverton, which took place after the engagement.

At one time during the battle of Butts Hill, the opposing sentries were only two hundred yards apart, and the two lines were so close that it was a difficult matter for our troops to retire without being noticed. General Sullivan, however, ordered the tents to be set up, which fortunately deceived the enemy and made the crossing of the east passage to the Tiverton shore less difficult. Another interesting fact is that a company of negro troops for the first time in American history fought here for liberty and independence.

The visitor on the way to or from Newport will do well to stop at Sprague Lane, a mile or so from the stone bridge between the island and Tiverton, and by continuing up that road he will notice a rough path leading past a small farmhouse direct to the old fortifications, the centre of the action referred to by Lafayette. Two entrances have been made in the earthworks, doubtless done in order to gather more easily the hay within the walls of the fort and in the fields beyond. One notices particularly the quantity of slate composing the banks, which in places reach a height of fifteen or twenty feet. Indeed, they seem higher than this, for in many spots the moat is still extant, and of considerable depth at many points. This slate, which resembles coal to some extent, reminds one of the defunct Rhode Island coal properties nearby, of which a geologist said that, were all the

Photographed through the courtesy   *From a picture in the collection*
of the late John R. Hess   *of the late George L. Shepley*

SOUTHEAST CORNER OF BUTTS HILL FORT,
PORTSMOUTH, RHODE ISLAND,

*showing the earthworks and the moat, both much as they were
during the war. This old fort and the one at Hull are
the best preserved of any of the Revolutionary defences in New
England that are associated with the French.*

world to catch on fire, the safest place to retreat to would be these coal fields at Portsmouth. This old fort, supposed to be in the best state of preservation of any of those of its time, is of considerable circumference; and, as the top of the bank is in most places three feet or so in width, it is a simple matter to walk entirely around it, a distance of about seven hundred paces. From the fort one gets a commanding view of the waters on both sides of the island, and realizes what a strategic position it was during those last few days of August, 1778. General Chastellux was so interested in this fort that he travelled, as he states in his "Memoirs," a considerable distance, on a frosty day, to visit Butts Hill. This elevation was once part of Quaker Hill, on which stands an interesting old Quaker meeting-house.

Fort Chastellux, now no longer visible,

Kindness of John W. Martyn, War Department, Washington, D.C.

SITE OF OLD DUMPLINGS ROCK BATTERY, ON CONANICUT ISLAND, OFF NEWPORT, RHODE ISLAND

Several detachments of French troops were stationed there under Count William de Deux-Ponts, Count de Custine and de Noailles. The fort was evacuated by the French on July 27, 1780. All the fortifications of Narragansett Bay, including this fort, were under the supervision of the French engineer, Major Tousard, who lost an arm during the Butts Hill engagement.

was situated on the site of Lorillard Spencer's house on Chastellux Avenue, which runs from Wellington Avenue on the border of the harbour over Hallidon Hill to Harrison Avenue. Part of the earthworks were levelled in order to build the house, and at that time some old cannon balls were dug up. One recently found is preserved by the family as a relic. This fort, which was the largest and most important on Rhode Island, was built by General Chastellux, one of Rochambeau's Maréchaux-de-Camp, who had command of the southern defences, and it was, therefore, very natural that it should be named for him. On this hill a battery was placed which commanded Brenton's Point and Goat Island. After the Revolution, the name of the fort was changed to Fort Harrison, as it became part of the Harrison farm, and since that time the name of Fort Denham has been applied to that locality. Today, Chastellux Avenue is the only visible reminder of the excellent work done by this Frenchman during our Revolution. General Cullum in his "Defences of Narragansett Bay" states that in 1884 part of the fort was situated in front of the Thorp Cottage, between Berkeley and King Streets, and remembers that his father was obliged to have a special act of Congress passed in order to clear his title, as our Government had some lien on the property in case of war.

Photographed through the courtesy of the late John R. Hess   *From a picture in the collection of the late George L. Shepley*

INTERIOR OF BUTTS HILL FORT, AT PORTSMOUTH, RHODE ISLAND,

where the battle of Rhode Island took place. Rochambeau later had the defences fortified more strongly.

From a photograph taken by Mrs. John M. Whitall shortly before the demolition of the fort   *Kindness of Anna Wharton Wood*

FORT LOUIS, NOW KNOWN AS FORT WETHERILL, A SUB–POST OF FORT ADAMS, ON DUMPLINGS
ROCK, A PART OF CONANICUT ISLAND, IN NEWPORT HARBOUR

A temporary fortification was placed on Conanicut Island about the year 1775, and in 1777 a more permanent fort, called Dumplings Rock Battery, was erected. About twenty years later this battery was still further strengthened by this stone construction. The older fort was occupied by some French soldiers in July, 1780, under Lieutenant-Colonel de la Valette of the Saintonge regiment. Rochambeau, a few days later, sent as re-enforcements to the island the second battalion of the Soissonnais under Colonel de Noailles, brother-in-law of Lafayette. De Closen mentions that the fort was in a few days evacuated and that later the navy established there its hospitals and workshops. When Admiral d'Estaing entered Newport Harbour in August, 1779, he landed temporarily 4,000 of his troops on the island. This fort, named probably for the King of France, was strengthened under the supervision of Major Louis Tousard, and was demolished in 1896 to give place to a more modern fortification. A sign has been placed nearby marking the site of the original fort.

Still another fortification, sometimes called Fort Louis in honor of the King of France, but now known as Fort Wetherill, a sub-post of Fort Adams, is associated with the French. It was situated on Dumplings Rock, a part of Conanicut Island, almost opposite the attractive Agassiz place called "Castle Hill," at the entrance to Newport Harbour. Here a temporary earthworks was thrown up about the year 1775; and two years later a more permanent fort, called Dumplings Rock Battery, was erected. About twenty years later, this battery was further strengthened by the stone construction shown in the accompanying illustration. The older fort was occupied in July, 1780, by some French soldiers under Lt.-Col. de la Valette of the Saintonge regiment. Believing that an attack was imminent, Rochambeau a few days later sent as re-enforcements to the island the second battalion of the Soissonnais under Colonel de Noailles, a brother-in-law of Lafayette. De Closen in his diary mentions that this fort was in a few days evacuated, owing to the fear that it could not be successfully defended, and that later the navy established there its hospitals and workshops. Comte de Deux-Ponts for a short time occupied batteries on the island. It has also been ascertained that in August of 1778, when Admiral d'Estaing entered the harbour, he landed temporarily four thousand of his troops on the island. Claude Blanchard mentions that on June 4, 1781, he spent part of the day there with some naval officers and de la Grandière and had dinner.

The later round stone fort, shown in a cut, such a well-known landmark of Newport for years, was entirely the work of Major Louis Tousard, a French officer who also superintended the whole system of Narragansett Bay defences after the war. While fighting at Butts Hill side by side with our troops, he had the misfortune to lose an arm. Later he served as French Consul at New Orleans, where he died. It has been said that the Dumplings Tower nearby served as a target for one of the commanders of Fort Adams in order to furnish practice for his artillery. In 1898 this old stone fort was destroyed to give place to a newer and more up-to-date fortification.

Conanicut is named for the great sachem of the Narragansett Indians, Quononicus, and it is said that the island was his favorite summer home.

VUE DE PASSY

Prise dans l'Isle des Cignes vis-à-vis les bons Hommes.

Photographed by Giraudon, Paris, from an old print in the Musée Carnavalet, Paris, France

THE HEIGHTS OF PASSY IN FRANKLIN'S DAY

from a drawing made from the Isle des Cignes in the Seine, showing the location of the house where Franklin lived nearly eight years. This is the only good view of Passy at the time of his sojourn there.

MEMORIES OF FRANKLIN IN PASSY AND PARIS

IN the introduction to his "Everybody's Life of Franklin," dated Paris, 1848, François Auguste Alexis Mignet, the French historian who wrote a history of the French Revolution in 1824, and many other works relating to French history and politics, writes:

"No one better than Franklin could have gone to plead the cause of America in France. As a free-thinker he would find there the zealous support of the philosophers who were directing public opinion at that time; as a shrewd negotiator he would hasten a decision of co-operation from the capable and farseeing minister who was then conducting the Foreign Office; as a humorist he would please everyone; and as a noble old man he would add to the sympathy of the people for his country by the respect which he commanded for himself."

This is a sound résumé of the rôle that Franklin played in France, and it is as accurate as it is concise.

It may be presumptuous to attempt to add anything to the exhaustive study of this subject which was made some thirty years ago by Edward Everett Hale and his son. The record of his keen and successful diplomacy is therein written; but, even if there is little new to tell, the story of Franklin's daily life in France is so rich and so noble in its simplicity that it will well bear repetition.

Franklin's mission to France was one that demanded a high type of diplomacy. Although he was the official delegate to the Continental Congress, that body had a flimsy status in America and had none at all in Europe. At the very outset, Franklin was decidedly *persona non grata* to the British Diplomatic Corps in Paris; in fact he was accused by the members of that corps of being a traitor and a spy. Throughout many long months he was harassed by the uncertainty of the American cause and by the difficulties of secret diplomacy. When, in 1778, the treaty of alliance with France was signed, he stepped modestly out of his seclusion and was everywhere acclaimed the Minister of the New Republic; and his home was recognized as the seat of the American Legation, the First American Embassy in France. Mignet judged him rightly: he was a "shrewd negotiator"; but while the negotiations were going on, the "humorist," the "philosopher," and the "noble old man" went straight through the "closed doors" of French society, made a host of beautiful friendships, and took time from the burdening cares of state to live largely and humanly in what was one of the most brilliant epochs in the social and intellectual life of the French capital.

During the reign of Louis XV and of Louis XVI, there was a certain man of letters, by name Louis Petit de Bachaumont. This keen observer, critic, wily man-about-town, apparently went everywhere, saw everything, and set down his opinions in no uncertain terms. He left an astonishing journal which he called: "Mémoires pour servir à l'histoire de la République des Lettres," a kind of diary of criticism and comment. He died in 1771; nevertheless, his Mémoires were continued by some of his literary friends with less genius, but in the same form and style. So popular and general an organ of criticism could not fail to comment frequently on the presence and personality of the philosopher-statesman who was the constant object of curiosity and interest throughout his entire sojourn in France. On the occasion of Franklin's first visit to France, the author himself makes this entry: "September 19, 1767. Monsieur Franklin, the Doctor, renowned for the experiments which he has made in electricity, the which he has pushed to an astonishing degree of perfection, is in Paris. All the savants are anxious to see him and confer with him."

Ten years later Franklin came back to Paris as the official delegate of the Continental Congress. On December 4, 1776, he debarked with his two grandsons, at Quiberon Bay, the tiny port near the mouth of the Loire which was so soon to serve as one of the principal bases for the naval operations of John Paul Jones. For diplomatic reasons, every effort was made to conceal his presence in France; consequently on January 17, 1777, even the keen continuator of Bachaumont's journal is ignorant of his arrival, for he sets down this casual comment: "The mode today is to have an engraving of Franklin over the fire-place, just as one used to have a jumping-jack. The portrait of this grave personage is indeed turned into derision in the same manner as was this toy of thirty years ago."

Then suddenly the story is out, and we find this crisp entry: "February 4, 1777. Doctor Franklin has arrived recently from the American Colonies. He is much sought after and fêted by the savants. He has a fine face, little hair, and a fur cap which he wears constantly on his head. He is very reserved in public as to the news from his country, which he praises highly. He says that the heavens are so jealous of her beauty that they have sent her the scourge of war. Our great men have been probing him about his religion; they thought to find him of theirs—which is to say that he had none at all."

One writer tells how he "slipped" into Paris and took up a very modest residence in the little Hôtel d'Hambourg in the Rue de l'Université; but there were many reasons why it was not best for him to remain in the capital, and he must have been heartily glad to accept the generous invitation to be the guest of one of his admirers, Jules Donatien Le Ray de Chaumont, at his suburban villa in Passy.

Passy boasts a long list of immortal sons, which number includes such names as Molière, Turgot, Mirabeau, Béranger, Rossini, Lamartine, Victor Hugo, Henri Martin, d'Estaing (so closely identified with our Revolution); not least among these is the name of our own Franklin. In fact, after the village had been absorbed by the city, there was a definite proposal to call it the Franklin District, and this appellation appears on at least one of the plans of the epoch. During the Revolution, the gate of the city which opened toward Passy and Versailles was called the "Barrière Franklin." In Louis XVI's day Passy was a "fashionable suburb," a "better-residence district" a half-mile or so outside the city wall. The villas and "hôtels" were built on the hills or the heights which overlooked the city and which sloped gently down to the Seine.

When Quillet wrote his history of Passy

Photographed from an engraving in the Cabinet des Estampes in the Bibliothèque Nationale, Paris *Kindness of Paul F. Cadman*

FRANKLIN'S HOST AT PASSY, FRANCE, JULES DONATIEN LE RAY DE CHAUMONT

He accompanied Franklin part of the way to Havre on his final departure for America.

and its environs in the year 1836, he made the preface sound dangerously like an advertisement for a health resort. He claimed that all the best Parisian doctors sent their patients there for convalescence; furthermore, there were numberless residents who lightly bore the burden of eighty or ninety years, and even one centenarian was reported as enjoying excellent health and all of his faculties. To be sure, there were mineral springs, "les eaux de Passy," which were famous long before the village was founded; but the real glory of Passy is told in the biographies of its "grands hommes" rather than in its thermal advantages.

The Hôtel Valentinois was built on one of the most favorable slopes, and its terraced gardens extended well down toward the river. It was interesting even in Franklin's day because of its history, and also because of its distinguished owner. At one time it belonged to the Duc d'Aumont, one of the two "maréchaux" of France who bore that name in the fifteenth century. Later it housed the beautiful but careless Countess of Valentinois, whose extravagant debaucheries with the dashing Count d'Artois, brother of the King and later

Photographed for the State Street Trust Company by George B. Brayton

TWO SUPPOSED VIEWS OF HÔTEL VALENTINOIS, FRANCE,

the property of Jules Donatien Le Ray de Chaumont, where Benjamin Franklin lived while in France between the years 1777 and 1785. The owner gave him part of this large dwelling for his use, and never would accept a franc of rent. Here Franklin transacted his business and received his many friends.

Charles X, are quite beyond telling. As one writer, however, states: "In France the walls do not speak; in fact they alone have nothing to say." Needless to say, the wags of the time were quick to catch the contrast between the wild license of the gay Countess and the solemn simplicity of the gentle Doctor.

Le Ray de Chaumont is described as "another Franklin." He had been at one time Intendant of the Hôtel des Invalides, but upon his retirement he had withdrawn from public life and lived with his daughter Sophie in quiet comfort at his Passy home. He was an ardent supporter of the American Cause, and was also particularly proud to be the host of the great Franklin. Bouchot says that the three drove frequently in the family carriage and that they maintained the most cordial and happy relations. His sincerity found ample proof in that he would never accept a penny of rent although Franklin lived for more than eight years beneath his roof.

How much more we should like to know about those eight years! An astonishing capacity for work and play was one of Franklin's rare gifts. We are told that he received hosts of callers, ranging from beggars to men of the highest genius; one man tried to interest him in a machine for cutting tobacco; another had an extraordinary scheme for landing a force of gentlemen-bandits in England to pillage and burn the coast villages; the Pope's emissary came to bring him the good wishes of the Saint Père toward America; and even the fiery Marat, already under suspicion, was generously accorded an interview. He entertained royally, and was

From an old print in the possession of M. Louis Batcave, Auteuil, Paris   *Kindness of Paul F. Cadman*

FRANKLIN'S HOUSE AT PASSY, FRANCE,
where he made his first balloon experiments.   Possibly not an authentic picture.

himself fêted constantly.   He kept up an enormous correspondence, had time for his lodge, time to write scientific papers, time to walk, time to study the new science of ballooning, and all the while he was launching, directing and concluding negotiations of the utmost importance. We are even told he had time to play at cards with his host: "Every night he played at cards, but always for the honor of winning.   He sometimes reproached himself for wasting his time; but, said he: 'Something whispers in my ear—you know that your soul is immortal; why are you stingy with your time when you have all eternity before you?'"

On June 10, 1778, there is an entry in Bachaumont's Mémoires that throws a rare light on his intimate hospitality:

"La Veille des Rois (which might be translated Epiphany): Monsieur Franklin who is still residing in Passy, decided to offer *le pain bénit* (blessed bread).   Since he was a Protestant and was not the owner of the house, which belonged to Le Ray de Chaumont, he need not have done so.   He procured thirteen brioches (a kind of sweetened bun) which had been blessed, representing the thirteen states of the United States.   He wanted to put a label on each one of them on which was to be written the word 'Liberty'; a certain priest who was dining with him greatly disapproved of this label, and the word 'Liberty' particularly frightened him.   The Bishop of Saintes (Charente-Inférieure) who was also present, disapproved highly and stated that it would not be possible for a clergyman to tolerate such an innovation.   Mademoiselle d'Eon, who was there, was asked her opinion.   Her answer was that she had nothing to add to what the members of the Church had already decided, but that to their opinion she would add a political reason, not less important; being only eight miles from Versailles, it was not right to use a word which was in such ill repute (at Court)."

The institution of "offering the blessed bread" dates from a very early epoch of Christian history and it is still in common use in France.   At stated seasons of the Christian year, such as Easter or Christmas, certain individuals in each parish subscribe to a fund which is used to purchase bread, usually in the form of small sweetened buns, which are piled in baskets and placed inside the chancel near the altar. After the Mass, the priest blesses the bread, and the acolytes or the choir boys, or both, distribute it to the audience. Frequently this bread is carried home to be eaten at a solemn gathering of the family circle as a token of solidarity and friendship. Formerly it was thought to have miraculous qualities; it would cure certain maladies; if a litigant carried a bit in his pocket, he was sure to gain his cause. In fact, its powers became so renowned that the distributors used to smuggle away large quantities to be sold at fabulous prices. A rigid legislation was required to correct this evil. This custom with all its quaint imagery and charming superstition appealed to the imaginative genius of Franklin, who was quick to make it serve the cause of liberty and the New Republic.

On February 5, 1778, there is this entry:

"Doctor Franklin grows more human and is appearing even in gallant society, which proves more and more his good relations with our government and the satisfaction over the happy news received from his country. Recently he attended a ball given by Madame de Floissac, the wife of the financier. There were many young and beautiful ladies there and they all went one by one to present their respects and to kiss him in spite of the glasses he always wears.

One is, in fact, rather scandalized by the luxury he allows and tolerates in his grandsons, which is in striking contrast with his own simplicity. They even wear 'red heels'—a frivolous fashion which is permitted at Versailles, but is unreasonable and undignified for the heirs of one of the chiefs of the Philadelphia Congress."

"Talons rouges," or red heels, were the mark of one who wanted to make a splurge. During the Revolution the term was frequently applied to the former nobility.

"March 20, 1778. . . . Doctor Franklin begins to appear more often in public. He came on Wednesday to the amateurs' concert and was applauded vociferously."

"July 17, 1778. . . . One was much surprised to see Doctor Franklin, who has such momentous affaires under his direction, take part in the fête which the Loge des Neuf Sœurs gave him recently and to pass the whole day among a lot of young men and poets who vied with each other in stupid and childish flattery. He was presented with the apron of Monsieur de Voltaire."

From a photograph taken for the State Street Trust Company   *Kindness of Paul F. Cadman*

THIS GATE IS THE LAST VESTIGE OF THE HÔTEL VALENTINOIS, IN PASSY, FRANCE,

where Franklin lived. It marks the entrance to the old château. Madame Valentinois sold the property to Le Ray de Chaumont, Franklin's friend. It was approached from Rue de L'Annonciation.

The Lodge of the Nine Sisters then in Rue Bonaparte is said to have been one of the most famous in the world. Freemasonry was introduced into France in 1720, and by 1778 there were more than three hundred lodges. If its history is turbulent, it is because it lived in turbulent times; but under a confusion of republics, empires and monarchies it ran a long, interesting and useful course. The lodge had a decidedly literary and philosophical atmosphere and gave no evidence of the prejudice which later sprung up against Catholicism, for it numbered many priests and abbots in its membership. There is a note which says that the beautiful and virtuous Princess de Lamballe was at one time the "grande maîtresse" of the lodge. Marie Antoinette wrote to her sister, Marie Christine, on February 26, 1781:

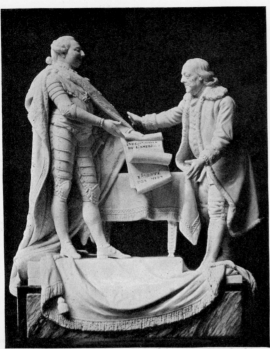

From a statue in the   *Photographed through the kindness of*
Providence Atheneum   *the late John R. Hess*

STATUETTE OF LOUIS XVI AND BENJAMIN
FRANKLIN,

made at the Niderviller factory owned by Comte de Custine,
who was with the French army in the American
Revolution, and who doubtless knew Franklin. It com-
memorates the treaty with France in 1788, and
is one of the four in the United States. It is a price-
less possession of the Providence Atheneum.
On the scroll are the words "Indépendance de l'Amérique."
De Custine as well as de Noailles walked at the
head of their regiments from Providence to the North River
(Hudson River). It was modelled by Lemaire,
the French sculptor.

". . . the free masons are not as bad as you make them out to be. (At their meetings) they eat and drink a great deal and they talk and sing also, which tells the king that people who sing and drink are never guilty of conspiracy."

An historian of the lodge says that it was the "fille posthume" of Monsieur Helvétius. Helvétius was a very ardent Mason and was surely instrumental in the forming of the lodge. Voltaire was probably the most distinguished member, and among others were John Paul Jones and the celebrated sculptor Houdon. Franklin was at one time its grand master, although he accepted the title as purely honorary, as can be seen from these two entries in Bachaumont:

"May 26, 1779. . . . It is wonderful to see Franklin in spite of the important and numerous business affairs which he has to direct, find time enough to come and play at the chapel and follow masonic meetings as if he had nothing to do. Last Thursday he was elected an honorary member of the Lodge of the Nine Sisters and a deputation was sent to Passy to inform him accordingly.

The brothers, Count de Milly and Count de Gebelin, first and second supervisors, brother la Dixmarie, orator, and brother abbé Cordelier de Saint-Firmin, general agent of the lodge, composed the deputation.

This election came at the right time and at a very critical moment when the lodge was being severely criticised because of a pamphlet in its favor which had just appeared. The Keeper of the Seals had written to Monsieur Noir to suppress it, to prevent its distribution and to make every effort to discover the printer. This is something to give an opportunity to a new 'vénérable' member to show his zeal."

"August 25, 1779. . . . Although Monsieur Franklin has accepted the position of 'Vénérable' he made the condition that he should not have to fill the rôle with the scrupulous exactitude which it demanded, and since it was his name that was wanted for the list of grand masters, he was exempted from all duties."

The Lodge of the Nine Sisters was finally disbanded in 1848.

Of the many friendships which historians have recorded and which his correspondence proves, none is more beautiful than that of Madame Helvétius, the widow of the famous author and philosopher. This good lady lived in Auteuil, a small town just beyond Passy, and one sharing the same distinctions. Hers was the home of all people of letters and learning. Her salon was one of the most typical, the most finished, of any of the famous literary salons of the times; the rendezvous of the encyclopedists, philosophers, and the glorious geniuses of the late eighteenth century. It was there that Franklin met Turgot, "the philosopher-prophet" of American Independence; it was there that he began his acquaintance with Diderot,

D'Alembert and possibly Rousseau. It was there that he met Cabanis and Volney. In fact, it is told that he once saw these two young men talking ardently in one corner of the salon, and because he loved to talk to young people, he approached them and joined in the conversation:

"At your age the soul is abroad—at mine it is within, looking out on the passersby and listening to their quarrels without taking part in them."

Later he became greatly attached to young Cabanis and willed to him the Court sword which he had carried at Versailles.

One of Franklin's greatest delights was to take his gold-headed cane, that famous cane which he willed to Washington, and walk over to Madame Helvétius' home, where he found "such good company" as Condorcet, that wonderful scientist-philosopher who took poison to escape the guillotine; Malby, the abbot-historian, and Morellet, the abbot-economist and encyclopedist, not to mention the two charming daughters of Madame Helvétius whom Franklin christened "Les Étoiles." It is said that in this company he was at his best, "simple, gentle, genial, listening or telling anecdotes, and always looking for a philosophical turn in the conversation."

Photograph of a rare miniature kindly lent by Calman-Levy, Editors, in Paris   *Kindness of Paul F. Cadman*

MADAME HELVÉTIUS OF AUTEUIL, FRANCE,

the closest and best friend of Benjamin Franklin while at Passy. She had been a widow a few years when Franklin arrived. Her salon was one of the most famous of her day. He proposed marriage to her.

And there were dinners—famous dinners—now "chez" Madame Helvétius and then at Franklin's hospitable board. Those of us who are wont to think of Franklin as the frugal lad who marched the streets of the town at an early morning hour munching a roll for breakfast, will be astonished to learn that in France the kindly old man was a real epicurean, with not the slightest tendency to despise dainty viands and noble vintages. There is today, in the possession of Mr. Rosengarten of Philadelphia, the original copy of a notebook in which are entered the daily expenditures of the "maître d'hôtel" of the Franklin house in Passy. Such a list would have gladdened the heart of Brillat-Savarin: poulets, capons, pigeons, partridges, turkeys, are common, everyday entries. Sea fish and shellfish are in abundance; grapes from Málaga, oranges from Malta, asparagus, mushrooms, green peas, sweetbreads, spring lamb, filet, and whole columns of spices, cheeses, fruits and vegetables for preserving. And there are flowers for the table and scores of candles and all the knickknacks that are dear to the caterer's art; and wine of mark and "eau-de-vie" and excellent spirits appear on every page. This treasured document also contains some curious agreements with the merchants, and especially with his cook and "maître d'hôtel" whereby they are to receive a bonus for good management.

Such an array lends much weight to the charge of extravagance which John Adams laid at Franklin's door. Our judgment, though, must be tempered by many facts: John Adams did not like Franklin; furthermore, Franklin had honestly amassed a very comfortable personal fortune by a lifetime of remarkable diligence and effort; and, finally, he found himself in a gay and luxury-loving society whose friendship he needed and whose good tastes he

STATUETTE OF BENJAMIN FRANKLIN
*by the famous Luzanne, in the private collection of David
Weill at Neuilly, on the Seine, France.*

genuinely appreciated. It is rather disconcerting to check the record of his conviviality with the rigid philosophy of his Poor Richard; but in the end there is not a little comfort in finding a warm, genial, fun-loving side to the good Doctor who is so often painted as puritanically solemn.

At one of these rare dinners where good cheer mingled with good viands, worthy wines, and inimitable intellects, the Abbot Morellet composed this bit of verse which has long since become historic. It might be translated as follows:

> Let history write Franklin's name;
> Let tablets bronze blaze forth his fame!
> As for me, to his praise
> A drinking song I shall raise.
> Fill your glasses, everyone,
> And sing to our good Benjamin!
>
> In politics, he's ever noble;
> At table, gay and free from trouble.
> While an empire he is founding
> You hear his toasts with mirth abounding.
> Serious, yet full of fun,
> Such is our good Benjamin.

Every Wednesday, "Notre Dame d'Auteuil" and the whole company came to dine "chez le patriarche de Passy." This was a mark of special favor, for since her husband's death Madame Helvétius had steadfastly refused all invitations. This friendship, founded on true kinship of thought and taste, grew to be one of rare and beautiful intimacy. Franklin had been a widower for many years. We are told that despite his seventy years he offered his heart to the good widow and pressed his suit with zeal. Madame Helvétius had already refused the hand of Turgot. Her greatest joy was to keep open house for the many illustrious souls who graced her salon, and her constant choice was to continue her devotion to her honored husband. Franklin took the refusal in excellent grace, and at once wrote her the letter which has been repeated in every work concerning him, but it is such a gem of wit and good humor that it suffers nothing in retelling:

"Chagrined at your resolution, so honestly pronounced last night, to remain single during all your life in honor to your beloved husband, I went home and threw myself on my bed. It seemed to me that I was dead and that I had arrived at the Elysian Fields. Someone asked me if I wanted to see any important personages. 'Take me to the philosophers,' said I. 'There are two who live near in this garden,' was the reply. 'They are good neighbors and very dear friends.' 'Who are they?' I asked. 'Socrates and Helvétius.' 'I hold them both in great esteem,' said I, 'but let me see Helvétius first, because I know a little French and not a word of Greek.' He received me with much courtesy, having known my character, so he said, for a long time. He asked me a thousand things about the war and the present state of religion, of liberty, and of the Government of France. 'You ask me nothing of your friend Madame Helvétius, notwithstanding the fact that she still loves you ardently and that only an hour ago I was in her presence.' 'Ah,' said he, 'you call to my mind my old happiness;

"CHÂLET" OF ÉTIENNE DELESSERT,

the great financier at Passy, France, situated near Franklin's residence, Hôtel Valentinois. Both Delessert and his wife had a high regard for Franklin, and the two families often exchanged calls.

but one must forget that if one wants to be happy here. For a good many years I thought only of her; then I consoled myself and took another wife—one the most like her I could find. She is not, to be sure, so altogether beautiful, but she has good sense and spirit and she loves me infinitely. Her continual study is to please me. For the moment she has gone out to buy some of the best nectar and ambrosia for the evening cheer. Stay here with me and you shall see her.' 'I see,' said I, 'that your old friend is more faithful than you are; for although a number of interesting proposals have been made to her, she has refused them all. I confess to you that I myself loved her to a point of madness; but she was unresponsive to my attentions and she refused me absolutely because of her love for you.' 'I sympathise with you,' he said, 'in your misfortune, for truly she is a good woman and very kind. But don't you still find the Abbot Morellet and the Abbot La Roche occasionally at her house?' 'Oh, yes indeed, for she has not lost one of your friends.' 'If you had bribed the Abbot Morellet with "café à la crème," to speak for you, you might have succeeded, for he is a reasoner as subtle as Scotus or Saint Thomas, and he puts his arguments in such good order that they are almost irresistible. Or if you had employed the Abbot La Roche, for the consideration of some beautiful edition of an old classic, to talk against you, that would have been better. For I have always observed that when he gives her advice, she has a strong penchant to do the very opposite.' At these words, in came the new Madame Helvétius with the nectar; I at once recognized her as Madame Franklin, my old American friend. I attempted to assert my devotion, but she coldly replied: 'I was your good wife for forty-nine years and four months, nearly a half a century. Be content with that. I have formed a new connection that will last forever.' Unhappy over the refusal of my Eurydice, I at once decided to leave these ungrateful shades and to return to this good world and to see again the sun and you. Here I am. Let us avenge each other."

There were many other Passy and Auteuil firesides where Franklin was a frequent and

VUE DE LA TERRASSE DE M.ᴿ FRANKLIN A PASSI.

Premier voyage Aérien en présence de Monseigneur le Dauphin. Cette Expérience c'est faite sous la direction de M.ʳ Montgolfier, dans le jardin de la Muëtte, ce Globe portant 70 pieds de hauteur sur 46 de dia-
metre, le poids qu'il a enlevé étoit d'environ 16 à 1700 livres, fut construit par M.ʳ le Marquis d'Arlande et
M.ʳ Pilâtre des Rosiers, ces deux intrépides Voyageurs partirent le 21 Novembre 1783, à une heure 54
minutes après midi, ils s'élevérent à 270 pieds de hauteur, ils arrivérent à bon port sur la Butte aux
Cailles entre le moulin de Merveilles et le moulin Vieux, ayant vogué dans l'air un intervalle de 400
toises en 20 ou 25 minutes sans avoir éprouvé la plus legere incomodité.
A Paris chez Vachez, quai de Gevres, à l'Esperance.
A.P.D.R.

Photographed from an old print for the State Street Trust Company by Giraudon, Paris   *Kindness of Paul F. Cadman*

THE FAMOUS BALLOON OF THE MONTGOLFIER BROTHERS,

*viewed from the terrace of Franklin's residence at Passy, France, showing the River Seine.   The exhibition
may have been made for his benefit.   The Montgolfiers were the inventors of balloons in their day,
and there was intense rivalry in this pursuit, all of which greatly interested Franklin.*

welcome guest. Madame Brillon was his near neighbor. It was for her that he wrote the famous story of the whistle, and to her he dedicated many of his moral epigrams, such as, "A penny saved is a penny earned." He frequently referred to her as "l'aimable brillante." Vigée-Lebrun says of him in her autobiography: "I have often seen him at Madame Brillon's, who lives in Passy. Franklin spends his evenings there. Madame Brillon and her two daughters often have music of an evening, and Franklin listens with pleasure; but between the selections I have never heard him say a word, and I felt inclined to believe that the Doctor was forever sworn to silence."

This charming portrait-painter was born in 1755 and was therefore only twenty-two years old when Franklin took up his residence in Passy. Her father had a little summer villa there.

Very near the Hôtel Valentinois was the beautiful chalet of Étienne Delessert, the great financier who established the bank which later became the Bank of France. This man of large vision was constantly engaged in agricultural, industrial and financial reforms, for which he enjoyed the comments and criticisms of his philosopher neighbor. Madame Delessert was a woman of unusual character and charm, her life being devoted to the education and training of her children. We shall see later how highly she regarded Franklin's friendship.

On Sunday Franklin kept open house for the Americans. Little Benjamin Franklin Bache, who was attending a French boarding school, came home for the week-ends and often brought some of his little schoolmates with him. The great philosopher adored his grandchildren.

From the terrace of his garden Franklin could look out over the Seine and up to the beautifully wooded heights of Meudon. Just across the river was the famous Champ-de-Mars, where the first balloonists of France were conducting their initial experiments. The Montgolfier brothers, like the Wright brothers in our day, were the inventors of the balloon, and Alexandre Charles, a noted physician, perfected their work by the application of hydrogen to aërostatics. A great quarrel and an intense rivalry, which was at its height during Franklin's stay at Passy, had sprung up between these famous inventors. His own inventive genius and his interest in popular mechanics and science gave singular force to his enthusiasm for the new science of aërostatics. Someone asked him rather scornfully what could be the use of such a thing as a balloon. His reply is reported as: "Of what use are new-born babies!" On December 5, 1783, Bachaumont's "Mémoires" record: "Monsieur Franklin was greatly impressed by the experiments of Monsieur Charles. Enthused by what he saw, he cried out that the first balloon was an infant, but that this one was a giant. He said also that the aërostatic machine was a child whose father was Monsieur de Montgolfier and whose mother-nurse was Monsieur Charles."

One of the most famous engravings of this Montgolfier balloon was made from Franklin's terrace and signed accordingly. It appears in an illustration.

Franklin was made a member of the Academy of Science and was, of course, greatly honored and respected by his fellow academicians.

Bachaumont's "Mémoires" say:

"April 15, 1779. . . . From the public assembly of the Academy of Science which was held yesterday, one must not omit two precious anecdotes: One is a paper on the Aurora Borealis by Monsieur Franklin. When someone spoke to the King of this paper, he observed that it was singular that the Minister of the New Republic, who was busy with the weightiest affairs, could still find time to amuse himself with studies in physics. The paper, clear, simple and methodical, is written in perfect French.

Photographed especially for the   *Kindness of Paul F. Cadman*
State Street Trust Company from
"*La Revue des Lettres et des Arts*"
in the Bibliothèque Nationale,
Paris

CURIOUS SKETCH OF FRANKLIN
presenting his grandson to Voltaire to receive his blessing.
This picture appeared in the "La Revue des Lettres
et des Arts" published in 1889, but now out of print.

It is true that the members of the Academy were notified that Monsieur Franklin had consulted and taken advice of a second for his style."

It seems that Franklin did learn to use the French language very effectively; yet if the following anecdote has good foundation, it is evidence that he had some serious difficulties. He one day attended a lecture in company with his little grandson, who had been studying at a French school. He was unable to understand the speaker, yet he wished to join in the applause; so he decided to watch a friend, Madame de Boufflers, who was one of the Auteuil circle, and to applaud when she did. As soon as the lecture was over, his grandson said to him: "But, grandfather, you applauded always and louder than all the rest when the speaker was praising you." This story does not check up very well with the one that is frequently quoted about Franklin's visit to Voltaire. The latter, then eighty-four years of age, had come back to Paris after twenty-seven years of exile, and, like all other philosophers, Franklin wanted to see him. On the occasion of the visit, Voltaire greeted Franklin with a few words of English, whereupon Voltaire's niece, Madame Denis, asked him to speak French so that everybody present could understand, reminding him at the same time that Franklin spoke French very well. "Oh, I know it," he replied, "but I could not resist the temptation to speak a few words in Monsieur Franklin's tongue." When Franklin presented his grandson to the old philosopher, Voltaire placed his hands on the lad's head and gave him this blessing: "God and liberty, that is the only benediction that is fitting for a grandson of Monsieur Franklin." We have included a picture of Voltaire blessing Franklin's grandson.

Soon after this, these two grand men appeared together at an open meeting of the Academy of Science; they were seated side by side. The audience was greatly moved at seeing the two great souls together and applauded them enthusiastically. They themselves felt the same emotion and, yielding to it, Franklin turned and shook Voltaire's hand passionately; whereupon the audience shouted: "Pas à l'anglaise, non, non, mais à la française." Then the two old men embraced each other tenderly amid the tumultuous applause of the entire assembly. Someone said that it was Solon embracing Sophocles, but Mignet puts it well in telling: "It was the brilliant genius and renovator of the old world embracing the simple and industrious genius of the new."

Another interesting public appearance is recorded by Bachaumont's successors:

"March 11, 1783. . . . The Paris Museum held, on Monday the sixth, a public and general assembly, more solemn than any yet held, and that is proper since the Peace was the object of the session. It was to celebrate the birth of the New Republic of the United States to which homage was rendered in the presence of Monsieur Franklin, its representative. This great man, there in the midst of society, listened eagerly to the different works in prose and poetry which were rendered on the subject. His bust, presented by Houdon, was inaugurated amid the acclamations of all the spectators. The affair terminated with a concert and supper . . . the master of ceremonies, with a friendly freedom, crowned the head of Franklin with laurels and myrtle. It was not an altogether philosophical spectacle to see a personage as grave as Monsieur Franklin, who is at this moment overburdened with the business of the utmost importance, taking part in such literary foolishness and attending such childish performances and apparently enjoying himself in them."

The author seems to have been much impressed with Franklin's ability to play, despite his onerous duties of state.

In 1782, when Lafayette had returned to Paris for a short visit, he was a frequent visitor and a welcome guest at the Passy villa. Bachaumont's diary says of him:

"September 29, 1782. . . . Monsieur le Marquis de la Fayette is still here . . . he is daily in conference with Monsieur Franklin and other insurgents. Monsieur de la Fayette is so enthusiastic over the New Republic, to whose existence he has

Photographed from an old print in the Trust Department of the State Street Trust Company　　*Kindness of Paul F. Cadman*

FRANKLIN'S RECEPTION AT THE PALAIS ROYAL
by the Duc d'Orléans (Louis Philippe) in 1778.

contributed not a little, that he has named his baby daughter Virginia; and his son George, because it is the name of Washington. The first word that he has taught him to pronounce is the name of this general who has inspired him with so great an admiration for everything connected with the United States of America, that the child looks on every voyager who comes back from that country, with a profound respect.

When Monsieur de la Fayette announced the birth of his daughter to Monsieur Franklin and told him the name he had given her, the Doctor replied that he wished him enough children so that there would be one to carry the name of each province (state); but that certain of them were not very harmonious (as to name) and that Monsieur Connecticut and Mademoiselle Massachusetts Bay would be little satisfied."

What a strange figure the good Doctor must have presented at the gorgeous Court of Versailles! His first presentation was a tremendous event and caused considerable worry to those in charge of the arrangements. He was amazed at the astonishing number of preliminaries and at the rigid rules of etiquette. After much argument he was persuaded to order a wig, and forthwith a famous "perruquier" came out from Paris to fit him. "Your head is too large," said the artist. "No, your wigs are too small," replied Franklin. Finally he refused all adornment, and his sponsors were obliged to present him in the simple, unaffected garb of his choice. Nevertheless, he was most graciously received at Versailles and was invited to dinner—an unexpected honor. It is said that the Queen was so charmed with his genuine geniality and good humor that she had him seated beside her at table. Later, when sick in body and weary in spirit, Franklin was starting on the long and trying voyage to America,

DÉROUTE DE PASSY.
le 15 Juillet 1-95, ou 25 Messidor An 1ᵉ de la République.

Photographed for the State Street Trust Company   *Kindness of Paul F. Cadman*

A RARE VIEW OF PASSY, NOW PART OF THE CITY OF PARIS,
showing the "Retreat of Passy," an event in the history of the place.   Franklin lived not far from there.

the Queen sent her own litter to carry him to Havre and the King presented him with his picture, framed in four hundred and eight brilliants.

The news of his going weighed heavily on the light heart of Parisian society.   Flourens, in his "Éloge Historique, O. B. Delessert," gives this delicate touch, which illustrates how dearly Franklin was loved and how sincerely his departure was regretted:

"Madame Delessert writes to her two children.   In these letters, piously conserved by her family, Madame Delessert tells her sons everything that is happening in Paris.   France has been happy enough, as everyone knows, to have Franklin during a few of the last years of his life."

Franklin and the Delessert family saw each other often.   At this time he was on the point of leaving France.   This is the way Madame Delessert speaks of Franklin to her children:

"I cannot tell you (she writes) with what emotion I look upon this venerable old man whose life has been so honorably complete.   He is very amiable and always has something spiritual and pleasant to say.

Someone was telling him how much we regretted seeing the preparation for his departure; he answered: 'I have spent a very pleasant evening, but, when bedtime comes, one must go home.   It is very hard for me to leave and often I am tempted to stay.   But I hope and believe that I am doing what is for the best.'   A touching silence followed these words.   Then someone mentioned that his compatriots did not seem as grateful to him as they should be; and that he had enemies among them. 'Their injustice does not surprise me at all: I know mankind.   I will not feel angry toward them and I will not be less pleased by the sight of their happiness.' "

Madame Delessert adds:

"With Franklin there is a youth of sixteen years, bright and intelligent, who looks like him physically and who, having decided to become a printer, is working to that end.   There is something very imposing in the sight of the American Legislator's grandson taking part in so simple a task."

What a charm there is in these words and, at the same time, what science, what art of motherhood!   How well the author of these letters shows the great gifts of Franklin and gives an insight into the largeness of his character and of his life!

Bouchot gives a very sympathetic picture of the little procession that started from Passy on the morning of July 10, 1785. The first stop was at Auteuil for the sad leavetaking which was so surely to be the last, and Franklin and Madame Helvétius wept "tears that were honorable of both." At Nanterre, the worthy Le Ray de Chaumont and his daughter Sophie said their farewell with unrestrained emotion. The generous host and the gentle guest had grown deep into each other's hearts. Not least among Franklin's Passy friendships was that of the young Monsieur Le Veillard, the director of the Passy mineral springs and later Mayor of Passy. Condorcet says that this good man had lavished all the cares of filial tenderness on Franklin and that to the last he wished

Photographed from an old engraving owned   *Kindness of Paul F. Cadman*
by the State Street Trust Company

CHÂTEAU DE LA ROCHEFOUCAULD,

*where Franklin is supposed to have spent the night on his way
to Le Havre on his homeward journey from Passy.
He was the guest of the well-known
La Rochefoucauld.*

to postpone what was to be an eternal separation. Le Veillard accompanied Franklin all the way to Le Havre. The overland voyage was uneventful. Franklin soon accustomed himself to the motion of the litter loaned by the Queen, which was carried by two small mules, and it is certain that with the condition of the roads at that time he enjoyed a far greater degree of comfort because of her bounty. The party spent the first night at Saint-Germain, one night at the château of the well-known La Rochefoucauld, and another "chez" Monsieur Holker at Rouen. At Le Havre there was a tremendous ovation prepared for him, and the entire city turned out to wish him Godspeed and "bon voyage." Franklin was particularly pleased to find Houdon, the celebrated sculptor, on board the vessel, and he remarked that he felt as if he were taking a little of France back with him.

The last entries concerning Franklin in Bachaumont's "Mémoires" are headed:

"Extracts from a letter received from Philadelphia. . . . Mr. Franklin arrived here the day before yesterday, the 15th of September, in better health than when he left Paris. He has been received like a titulary god—it was a general holiday. The vessels in port were all in flags, even the British. He was forty-eight days in crossing. Monsieur Houdon was with him.

Monsieur Franklin has returned his grandson, already full grown, to the lad's mother. This child was only a boy when he was taken to Paris in 1776."

In the crowded months of his last busy years in America, Franklin took time to care for the precious memories of his long sojourn in France. In his correspondence there are many tender and even affectionate letters to and from his old Passy friends and those of the salon Helvétius, which he always called l'Académie des Belles-Lettres d'Auteuil. Soon after his arrival in America he wrote to Madame Helvétius:

"I stretch my arms toward you, despite the immensity of the seas which separate us, awaiting the celestial embrace which I confidently hope to one day give you."

In his delightful book, "Le Salon de Madame Helvétius," Antoine Guillois tells us that "le patriarche" never lost touch with the "hermitage d'Auteuil":

"He recalled with happiness the birds and the flowers, the dogs and especially the cats which

L'AMÉRIQUE INDÉPENDANTE

Dédiée au Congrès des Etats unis de l'Amérique

From an old engraving in the Bibliothèque Nationale

Kindness of Paul F. Cadman

ALLEGORY OF THE INDEPENDENCE OF AMERICA

Franklin is shown in the centre of the picture.

last had invaded the whole house. There were eighteen, lazy, voluptuous, eating everything that came their way and doing nothing except to tuck their paws in their furry coats and warm themselves in the sun, leaving the whole house to be infested with mice. They were not even disturbed for their meals which were served to them in large flat plates and which consisted of breast of chicken and partridge. At the sight of these victuals, all these personages forgot their dignity, and quarreled over each morsel with snarlings and scratchings. Then they took up their places on the best chairs which they starred with spots, much to the despair of the visitors who never knew where to sit."

This smacks of Morellet, for the good Abbot wrote Franklin in February, 1786:

"Notre Dame d'Auteuil is in excellent health, notwithstanding the fact that she drinks too much coffee, which is contrary to the orders of Doctor Cabanis, and that she always steals my share of the cream which is against all the rules of justice. The bulldog which your grandson brought us from England has become positively unbearable and even vicious. He has already bitten the Abbot de La Roche and he shows signs of a ferocity which is really alarming. We have not yet been able to persuade his mistress to enter him as a combatant at the bull fights or else to drown him; but we are hard at it. We have also some other domestic enemies, less ferocious, but very harmful. A great number of cats which keep on multiplying both in the woodshed and in the poultry-yard, thanks to the generous care that she gives to their feeding. Today there are eighteen but there will soon be thirty. One of us proposed to rid ourselves of them either by throwing them in the river or by catching them in a trap, but some sophist has composed a petition for them which might serve as the counterpart of the 'thanks' which you wrote for the flies in your apartment after the destruction of the spiders which had been ordered by Our Lady."

Guillois goes on to quote the reply to this delightful letter which was addressed to l'Académie des Belles-Lettres d'Auteuil in April, 1787:

"Your project to deport the eighteen cats of Our Lady of Auteuil rather than to drown them, is very humane. The kind treatment which they enjoy at the hands of their present mistress may keep them from wishing to change their situation. Nevertheless if they are of the race of Angoras and if one can make them understand how two cats of their tribe, brought here by my grandson, are caressed and nearly adored, you may be able to persuade them to emigrate of their own accord rather than exposing themselves to the hate of the abbots who will surely succeed sooner or later in obtaining their condemnation. Embrace very tenderly for me the good Notre Dame whom I love as much as ever . . . present my compliments to Monsieur Le Ray, and to all the Wednesday diners and to Les Étoiles (the daughters of Madame Helvétius). . . ."

And in another letter to Morellet written in December, 1788, Franklin says:

"In this poverty of news from l'Académie d'Auteuil, I read and re-read with a pleasure always new, your letters, those of the abbot de La Roche and the articles which you sent me in July 1787 and the scrawl as she herself called it from the good Dame whom we all love and of whom I will always cherish the memory as long as there is a breath of life in me; when, in my dreams, I fly to France to visit my friends, I always go first to Auteuil. . . ."

Franklin must have realized the great part that he had played in the foundation of America. His patriotism and loyalty were well-nigh perfect; yet eight years in Paris had made him a citizen of France in spirit at least. The glorious friendships of those years had been among the most precious acquirements of his long life. Scarcely four years passed after his return to America before the country of his adoption fell into a sorry plight. The news of the Revolution of 1789 was long in reaching the States, and no doubt the first reports were fantastic in the extreme. When word did come, his noble old heart must have been torn between the triumph over the oppressions and abuses of the old régime and his anxiety for the many children of France who had taken a lasting place in his life. No doubt he thought how that wild mob, which had marched on Versailles to demand bread of their King, had taken the very road which skirted the garden of his Passy home. Fortunately, he was spared the horrors of the Reign of Terror, during which terrible days most of his old friends of Auteuil and Passy were driven into exile, were imprisoned, or paid for their convictions with their

Photographed from an old print in the collection of the State Street Trust Company   *Kindness of Paul F. Cadman*

HALLE AU BLÉ, OR WHEAT MARKET, IN PARIS,

where a commemorative ceremony was held on July 21, 1790, upon learning of Franklin's death. The building was decorated in black, and mourning was voted by the Assembly. Seven years before, a great ball was given there to celebrate the Peace of Versailles, and all Paris was illuminated for the occasion.

lives. Condorcet, as we have said, took poison to escape the guillotine, and Le Veillard perished on the scaffold. Madame Helvétius survived the Terror, and her salon remained the headquarters of the cultured, the learned and the geniuses of France. She died on the 13th of August, 1800, at the age of eighty-one.

Franklin died on April 17, 1790. It took nearly two months for the news to reach Paris. On the eleventh of June, in the same year, Mirabeau addressed these words to the Constituent Assembly:

"Franklin is dead! He has returned to the bosom of the Divinity—this genius who freed America, and who poured out on Europe such torrents of light; this sage whom two worlds acclaim; this man whom the history and science of two empires is discussing, holds without doubt a very high rank among his fellowmen.

Too often political cabinets have announced the death of those who were great only in their funeral eulogies; too often the etiquette of courts has decreed hypocritical mournings. Nations should go into mourning for their benefactors only; the representatives of Nations should alone propose homage to the heroes of humanity.

Congress has ordained throughout the fourteen States of the Confederation two months of mourning for Franklin and America is now paying that tribute of veneration to one of the Fathers of Her Constitution. Would it not be fitting, gentlemen, for us to unite in this religious act, to participate in this honor, which is given in the face of the whole universe, to the rights of man and to the philosopher who has contributed most to propagate their conquest over all the earth! Antiquity would have built altars to this vast and powerful genius—who, to the profit of mortals—embracing in his thought both the earth and the sky, knew how to overcome both lightning and tyrants. France, enlightened and free, owes at least a witness of remembrance and regret to one of the greatest men who has ever served philosophy and liberty.

I propose that it be decreed that the National Assembly wear mourning for three days for Benjamin Franklin."

Lafayette and Rochefoucauld seconded this motion. The official decree was as follows:

"The National Assembly decrees that its members shall wear mourning for Benjamin Franklin for three days, beginning next Monday; that the discourse delivered on this occasion shall be printed; and that the President shall write to the American Congress in the name of the National Assembly."

The City of Paris held a commemorative ceremony in the "Halle au Blé," the Wheat Market, which building was draped in black. (A picture is shown herewith.) The Society of the Printers of Paris met together in a great hall in the middle of which the bust of Franklin had been placed on a high pedestal. While one of the members pronounced a funeral oration about the great printer who had become a statesman and the godfather of liberty of two worlds, other members were setting up the speech which was printed and distributed to all the members before they left the hall.

For more than a century and a half, historians, literary men, artists, and diplomats of

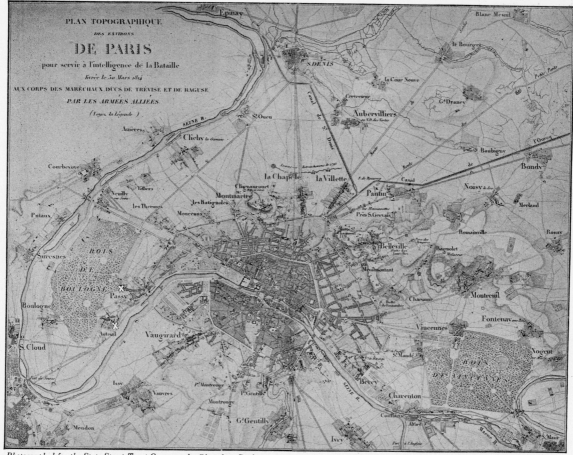

Photographed for the State Street Trust Company by Giraudon, Paris   Kindness of Paul F. Cadman

MAP OF PARIS AND ENVIRONS
made twenty years or more after Franklin left France, showing Passy and Auteuil (near the Seine and not far from the Bois de Boulogne). Those who know Paris well will be interested to see how far removed Clichy, Montmartre and Neuilly were in those days.

France have combined to preserve the memories of Franklin, not only for France but for all. There is one organization which has been particularly zealous in this labor, and justly so. La Société Historique d'Auteuil et Passy has, since the day of its foundation, pursued every trace and conserved every bit of evidence about Franklin's sojourn in France, and from the valuable bulletins of this society, now in its twenty-fifth year, a real biography could be gleaned.

Auteuil and Passy have long since merged into one, and the twain find themselves today well inside the city limits, forming the sixteenth "arrondissement," or ward, of Paris. The district, which is still that of the "better residences," is bounded roughly by the Bois de Boulogne, the Avenue de la Grande Armée, the Avenue Marceau and the Seine. It contains many interesting streets and monuments, and a part of it is sometimes called "Little America," because of the numerous souvenirs of Franco-American amity. In the Place d'Iéna is the magnificent equestrian statue of Washington by Daniel French. In the Place des États-Unis is the bronze group of Washington and Lafayette which was the work of Bartholdi in 1895. Near this are the present American Embassy and the American Naval Headquarters in Europe. Besides these American souvenirs, there is the great Palace of the Trocadéro, built for the Exposition of 1878 and conserved as a museum, theatre, and public garden. The Place Victor Hugo celebrates the great author with an imposing statue. Then there is the beautiful park La Muette. At one extremity of the Passy district is the Avenue du Bois de Boulogne, the most beautiful residence highway in the city; at the other extremity is the main road to Versailles. At a point very near the former gardens of the Hôtel Valentinois, the Seine is bridged by the Pont de Grenelle, in the middle of which stands a replica of Bartholdi's Statue of Liberty, erected by the Paris American Colony.

How have Passy and Auteuil commemorated Franklin? As far back as 1792 the suburb of Auteuil honored Franklin by placing his bust on the façade of the town hall. This building, which was dedicated on August 5th of that year, was called a veritable Pantheon, for it was decorated with the busts of Rousseau, Voltaire, Helvétius, and Mirabeau as well as others of less fame. During the ceremonies, when the bust of Franklin was placed in its niche, the Mayor made this astonishing comment:

"Honor to the genius Franklin—that good patriarch who knew how to apply science, so often useless, to the needs of humanity. He perfected the art of printing, agriculture, and physics; he invented the lightning rod; he established the Independence of America, his country, and he prepared the way for our liberty. Honor to Franklin the author of the Science of Poor Richard."

In a hundred and fifty years most of the ancient monuments of Auteuil and Passy have disappeared, with them the town hall just mentioned and the famous old "hôtel" of Madame Helvétius. The Hôtel Valentinois has literally vanished from the face of the earth. After the death of Le Ray de Chaumont it passed into other hands, the beautiful gardens were subdivided, and before long the fine

*Photographed for the State Street Trust   Kindness of Paul F. Cadman
Company by Giraudon, Paris*

ORIGINAL PLAQUE WHICH AT ONE TIME WAS PLACED ON THE SITE OF THE OLD HÔTEL VALENTINOIS, AT PASSY, FRANCE,
where Franklin once lived. A new house has been erected here, and a new plaque, shown in another illustration, placed on the corner. This plaque is now in the Musée Carnavalet, in Paris, which is dedicated to memorials of interest to the City of Paris.

old house was torn down to make room for modern dwellings which have neither history nor charm. For many years the Société Historique d'Auteuil et Passy has been trying to find means to locate definitely the former site. Up to the present time they have not succeeded, but the controversy has and will furnish great interest to those who hold large pride in the history of their "arrondissement."

In 1896, there was a small chapel on what was thought to be the site of the old Hôtel Valentinois. The Society held a very dignified ceremony on March 5th of that year and placed a plaque (shown in an illustration), on the door of this little chapel. Anatole France was then vice-president of the organization, and many other distinguished men were members. These and many others, including ambassadors and representatives of foreign lands and of France, met to pay homage to Franklin. There were many brilliant speeches, in which high tribute was offered to the American who, in the words of the great abbot-politician Sieyès, of Napoleon's time, was "particularly dear to a land where he knew how to make an infinite number of friends in a very short time." A certain Monsieur Faye, a former minister and member of the Institute, gave a scientific discourse on the history of the invention of the lightning rod; he also gave a short eulogy of Franklin, and closed his remarks with Turgot's famous phrase:

Photographed for the State Street   *Kindness of Paul F. Cadman*
Trust Company by Giraudon, Paris

LOCATION OF THE PAVILION OF THE OLD HÔTEL VALENTINOIS, PASSY, FRANCE,

where Franklin lived most of the time between the years 1777 and 1785. He lived also at the Hôtel de Valentinois itself part of the time. This modern apartment house, called Maison d'Angle, has been erected here, on the corner of Rues Raynouard and Singer. The former building was owned during Franklin's time by Le Ray de Chaumont. On the corner of this new structure can be seen a tablet placed there in commemoration of Franklin's residence.

Eripuit coelo fulmen sceptrumque tyrannis—

which he translated:

"Il arracha la foudre aux cieux et le sceptre aux tyrans"—

and which we can translate again:

"He snatched the lightning from the heavens and the scepter from tyrans."

Another speaker recalled the fact that Franklin had placed the first lightning rod ever installed in France on the Hôtel Valentinois.

The little chapel has, too, disappeared, and the plaque which was placed with such grace and sincerity is now safe in the keeping of the fine old Carnavalet Museum of Paris. A spacious modern apartment house now stands on the corner of the Rue Raynouard and the Rue Singer,

Photographed by Giraudon, Paris

PLAQUE PLACED ON THE END OF NEW BUILDING ON THE CORNER OF RUES RAYNOUARD AND SINGER IN PASSY, FRANCE,

to commemorate Franklin's residence.

which junction marks, if not exactly, at least the general area of the lost site. The landlord has decorated one corner of his building (shown on page 87) with a very generous plaque which speaks for itself. Just in front of the Trocadéro Palace there is a short street which runs up over the gardened hill which was once one of the principal heights of Passy, and this is the Rue Franklin. Below it on a beautiful plot of lawn, which is happily decorated with plants and shrubs, is the splendid statue of Franklin which was presented to the City of Paris by the late John H. Harjes. On either side of the base of the statue are bas-reliefs, one representing Franklin signing the treaty of Paris and the other showing his presentation at the Court of Louis XVI, pictures of which are shown on pages 90 and 91. In the Salle des Fêtes of the present town hall of the sixteenth "arrondissement," Franklin's name occupies a large panel in the ceiling, as do those of the other great sons of Passy.

Throughout Paris there are many other souvenirs of the first American minister. In the entrance hall of the Bibliothèque Mazarine there is the well-known bust by Caffieri, while in the Louvre there is the nearer perfect and better-known bust of Houdon. At Carnavalet there is a large painting by Duplessis. There have been more than one hundred and fifty engravings of Franklin, and there are still copies of these often fine works for sale at all the "marchands des gravures." The Cabinet des Médailles of the Bibliothèque Nationale has an admirable collection of Franco-American medals, among which there are many of Franklin. In the private collection of Monsieur David Weill at Neuilly there is a rare and beautiful miniature of Franklin, which is no bigger than a thumbnail— a veritable bijou. In the same collection is a statuette, perhaps twelve or fourteen inches high, which is probably the work of the famous Luzanne.

In the old cemetery of Père-Lachaise is the tomb of William Temple Franklin, who was with his grandfather throughout his entire stay in France. He died in Paris on the 25th of May, 1823. On his tomb is this inscription: "He was ever worthy of a name which dies out with him."

We opened this chapter with the generous résumé of Franklin's rôle in France by Mignet; we can do no better than give here another quotation from the same author, which presents not only a sketch of Franklin's life but tells how high a place he held and holds and will hold in the history and thought of France:

"Few careers have been so fully, so virtuously, and so gloriously complete as that of the son of the Boston dyer, who began by pouring the tallow into candle moulds, then made himself a printer,

STATUE OF BENJAMIN FRANKLIN IN FRONT OF THE TROCADÉRO PALACE,

presented to the City of Paris by John H. Harjes. It was officially dedicated on April 27, 1906, on the bicentenary of Franklin's birth. The Rue Franklin runs just behind the iron fence which is seen in the picture. Details of two bas-reliefs appear in other illustrations.

THE SIGNING OF THE TREATY OF PARIS
Bas-relief on the pedestal of the Franklin statue in front of the Trocadéro.

edited the first American newspapers, established the first paper factory in the Colonies, discovered the identity of electricity and lightning, became a member of the Academy of Science of Paris and of nearly every organization of savants in Europe; was the courageous representative of the submissive Colonies at the Metropolis; the negotiator of the insurgent Colonies both in France and in Spain; took his place beside Washington as the founder of their independence, and at last, after having done good throughout eighty-four years, died surrounded by the respect of two worlds; a sage who had spread the knowledge of the laws of the universe, a great man who had contributed to the freedom and the prosperity of his country and who merited not only that America should go into mourning for him but that the Constituent Assembly of France should share in that mourning by a public decree.''

There are also some interesting facts regarding Franklin's suggestions for daylight saving, and these we quote:

"The following delightful letter from the pen of Franklin appeared in the *Journal de Paris* Nonidi 9 Frimaire An IV, according to the Revolutionary calendar, or November 30, 1795, according to the Julian reckoning. The editors stated that it had been copied from the *Décade Philosophique*, and remarked that although it was more than eleven years since its writing, it still had some very useful applications:

'Letter from Franklin to the editors of the *Journal de Paris*, written at Passy in 1784.

Gentlemen: You frequently inform us of new discoveries, permit me to make known to you one of which I myself am the author and which I believe can be of great use.

I passed an evening recently in a house which is lighted by the lamps of Messrs. Quinquet and Lange—we experimented and speculated a great deal as to whether or not they burned more oil than ordinary lamps.

I noted this taste for economy with a great deal of satisfaction, for economy is one of my chief interests. I returned home and went to bed about three hours after midnight, my head full of the subject of our conversation. About six o'clock I was awakened by a noise over head and I was greatly astonished to find my room brilliantly illuminated; I thought someone had lighted a dozen of Monsieur Quinquet's lamps—but on rubbing my eyes I plainly perceived that the light was coming in through my windows. I got up to see where it was coming from and discovered that the sun which was just

FRANKLIN'S PRESENTATION AT COURT
Bas-relief on the pedestal of the Franklin statue in front of the Trocadéro.

rising above the horizon, was flooding my room with an abundance of rays, since my servant had forgotten to close the shutters.

You surely have, Messieurs, many readers of both sexes who will be as astonished to hear that the sun is up at such an early hour as they will to know that I was up to see it; they will be none the less astonished to hear my assurance that the sun gives its light as soon as it gets up, but I have proof of the fact, it is impossible to doubt it, I was an eye-witness, and on repeating the observation the three following mornings I obtained the same result. This phenomenon caused me to make several serious reflexions: If it had not been for the accident that awakened me on that morning, I would probably have slept six hours longer during which time the sun would have been shining—consequently that evening I should have passed six hours more by candlelight. This last manner of lighting is much more expensive than the first, and my taste for economy led me to make use of the little arithmetic which I possess to make some calculations on the subject . . . and I have found . . . the city of Paris alone would save 96,075,000 livres Tournois [the pound of the city of Tour was current and was worth about the same as a franc at par] of wax, tallow, and oil, by making use of daylight instead of candles during the six months of summer. There you have it, Messieurs, the discovery and the reform which I propose.

I believe that all reasonable persons who learn through this letter that there is daylight as soon as the sun gets up, will resolve to get up with it, and as for the others, in order to make them follow the same course, I propose that the government make the following rules:

1.—A tax of one Louis on every window that has a shutter.

2.—Guards at every wax and candle shop to prevent any family from using more than one pound of candles a week.

3.—Guards who will arrest every carriage which is found on the streets after nightfall.

4.—Have all the church bells rung at sun-rise and if that is not enough, fire a cannon in every street so as to open the eyes of the lazy to their best interests.

The first two or three days would be the hardest—after which the new way of living would be as natural and as easy as the irregularity in which we now live—the first steps would be the hardest. If you make a man get up at four in the morning, it is more than likely that he will go to bed at eight at night—and he will get up without any trouble at four the next morning.

Although my discovery may have great advantages, I ask neither reward nor pay for having thus frankly made it public. . . . I foresee plainly that certain narrow and jealous persons will dispute

TOMB OF WILLIAM TEMPLE FRANKLIN AND
HIS WIFE IN PÈRE–LACHAISE CEMETERY,
PARIS

William Temple Franklin was a grandson of Benjamin
Franklin, and lived with him while he was in Paris.
He died there on May 25, 1823. His tomb, the one on the
left, bears the following inscription: "He was ever
worthy of a name which dies out with him." He lived at
No. 8 Rue Saint-Georges. His wife is buried in
the other tomb.

this matter with me and will say that the ancients had the idea before I did. I do not deny that the ancients knew the hours of sunrise, but it does not follow from that, that they knew that which I pretend to be the first to teach, namely, THAT IT GIVES LIGHT AS SOON AS IT RISES. It is that which I claim as my discovery.

At all events if the ancients did know the truth, it has been well forgotten. All Parisians have with me a great taste for economy—everyone has good reason to like it. If this is granted, I say that it is impossible that a wise people under such conditions, who have so long used a smoky and unhealthy candle should continue to do so when they can light up for nothing with the beautiful and pure light of the sun.

I have the honor to be . . . '

"On the twelfth of the same month in which this letter appeared, an indignant citizen, who signed himself 'a subscriber,' published a letter in the same *Journal* bitterly assailing the paper for publishing such rot, 'froide et insipide,' and stating that if great men had to write such stuff in their off moments it was a pity that their people could not keep such letters concealed with the family treasure.

"However, the good gentleman who invented the lamp mentioned in the letter, one Dr. Quinquet, pharmacist, did not take any offense at the writing at all, but was quick to turn it into a bit of advertising from which he no doubt drew large benefits. On the eighteenth of the same month he published the following letter:

'Paris le 18 frimaire An 4.

Aux Auteurs du Journal.

It was with great surprise, citizens, that I read in your *Journal* of the twelfth instant, the letter from one of your subscribers, who pretends to reply to that of the celebrated Franklin which appears in the issue of the ninth.

I have not time to waste so I will come to the point at once.

I do not know anything about Franklin's idea—but more than six months ago, I made known to several persons and special commissions, my views tending to economise materials which are becoming extremely rare and which we may run out of at any moment by reason of the extravagant use which goes on all the time. These views are the same as those of the Homme Célèbre, which someone is trying to ridicule.

I proved by definite results that my lamps made possible the greatest economy since they served the triple functions of lighting, heating and cooking. Nevertheless if the necessary elements were becoming too rare and too dear, there was still another way of economizing, viz.—to go to bed at dark and to get up at sunrise.'

He then goes on to quote a lot of statistics on wax and oil and draws the conclusion that by 'daylight saving' Paris alone could save some 72,000,000 francs a year; and with a bit of real irony he adds:

'If you express this in terms of "assignats" at one hundred to one, the economy would amount to six billions, twelve hundred millions. . . . I do not see anything foolish in that nor does it seem a clumsy joke.

Do we live in the same conditions during the day as during the darkness?

Does our body suffer from absence of light? Are we constituted to move about, to act, to work in the darkness? On the contrary Nature seems to indicate that the very absence of this living light is provided for our repose. The flowers close their chalices and hold back their perfume when the sun goes down; the animals give themselves to sleep.

Furthermore, I am sure that these ideas will find contradictors. . . . Our too numerous spectacles—who will attend them? . . . to which one might reply: what difference does it make to the working man what the idle do! We will have less spectacles, they will be better, and thereby another economy . . . we will be in less danger of demanding with the Romans, so unworthy of their ancestors, only bread and comedians. . . .

Salut et fraternité.

QUINQUET, Pharmacien.'

"To this droll correspondence it remains only to add that Quinquet's lamp, however economical it may have been, left such a bad impression that to this day the name is employed to stigmatize a lamp as a failure; and one frequently hears: 'Oh, that burns like a bad old Quinquet.' "

THIS ALLEGORICAL PRINT APPEARED IN PARIS AFTER FRANKLIN'S DEATH,

and depicts Philosophy and Innocence rendering the last rites to Franklin. Above appear the words, "Weep for the great men—they are rare." This museum contains many other relics of interest.

In looking over some of the books concerning Franklin, the compiler of this volume has picked up at random a few amusing anecdotes and incidents which he is adding to Mr. Cadman's interesting chapter.

Franklin's popularity shortly after his arrival caused him to write to a friend in America: "I am the absolute doll of the people of Paris, who call me, deck me out, crown me and play with me in the most agreeable manner in the world; they have lavished so much on my bust that if a price were put on my head it would be impossible for me to escape." In another letter, this time to a Bostonian, he said: "You mention the kindness of the French Ladies to me. . . . Somebody, it seems, gave it out that I lov'd Ladies, and then everybody presented me their Ladies to be embrac'd, that is to have their Necks kiss'd. For as to kissing of Lips or Cheeks it is not the mode here; the first, is reckoned rude and the other may rub off the

SIGNING OF THE TREATY OF AMITY AND COMMERCE AND OF ALLIANCE BETWEEN FRANCE
AND THE UNITED STATES, FEBRUARY 6, 1778

From one of the beautiful paintings in the Franklin Union, Boston, done by Charles E. Mills of Dedham.

Paint." At another time when a friend of his, Marquis de Tonnerre, called at Passy, Madame de Chaumont said to him: "Hélas! tous les conducteurs de M. Franklin n'ont pas empêché la tonnerre de tomber sur Mde. de Chaumont," to which the American replied that he would make no use of his lightning rod to prevent the match. In fact, the subject of electricity and lightning rods was so much discussed in Paris that at one time costumes were seen in the streets called "lightning conductor" dresses with a little steel point and two wires trailing to the ground. Coiffures, as we have heard, were arranged "à la Boston" and many articles were called "a l'Amérique." Franklin's name was also given to hats, gloves, dishes, and especially snuff-boxes, many of which bore his picture on the cover. One of these snuff-boxes is in our Bostonian Society.

Another of his favorite expressions became used a great deal, as James Hazen Hyde points out in his "Franco-American Historic Relations." When anyone asked America's representative how affairs were progressing, he was satisfied to reply: "Ça ira! Ça ira!" As Mr. Hyde further explains, one of the French Revolutionary songs of a few years later took this expression for its title.

The French looked upon the American as the "Sage of Passy," but never could really tell whether he were serious or joking. On a cold day he was sitting with some friends in Passy and the conversation naturally turned to the subject of cold and how best to keep warm. He told them in all seriousness that he could describe to them how a family could keep warm for a year on one piece of wood. He then explained in his quiet way that each member in turn could throw a piece of wood out of the window, then run downstairs, pick it up, run upstairs and repeat the performance. This he said was a sure way to keep warm even in the coldest weather.

His modesty, in spite of the many attentions and presents heaped upon him, made a great impression upon the French. On one occasion a gift of fruit was sent to him accompanied by an envelope addressed to "Le Digne Franklin." "This time," declared Silas Deane, "you cannot pretend it is not for you alone." "Not so," said Franklin, "the Frenchman cannot master our American names; it is plainly Lee, Deane, Franklin, that is meant." His fondness for jesting again made itself apparent, so it is said, for he stated that before his country decided to get its liberty he used to sign his letters "Free B. Franklin," and after America declared herself independent, he signed himself "B. Free Franklin."

Another well-known saying is attributed to him by Pontgibaud in his book on the war. Some friends called upon him at his home in Passy to condole with him on the fall of Philadelphia. "You are mistaken," ejaculated Franklin quite calmly, "it is not the British Army that has taken Philadelphia, but Philadelphia that has taken the British Army."

Madame Brillon told Madame Helvétius, as Franklin was leaving for his home, that his departure was all her fault, for if she would only consent to marry him Paris might always keep him. The former lady used to call Franklin's grandson by the affectionate title of "M. Franklinet."

Photographed for the State Street Trust Company by Giraudon, Paris   *Kindness of Paul F. Cadman*

TABLET ON THE BUILDING WHERE FORMERLY WAS SITUATED THE PAVILION OF LANGEAC, NO. 2 RUE DE BERRI,

where Thomas Jefferson lived from 1785 to 1789 during his residence in Paris. It was given by students of the University of Virginia, which was founded by him. In the year 1785 he served as minister to the Court of Versailles, succeeding Franklin. Jefferson is supposed to have said of his predecessor, "He is one of those men whom one succeeds, but whom one does not replace." Jefferson later lived in Têtebout Alley, now a part of Rue Têtebout.

In connection with Franklin, it is interesting to remember that Clemenceau and he both lived at Passy, and not only that but even resided on the same street. When Clemenceau was in this country on one occasion, he was introduced as a Pilgrim from Passy and Franklin was spoken of as a Pilgrim to Passy.

MARKER ON THE QUAY AT AURAY ON THE
BAY OF BISCAY, FRANCE,

*where Benjamin Franklin landed on December 4, 1776.
The quay on which this tablet was placed last December is
now named for this American diplomat.*

During his sojourn in France, many
visitors approached him with all kinds of
suggestions, but the most curious idea originated with a man who stated that if his
gambling debts should be paid by Franklin
he would be willing to "pray for success to
our cause." To Franklin, in addition to his
many other accomplishments, has been attributed, according to some authorities, the
invention of the first harmonica and the
institution of the first thrift campaign. He
also served as the first Postmaster-General
of this country, and was to all intents and
purposes the first American Ambassador to
France.

Benjamin Franklin left a lasting impression
in the hearts of the French people. Although
his stay in France was only for a few years
and he finally took leave of his new friends
and departed for home over one hundred and
forty years ago, his memory still lingers. Only
last December a commemorative marker, of
which we show a reproduction, was placed
on the quay at Auray, situated on the Bay
of Biscay, France, where Franklin landed on
December 4, 1776. This quay has since been
named for our famous statesman and diplomat.

DE FLEURY, THE ONLY FOREIGNER DECORATED BY OUR GOVERNMENT DURING THE REVOLUTIONARY WAR

AS far as we can learn, the only Frenchman, or in fact the only foreigner, to receive a medal from the United States during the Revolution was Lieutenant-Colonel François Louis Teisseidre de Fleury, of Saint Hippolyte, in Languedoc. His father was a nobleman, and acted as preceptor of the grandson of Louis XIV. The son was commissioned by his country a captain of engineers in 1776 and soon obtained a furlough to enter the American army as a volunteer, sailing for this country with Du Coudray in February, 1777.

He received an appointment as captain from our Congress on May 22, 1777, later serving as inspector, adjutant-general and lieutenant-colonel. He joined General Washington's army upon his arrival, and was soon wounded. At the battle of Brandywine his horse was killed under him, he himself again receiving a wound. Congress, on September 13, 1777, presented the gallant Frenchman with a new horse "as a testimonial of the sense they had of his merits," promoting him to a lieutenant-colonelcy in consideration of the disinterested gallantry he had manifested in the service of the United States. At Germantown this horse was shot under him. He also served with great distinction in Rhode Island, and was commended by d'Estaing. Later on, in the assault on Stony Point, de Fleury, leading one of the attacks, was the first to enter the main works, and with his own hands captured the flag of the enemy. For this brave deed Congress voted him the medal shown in an illustration, passing a resolution under date of October 1st, 1779: "That Congress entertain a high sense of the zeal, activity, military genius, and gallantry of Lieutenant-Colonel Fleury which he has exhibited on a variety of occasions during his service in the armies of these States, wherein while he has rendered essential benefit to the American cause, he has deservedly acquired the esteem of the army and gained unfading reputation for himself."

Chastellux wrote that "the attack was so brisk on the part of the Americans . . . that M. de Fleury, who was the first that entered, found himself in an instant loaded with eleven swords which were delivered to him. . . ." He also claimed that this attack was one of the most brilliant of the war. According to this French general, three commemorative medals were struck off, one of which was given to Colonel Fleury.

General Washington from his headquarters at West Point wrote to the President of Congress about this French officer under date of July 25, 1779, adding he "has acquitted himself in every respect as an officer of distinguished merit, one whose talents, zeal, activity and bravery alike entitle him to particular notice." General Washington begged the French Minister to report the gallant conduct of de Fleury to the French Court, and this he did. He returned to France on a leave of absence soon after the capture of Stony Point.

After the arrival of Rochambeau, he served under him in the campaigns of 1780, 1781 and 1782, receiving still another honor, this time bestowed by his King—a pension of four hundred livres in recognition of his bravery at Yorktown. He was a major in the Saintonge regiment. After the war he served in India, was made commander of the islands of Mauritius and of Bourbon, and returned to France in the year 1790. Later he was made a maréchal-de-camp in the Army of the North, and at the end of the war served under Rochambeau and Luckner. Mishaps continued to follow him, for during the retreat from Mons, his horse was shot and fell

Photographed by Giraudon, Paris, from a copy presented by Alexandre Vattemare to the   Kindness of Paul F. Cadman
Bibliothèque Nationale in Paris

MEDAL AWARDED BY THE UNITED STATES TO LIEUTENANT–COLONEL FRANÇOIS LOUIS TEISSEIDRE DE FLEURY,

the only foreigner to receive a medal from this country during the Revolutionary War. He was one of the earliest volunteers serving with Washington's army, first at Fort Mifflin, and later at Brandywine. This award was given to him for leading one of the attacks at Stony Point, where he himself captured the enemy's flag. He served with Rochambeau's army in the siege of Yorktown, and upon his return to France was made a Field Marshal. The medal is by Duvivier, one of the best of the French engravers, and represents de Fleury as a Roman soldier amid the ruins of a fort, a sword in one hand and a flag in the other. On the face are the words: "The American Republic presented this gift to de Fleury, French Knight, the first to mount the walls." On the reverse are, "Fortifications, marshes, enemies, overcome," with a plan of Stony Point and date of capture. General Washington had a high regard for him. He was born in St. Hippolyte, Languedoc, in 1749. He probably came to Boston, but no records have been found referring to his visit.

upon him, and as he was unable to extricate himself from this position the cavalry of the enemy rode over him. Upon his return to France he was made a field marshal, but after a long illness he resigned from the army, retiring to Rebais in the Seine-et-Marne.

The medal is by Duvivier, and represents de Fleury as a Roman soldier amid the ruins of a fort, a sword in one hand and the captured flag in the other. It is probable that he never received the medal, as it was lost somehow or other in Princeton, New Jersey. Although far from rich, he refused any pecuniary recompense from Congress upon leaving this country.

Congress awarded eight medals, but only one was given to a foreigner. One authority claims that another decoration was given to a Frenchman, but this cannot be verified. It is a curious fact that no medal was ever given to Rochambeau, Lafayette, de Grasse, or d'Estaing.

During the World War, Congress authorized the President to bestow American decorations on foreigners. One hundred and sixteen soldiers of France received our Distinguished Service Cross, and nearly all were attached to the American army.

DE LAUZUN'S CAVALRY AT LEBANON, CONNECTICUT

ROCHAMBEAU learned of the deep snows and the cold weather in Newport during the winter of 1780, and so determined to make a change before the following winter. About the first of November he withdrew his Bourbonnais and Soissonnais brigades from their summer positions to Newport, where they could protect the city, and then prepared to move the rest of his army to other places. The French Commander-in-Chief expected to send to Providence the Duc de Lauzun's celebrated Legion of Horse—"as fine a one as I have ever seen" according to General Heath; and a committee of that city was therefore chosen to select rooms for the officers and quarters for the men and horses. Rochambeau, in spite of the fact that the State of Rhode Island had prepared such excellent lodgings, heard also that some persons had raised the price of forage; and, therefore, after conferring with his agent, Colonel Wadsworth, he decided to have the Legion winter in Connecticut. "Good policy," he said, "would render it necessary that the corps should be in the same place under the inspection of its chief," upon whose "honesty every way," he assured Governor Trumbull, he might depend. "I am acquainted," he concluded, "with all the zeal that Your Excellency has for our common cause, and that you will do all in your power to receive that part of the French corps." The place chosen was Lebanon, spelled by Rochambeau "La Banon," chiefly on account of the abundance of fodder and wood to be had there. Lauzun was not on the best terms with his superior officer until after Yorktown, and this may have induced Rochambeau to send him "into the forests of Connecticut," as the French officer expressed it. "As I spoke English," he added, "I had to look after an infinite number of frightfully annoying but necessary details. I did not leave Newport without regrets; I found myself in a most agreeable society. . . . I left for Lebanon on the tenth of November; we had as yet received no letters from France. Siberia alone can be compared to Lebanon, which is composed only of some cottages scattered in the midst of a vast forest." He wondered why he did not hear more often from his many admirers in France, whom he mentions continually throughout his "Mémoires," which were written at No. 15 Place Vendôme, now owned by the Hotel Ritz. When he learned of the death of de Ternay, "of chagrin," as he uncharitably put it, he returned to Newport. In vain he endeavored to persuade his chief to include him among a detachment of the army which he thought might be sent out on a "sortie" with the squadron. He had been sent just previously, however, to Washington's headquarters on the North (Hudson) River, where his boat was sunk, de Lauzun and his friends reaching shore by running "tiddledies" as the boys call it, jumping from ice floe to ice floe till they reached shore.

On the tenth of November the Legion, numbering over two hundred and twenty, with an equal number of horses, reached Providence, presenting, as an eye-witness expressed it, "a very martial appearance"; and while there the Duc de Lauzun, who was a great favorite wherever he went, gave a ball in Hacker's Hall, "made brilliant," according to Stone's description, "with beautiful women and with the showy uniforms of French officers." Every soldier of the Legion wore a moustache. On the 12th, the corps left Providence, stopping on their march at Windham for a week. While there the Marquis de Chastellux, a major-general in the army, visited de Lauzun, and again with Baron de Montesquieu when the Legion reached Lebanon, where the Duc entertained his guests with a squirrel hunt—"a diversion which is much in fashion in this

HOME OF DAVID TRUMBULL, LEBANON, CON-
NECTICUT, KNOWN AS "REDWOOD"
*Here the French officers had their headquarters and were enter-
tained during the winter of 1780–81.*

country." "I was not sorry," Chastellux says, "to find myself in the French army, of which these Hussars formed the advanced guard, although their quarters be seventy-five miles from Newport, but there are no circumstances in which I should not be happy with M. de Lauzun. . . . It must be allowed that conversation is still the peculiar forte of the amiable French." Continuing, Chastellux writes: "It is told of an Englishman accustomed to be silent, that he said 'Talking spoils conversation.' This whimsical expression contains great sense: everybody can talk, but nobody knows how to listen, insomuch that the society of Paris, such as I left it, resembles the chorus of an opera, which a few *coryphées* alone have a right to interrupt."

The leader of the Legion also gave them a dinner at David Trumbull's house, at which the father, Governor Jonathan Trumbull, was also present, this occasion being well described by Chastellux:

"On returning from the chase, I dined at the Duke de Lauzun's, with Governor Trumbull and General Huntington. The former lives at Lebanon and the other had come from Norwich. I have already painted Governor Trumbull. You have only to represent to yourself this small old man, in the antique dress of the first settlers in this colony, approaching a table surrounded by twenty Hussar officers, and without either disconcerting himself, or losing anything of his formal stiffness, pronouncing, in a loud voice, a long prayer in the form of a Benedicite."

On another evening the French officers were invited to dine with General Huntington at his home in Norwich, the occasion being well described in the "Life of Governor Trumbull": "They made a superb appearance as they drove into town, being young, tall, vivacious men, with handsome faces and a noble air, mounted on horses bravely caparisoned. After dinner the whole party, going out into the yard, huzzaed for liberty, and, in good English, bade the people to 'live free, or die for liberty.' "

Stuart, in his life of Trumbull, further describes the great contrast between de Lauzun and his men and Governor Trumbull: "What a picture this from a gay Frenchman to the worthy old Governor! He is grave in carriage. His manners seem ceremonious. He is preceptive in conversation. He courts business. He is the happiest of mortals when he has any to transact. He is profoundly considerate in its execution—is heedful of comparing opinions with his Council. He wears the peculiar, imposing dress of his ancestors—and there over a table where doubtless waited 'the brimming bowl'—in the midst of a party of volatile, laughter-loving French officers—to all of whom good-natured derision and merriment was an instinct . . . the Governor, in the true old Puritan style, 'says grace'—and with such imposing solemnity of manner, and sincerity of tone, as, for his Benedicite, to extort 'at once from the midst of forty moustaches' . . . twenty profound, complaisant Amens! Truly it was a scene for a painter.

"But we have another picture of the Governor from the same hand . . . one to which reference is made in the preceding extract . . . drawn when the Marquis met him on another occasion and while the Marquis was for a day or two the guest of Colonel Wadsworth in

Hartford, whose house he found 'a most agreeable asylum' . . . and whom he describes as then 'about two-and-thirty, very tall and well made' . . . possessed of a 'noble as well as agreeable countenance' . . . and of a name, he adds, which 'throughout all America, is never pronounced without the homage due to his talents and his property.'"

Governor Trumbull whose family, by the way, once lived in Roxbury and then in Rowley, Massachusetts, had a warship and a privateer named for him, both fitted out in Connecticut.

Near the first of December, just before the death of de Ternay, Rochambeau on his inspection tour visited Lebanon and then proceeded to Providence and Boston. General Washington also visited Lebanon on March 5, remaining there three days; and according to Stuart in his history of Trumbull stopped "long enough (on the village green with great satisfaction alike to himself, the French, and crowds of spectators) to bestow on Lauzun's imposing legion the compliment of a stately review." The American Commander highly complimented de Lauzun on the discipline and appearance of his troops.

From the latter part of November, 1780, to June 23, 1781, this French Legion of Horse was stationed in this Connecticut village, and during these seven months the quiet, simple people of Lebanon rose to the occasion and did their utmost to make the sojourn of these foreigners as agreeable as possible. It is related that only one house—that of David Trumbull, the Governor's son, had a carpet, used only as an ornament; of course, his father, the Governor, made him give his residence up to the visiting officers. The annals of the town also record that "the son very properly replied that he must consult Mrs. Trumbull, which he proceeded at once to do. To the question, 'Will you allow me to take you to your mother's house at Norwich and give up our house to the French officers?' Mrs. Trumbull promptly replied, 'Certainly.' She was informed that the troops were already on the march and was asked when she would be ready for her journey. 'In just one hour,' was the prompt reply; and at the appointed time, with her infant daughter, fifteen months old, leaving everything in the way of comforts in her house, this patriotic lady set out for her drive of twelve miles on a cold autumn day." On the second day of the New Year her second daughter, Abigail, was born. In the following spring, Mrs. Trumbull paid a short visit to her home. It happened that Lafayette was also there at the same time and insisted on meeting the "patriotic lady" and her "patriotic baby," kissing the child and handing her about to the other officers. It is of interest to know that the brocade wedding gown of Jonathan Trumbull's bride has descended to her great-great-great-granddaughter, Colonel Louis R. Cheney's daughter.

A VIEW OF THE VILLAGE GREEN OF LEBANON, CONNECTICUT,
near the encampment of de Lauzun's Hussars.

Colonel Wadsworth and David Trumbull spared no pains to provide for the comfort of the troops by taking over vacant houses, repairing vacant buildings and erecting barracks. Most of the troops

Photographed from the "Life of Jonathan Trumbull" by Stuart

MADAM FAITH TRUMBULL, WIFE OF THE GOVERNOR
OF CONNECTICUT, CONTRIBUTING HER SCARLET CLOAK
TO THE SOLDIERS DURING THE REVOLUTION, IN THE
FIRST CONGREGATIONAL CHURCH OF LEBANON

*It is said that this garment was a gift to her from Rochambeau. It was cut
into pieces to help clothe the Americans. This church is still standing at the head of the village green.*

were quartered in the fields still known as the "barracks" on the Governor Trumbull farm on the right of the road that leads to Colchester, and just west of the War Office and the First Congregational Church. This building was designed by John Trumbull from the work of Christopher Wren. Others camped at the southerly end of the long common and also on both sides of the broad and beautiful village street. Water for the troops came undoubtedly from Locke's pond nearby. Lebanon could not accommodate all the Hussars; therefore some were sent to Colchester and temporarily to Windham. The Duc de Lauzun, later known as the Duc de Biron, who was a rich nobleman, witty, and brave, occupied David Trumbull's house, which is situated nearly opposite the spot where the War Office stood before its removal, and on the opposite corner from the Congregational Church.

There he gave brilliant banquets and balls. In fact, the presence of the French at Lebanon during that winter, with their gayeties, parades on the common and the martial music, with the added attraction of their well-groomed horses, was a unique event in the town's history—one that will be passed down from generation to generation. De Lauzun himself was much liked by the townspeople, and appreciated a good joke. Rochambeau, in his "Mémoires," describes an amusing incident that took place there: "I will relate an anecdote, which will convey a just idea of his private character. One of the good villagers asked him of what trade his father was in France. 'My father,' replied de Lauzun, 'is not in business; but I have an uncle who is a maréchal' (literally a farrier), making allusion to the Maréchal de Biron. 'Ah, indeed!' said the American, giving him a hearty squeeze of the hand, 'there are worse trades than that. . . .'"

Stuart, in his "Life of Jonathan Trumbull," describes these days better when he writes that "here it was these gay and laughter-loving Frenchmen gathered about their watchful camp fires, and paraded in the common in their beautiful uniforms, making the neighborhood alive with activity and eager to do all in their power by way of entertainment during their brief stay." Of their encampment there the people of Lebanon have handed down a number of interesting tales. They relate that the French used to visit the bar at Alden's Tavern which then stood on the eastern side of the Green, and that the cavalrymen often rode up to the bar on horseback. When the old tavern was later torn down, it is said that many coins, some of them French, were found in the cellar, having slipped down through the many cracks in the floor.

An illustration from the same book just referred to shows Faith Trumbull, the patriotic wife of the Governor, placing on the pulpit of the First Congregational Church of Lebanon a cloak supposed to have been a gift of Rochambeau, as an offering to our army. It is said that this French garment was cut into pieces to help clothe the poorly-clad American soldiers. Madam Trumbull was a great help to her husband during the trying years of the war. A romantic story has been told of a little girl called Diffidence Wyatt, who, while walking along a lane in Lebanon, came upon a French officer lying on the ground, who had been thrown from his horse and had suffered a broken leg. She secured help and removed him to her house, where he remained until he had recovered, when, as a token of gratitude, he gave her a golden necklace. One Sunday, when the pastor called for offerings for the troops, she donated this treasure to the cause. The story goes on to relate how the officer returned and danced a minuet with this Lebanon girl at the home of Governor Trumbull. Somewhat fearful, she confessed what she had done with his present, but was consoled to find that he thoroughly approved of her action.

Another romance has been woven around a Frenchman who was shot for desertion and who lies buried on the left of the Colchester Road, just west of the pond and old mill, the exact location being marked by a pile of stones and a wooden tablet. (Joseph Stedman of Westerly, Rhode Island, is anxious to have a better memorial placed over the grave.) Mistress Prudence Strong, who does not appear on the town records, is supposed to have procured his pardon from Rochambeau, but unfortunately the bearer of the news arrived too late to save his life. It is true that there had been some stealing of poultry and sheep which much vexed the commander of the troop. Fearing his wrath, a few of his men deserted; but this soldier was soon captured, court-martialed and shot. It is said that de Lauzun had him tried at once and shot before sunrise the next morning; for he realized that if Jonathan Trumbull heard of the case, he would interfere to save the culprit's life and might actually succeed in doing so, as de Lauzun always held in great respect any suggestions coming from the worthy Governor of Connecticut.

Governor Trumbull's diary thus describes the departure of the French troops: "June 23, 1781—Duke de Lauzun marched early. Went to Pine Swamp, near Col. Champion's." (This house, still standing, is in Westchester Centre, and is the summer home of a Hartford lawyer.) From there they passed through part of Connecticut to join Washington on the Hudson (described in Volume I). At this time, the Governor and the Council issued the proclamation urging their fellow citizens "not to raise a single cent the price of provisions during the passage of the French troops." Rochambeau says that "the inhabitants obeyed this injunction so generously that each mess was able to add every evening, to the common allowances, every kind of provision at a low price."

The most historic place in Lebanon, once the store of Governor Trumbull's father, is the old War Office building dating back to 1727, the floors of which have been trodden upon by Washington, Rochambeau, Admiral de Ternay, de Lauzun, Lafayette, Chastellux, the Dillon brothers, who were later guillotined, and Generals Sullivan, Knox, Putnam; by Samuel Adams, John Jay, Thomas Jefferson and Benjamin Franklin. These verses by Miss Ellen C. Williams, of which we quote only a few lines, give an excellent idea of these Revolutionary days in the old War Office:

Photographed from the "Life of Jonathan Trumbull" by Stuart

THE OLD WAR OFFICE AT LEBANON, CONNECTICUT,

as it appeared during the Revolutionary War, showing also the residence of Governor Jonathan Trumbull. Previously, and during the conflict, this War Office building was used as a store, and here some of the greatest American and French officers came to consult with the Connecticut Council of Safety, which held over eleven hundred meetings. Both buildings since the war have been moved a short distance north on the west road running past the village green.

The shadow of our George Washington has slanted athwart that door;
And the Count, Marquis and Baron, whose voices will be heard nevermore,
Once mingled with Duke and Admiral, Generals and noted men;
But they have been called to the higher rank, even before the King.

Is it a marvel we prize each shingle and every time-brown beam
Of the office that is left us, from the past, near our village green;
And seek carefully for ancient relics amid the dust and nails,
Glad that it's shielded by "the Sons" of Revolutionary fame?

In this old building Governor Trumbull, who lived next door on the corner of the Colchester Road and Town Street, had his war office, and there were held the many sessions of the "Council of Safety":

The Governor's face grew sad,
   In his store on Lebanon hill;
He reckoned the men he had;
   He counted the forts to fill.

The brave State's sons were gone;
   On many a field they lay;
They were following Washington,
   Afar down Yorktown way.

. . . But Jonathan Trumbull never quailed,
   In his store on Lebanon hill.

> There was New London fort,
>   And the fort on Groton Height,
> And the rich and crowded port;
>   But where were the men to fight?
>
> . . . Nay, never a word of such grudge was heard
>   On Lebanon hill.

In fact, this historic building was for a time the Military and Naval Headquarters of the Colony, owing to its inland situation; and as Lebanon itself lay on the direct road from New York to Boston, and, as the latest news was usually first heard there, it has often been referred to as the "focus of Connecticut patriotism and vigilance during the Revolution." In order to perpetuate the American and French connections with this War Office, the tablet, shown on the next page, has been placed over the fireplace in the room where the council met, the unveiling taking place on June 17, 1896.

This ancient red building as well as Governor Trumbull's house used to stand near the corner of Town Street and the Colchester Road, and after the war its location was slightly changed, being used then as a country store. Under another change of ownership, it was again removed for some unknown reason to its present location a few rods further north of the Colchester Road, where it became a dwelling. Today it is much as it was in the war days, the lower story serving as a museum and meeting place for the Trumbull Chapter, D. A. R. A little cross in front of the building, to the memory of Louis Raymond Abel of Lebanon, who was killed in the Argonne in the World War, serves to link the past with the present. Father Cabanel, Chaplain of the famous Blue Devils of France, also well known to New Englanders, visited Lebanon during the latter part of the World War, and before partaking of luncheon insisted upon seeing the old War Office.

The War Office building has had many owners. It was given in 1890 to the town as a memorial by Mrs. Bethiah Wattles, an old lady of ninety-two, who was anxious to have the building preserved for all time. The formal ceremony of dedicating the historic house was held on June 15 of the following year, those present visiting in turn Governor Trumbull's tomb, the barracks lot, the French graves, and the ruins of the old French ovens. These ovens deserve more than a passing mention. Their location, on the east side of the village Green and almost opposite the War Office, was discovered by Ernest E. Rogers of New London, who came upon the brick foundations, the superstructures having probably been removed for building purposes. He has some of these bricks which he is keeping as relics. An interesting incident of the dedication was the raising of the Stars and Stripes by descendants of Jonathan Trumbull and General Huntington "to signify," as stated in the account of the proceedings, "that Trumbulls and Huntingtons could still pull together at the War Office as in the days of '76." Curiously enough, in the war days it is said that the people who frequented the War Office were too busy formulating plans to take the time to hoist the flag. The president of the Connecticut Society of the Sons of the American Revolution in his speech at the dedication mentioned among other things the work done at this office—"the ceaseless and tireless meetings of the Committee of Safety—the coming and going of couriers with despatches to and from Congress and the generals and the Commander-in-chief—the fitting-out of provision-trains and supplies of beef upon the hoof—the raising of recruits for the dwindling army —the ordering of militia regiments to threatened points of the State frontier; and to the relief of neighbor States—the equipping and commissioning and commanding of Connecticut's adventurous little navy—the councils of war and of state there held with Washington and other

TABLET IN THE OLD WAR OFFICE BUILDING AT LEBANON, CONNECTICUT,

recording the many meetings of the Council of Safety of the State. On each side appear the names of many American and French officers, including Washington, Putnam, Huntington, Rochambeau, Lafayette, Chastellux and de Lauzun. Adams, Jay, Jefferson and Franklin have also trodden the floors of the War Office which stood near the encampment of de Lauzun's Hussars.

Continental generals, with Rochambeau and the Duke de Lauzun and other French commanders, military and naval." Later on in his remarks, he spoke of the war days: "A contrast as startling and intense as the canvas of history has ever exhibited was that which was exhibited here on Lebanon green when the French regiments lay cantoned here in winter quarters. Where, in American history at least, could such subjects be found for romance, or for the pencil of the historical painter? These representatives of the gayest, most brilliant, most corrupt and vicious court in Europe, what kind of figure did they make in the midst of the severe simplicity of old Lebanon? We are not without some record of their impressions, in the journal of the Count de Rochambeau and the travels of the Marquis de Chastellux. . . . But the contrast between the foremost personage among the Frenchmen here, the gay Duke de Lauzun, who made his headquarters at the house of David Trumbull, and the serious, precise figure of the governor is drawn already to our hand by the graceful pencil of Donald Mitchell:

'And what a contrast it is—this gay nobleman, carved out, as it were, from the dissolute age of Louis XV, who had sauntered under the colonnades of the Trianon, and had kissed the hand of the Pompadour, now strutting among the staid dames of Norwich and of Lebanon! How they must have looked at him and his fine troopers from under their knitted hoods! You know, I suppose, his after history; how he went back to Paris, and among the wits there was wont to mimic the way in which the stiff old Connecticut governor had said grace at his table. Ah! he did not know that in Governor Trumbull, and all such men, is the material to found an enduring state; and in himself, and all such men, only the inflammable material to burn one down. There is a life written of Governor Trumbull, and there is a life written of the Marquis (duke) of Lauzun. The first is full of deeds of quiet heroism, ending with a tranquil and triumphant death; the other is full of the rankest gallantries, and ends with a little spurt of blood under the knife of the guillotine upon the gay Place de la Concorde.'"

THE WAR OFFICE AT LEBANON, CONNECTICUT,
as it looked four or five years ago, before repairs were begun.

Jonathan F. Morris followed with these words:

"The National Society of the Sons of the American Revolution has authorized the commemoration of 'Flag Day' by the State societies, and here to old Lebanon the Connecticut Society has come to celebrate the day. And what more fitting place could they have chosen? Lebanon! the home of patriots; the home of the Trumbulls, the Williamses, the Clarks and others. Lebanon! where so many plans were made and measures taken to carry on the Revolution. Lebanon! soil trodden by Washington, Knox, and Trumbull; by Lafayette, Rochambeau, de Ternay, de Lauzun and Chastellux, brave allies of the American cause.

Here in the old War Office of 'Brother Jonathan' they held councils which led to victory. Here on the spot where we are gathered, and on the broad field before us, the golden lilies of France bloomed in beauty on their white banners beside the stars and stripes of America. Surely no spot is more sacred to Liberty than this! There was no place in the whole land where the principles of the Revolution were better understood and maintained than here."

The French Minister, Roustan, was invited to be present at the dedication, but was unable to accept. Another celebration was held at Lebanon on the National Centennial, July 4, 1876.

Other buildings of interest are Governor Trumbull's house, occupied by Miss Ellen B. Huntington, now somewhat removed from its original site on the Colchester Road to the street west of the Green, about a quarter of a mile from the First Congregational Church, where he entertained many of the distinguished personages of the war; the Williams house on the east side of the Green, once the residence of Hon. William Williams, husband of Mary Trumbull, second daughter of the War Governor; another old building is the birthplace of Joseph Trumbull, Commissary of the American army, later the residence of David Trumbull, also a son of the Governor. This house is known as "Redwood," and is situated on the opposite corner from the church, and was used as the headquarters of the French army. On the Station Road in the old dilapidated burial ground is the Trumbull tomb, where Governor Jonathan and his sons Joseph and David and two other members of the important Connecticut family lie buried.

Photographed through the kindness of Perry Walton

THE TRUMBULL TOMB IN THE OLD TRUM-
BULL BURIAL GROUND AT LEBANON,
CONNECTICUT,

*where Governor Jonathan Trumbull, his sons Joseph and
David, and several other members of the family are
buried. It is situated on the Station Road and is sadly in
need of repairs. Governor Trumbull kept constantly in touch with the French officers, many of whom
came to the War Office at Lebanon to confer with him.*

Many years later, in 1794, John Trumbull, son of the Governor, was spending the night at Mühlhausen on the Rhine, and the town was crowded with French troops. He appealed to the innkeeper for a bed, the result of the interview being best described in his own words:

" 'I am afraid that will be impossible,' replied the innkeeper . . . 'but come with me, and I will do as well as I can.' I followed through a crowd of young officers, and at the door met the old General coming out. The veteran looked at me keenly, and asked bluntly, 'Who are you?—an Englishman?' 'No, General, I am an American of the United States.' 'Ah! do you know Connecticut?' 'Yes, sir; it is my native State.' 'You know then, the good Governor Trumbull?' 'Yes, General, he is my father.' *'Oh! mon Dieu, que je suis charmé;* I am delighted to see a son of Governor Trumbull; *entrez, entrez;* you shall have supper, bed, everything in the house.' I soon learned that the old man had been in America, an officer in the legion of the Duke de Lauzun, who had been quartered in my native village during the winter I had passed in prison in London, and had heard me much spoken of there. Of course I found myself in excellent quarters. The old General kept me up almost all night, inquiring of everybody and everything in America, and especially of the people of Lebanon, and above all, the family of Huntington, with whom he had been quartered." Trumbull visited Paris, where he painted portraits of some of the French officers who had campaigned in America. He saw, while there, Talleyrand and Lucien Bonaparte.

It is stated that de Lauzun refused to go into camp in France previous to embarking for America. Finally he persuaded the King to allow him to form a cavalry unit to take to this country. It is also said that he insisted on having a band to escort him to the seacoast. He sailed on the "Provence," and, as will be remembered, was one of the officers selected by Rochambeau to carry to France the news of the Yorktown surrender. As he was about to be guillotined, he showed his great bravery, for he would not allow his hands to be tied, declaring to the executioner: "We are both Frenchmen, we shall both do our duty."

HARTFORD AND WETHERSFIELD, WHERE WASHINGTON AND ROCHAMBEAU MET IN HISTORIC CONFERENCES

THE old Wadsworth house where Rochambeau and Washington first met is now no more, for it stood in the centre of Hartford and had to give way to a more modern and useful building called the Wadsworth Atheneum, named for the previous owner of the property, Rev. Daniel Wadsworth, pastor of the First Congregational Church and father of Colonel Jeremiah Wadsworth, who was the Commissary of the French army and also of the American army after Colonel Joseph Trumbull's death. The only relic of this historic house that has been preserved is a wooden panel from the wall of the room in which the meeting took place. This reminder of the conference between the Generals of the two armies now adorns the rooms of the Connecticut Historical Society in the Atheneum. The inscription reads as follows:

This panel was taken from the house which was removed from the spot where Wadsworth Atheneum now stands; the house was built and owned about the year 1730 by the Rev. Daniel Wadsworth, Pastor of the First Congregational Church in Hartford, and descended from him to his son Jeremiah, and his daughters Eunice and Elizabeth, and from them by will and by deed to Daniel, the son of Jeremiah Wadsworth. In the spring of 1842, Daniel Wadsworth executed a deed of the land and mansion house to the Corporation of Wadsworth Atheneum. The panel mentioned above was taken from the southwest chamber on the second floor, a room where our greatest benefactor, Washington, with officers of the French Army, Rochambeau, De Lauzun, Lafayette and other worthies of both nations, met more than once to plan and mature some of the great projects upon which the successful termination of the American Revolution seem even at this distant day to have depended. It was while on one of these visits of Washington, to Hartford on the 21st Sept. 1780, that Arnold's treason was discovered at West Point, and happily frustrated by the capture of André.

Hartford, September 17, 1845.

DANIEL WADSWORTH.

The Atheneum also has several boxes of vouchers and letters dealing with the many transactions which the Commissaries, Wadsworth and Carter (the latter's real name was Church), had with the French army. A careful perusal of them would undoubtedly bring to light some interesting facts. Another permanent reminder of the second conference is a bronze tablet on the right of the porch as one enters the building, bearing this inscription:

ERECTED, MCMXIII | COL. JEREMIAH WADSWORTH | BRANCH CONNECTICUT | S A R | HERE STOOD THE HOME OF | COL. JEREMIAH WADSWORTH | COMMISSARY GENERAL OF THE | AMERICAN FORCES IN THE WAR | FOR INDEPENDENCE AND A | TRUSTED FRIEND OF | GEORGE WASHINGTON | AND "BROTHER JONATHAN" | TRUMBULL | HERE IN 1775 HE | ENTERTAINED WASHINGTON | ON HIS WAY TO | CAMBRIDGE TO ASSUME | COMMAND OF THE | CONTINENTAL ARMY | IN THE SOUTHWEST CHAMBER | WASHINGTON MET THE | FRENCH COMMANDER | COUNT DE ROCHAMBEAU | AND OTHERS IN MAY 1781 | AND CONSIDERED THE PLAN | OF THE | YORKTOWN CAMPAIGN | WHICH IN OCTOBER RESULTED | IN THE FALL OF THE | BRITISH POWER IN | AMERICA.

[The conference itself was held at Wethersfield.]

Two months had passed since the arrival of our foreign allies at Newport and yet Rochambeau, de Ternay and Washington had not met, possibly owing to a slight difference of opinion as to the best use to be made of the French fleet. Lafayette, however, with his usual tactfulness, suggested to the American General that an interview might be profitable, and this was arranged for September 20, 1780. Hartford was the place selected and accordingly, on the

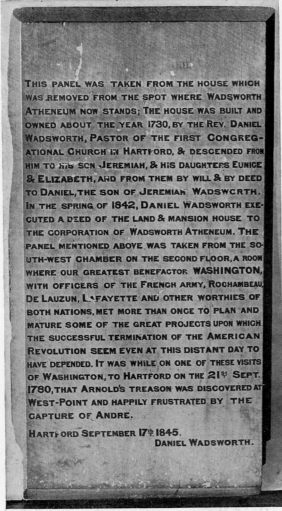

THIS PANEL WAS TAKEN FROM THE HOUSE WHICH WAS REMOVED FROM THE SPOT WHERE WADSWORTH ATHENEUM NOW STANDS; THE HOUSE WAS BUILT AND OWNED ABOUT THE YEAR 1730, BY THE REV. DANIEL WADSWORTH, PASTOR OF THE FIRST CONGREGATIONAL CHURCH IN HARTFORD, & DESCENDED FROM HIM TO HIS SON JEREMIAH, & HIS DAUGHTERS EUNICE & ELIZABETH, AND FROM THEM BY WILL & BY DEED TO DANIEL, THE SON OF JEREMIAH WADSWORTH. IN THE SPRING OF 1842, DANIEL WADSWORTH EXECUTED A DEED OF THE LAND & MANSION HOUSE TO THE CORPORATION OF WADSWORTH ATHENEUM. THE PANEL MENTIONED ABOVE WAS TAKEN FROM THE SOUTH-WEST CHAMBER ON THE SECOND FLOOR, A ROOM WHERE OUR GREATEST BENEFACTOR WASHINGTON, WITH OFFICERS OF THE FRENCH ARMY, ROCHAMBEAU, DE LAUZUN, LAFAYETTE AND OTHER WORTHIES OF BOTH NATIONS, MET MORE THAN ONCE TO PLAN AND MATURE SOME OF THE GREAT PROJECTS UPON WHICH THE SUCCESSFUL TERMINATION OF THE AMERICAN REVOLUTION SEEM EVEN AT THIS DISTANT DAY TO HAVE DEPENDED. IT WAS WHILE ON ONE OF THESE VISITS OF WASHINGTON, TO HARTFORD ON THE 21ST SEPT. 1780, THAT ARNOLD'S TREASON WAS DISCOVERED AT WEST-POINT AND HAPPILY FRUSTRATED BY THE CAPTURE OF ANDRE.

HARTFORD SEPTEMBER 17TH 1845.
　　　　　　　　　　DANIEL WADSWORTH.

Photographed through the kindness of Colonel Louis R. Cheney

PANEL FROM THE WADSWORTH HOUSE, NOW IN THE WADSWORTH ATHENEUM, HARTFORD, CONNECTICUT

It was taken from the southwest chamber of the second floor, where Washington, Rochambeau, Lafayette, de Lauzun and others met to discuss plans.

18th, Rochambeau, de Ternay, Rochambeau's son, de Lauzun, and aides de Fersen and de Damas, and engineer Desandrouins, and their suites set out from their headquarters, their journey being best described by the French General himself in his 'Mémoires'':

"I will here venture to intrude on the kind attentions of the reader an anecdote, which is strikingly characteristic of the manners of the good republicans of Connecticut. The conveyance in which I proceeded to the conference, in company with the admiral de Ternay, who, by the way, was very infirm, broke down. I dispatched my first aide de camp, Fersen, to get a wheelwright who lived about a mile from the spot where the accident occurred. He soon after returned to us, however, and informed us that he had found the man sick with the ague, and that he had positively declared to him that for his hat full of guineas he would do no work at night. I prevailed upon the admiral to accompany me to the man's shop, and we repaired thither; we told him that General Washington would arrive at Hartford the next evening to confer with us the following day, and that unless he could repair our carriage, we would be too late to meet him. 'You are no liars at any rate,' he replied; 'for I read in the Connecticut paper that Washington was to be there to confer with you; as it is for the public service I will take care that the carriage shall be ready for you at six in the morning.' He kept his word, and we proceeded on at the promised time. As we returned, another wheel broke, and we were once more obliged to have recourse to our old friend. 'Well,' said he, 'so you want me to work again for you at night?' 'Aye! indeed we do,' I replied, 'Admiral Rodney has arrived to reënforce threefold the naval forces against which we are contending, and it is of the highest importance that we should return without delay to Rhode Island to oppose him.' 'But what can you do,' he continued, 'with your six ships against the twenty English?' 'It will be the most glorious day of our life if

they attempt to break our line.' 'Come, come,' said he, 'you are good, honest fellows; your carriage shall be put in repair by tomorrow morning at five o'clock. But tell me, before I set to work, although I do not wish to inquire into your secrets, how did you like Washington, and how did he like you?' We assured him that we had been delighted with him; his patriotism was satisfied and he kept his word. I do not mean to compare all good Americans to this good man; but almost all inland cultivators and all land owners of Connecticut are animated with that patriotic spirit, which many other people would do well to imitate. . . ."

Washington, Lafayette and General Knox, with a number of aides, and an important French engineer called de Gouvion, arrived at the meeting place first, the French following soon after, their coming being best recorded in Stuart's "Life of Trumbull":

"The Governor's Guards . . . saluted Washington, as he entered the town, with thirteen guns. Trumbull, and Colonel Jeremiah Wadsworth, and other distinguished personages of the State, met him as he advanced. They gave him a cordial welcome—and, through crowds that rent the air with cheers, and strained to catch a sight of the illustrious Commander-in-Chief, the latter made his way, together with Knox and Lafayette, to the residence of their mutual friend, Colonel Wadsworth—there upon the site where the Historical Society of Connecticut now lifts its walls—and where, in a beautiful mansion, still standing, though upon another spot, himself and his principal officers were nobly entertained during their stay.

The same ceremony was repeated soon after Washington came, upon the arrival of the French commander and suite. They were formally received at the City Landing, after crossing the ferry—and marching to the area in front of the Capitol (called 'Court House' in those days), were there met by General Washington and his military companion. It was the first time that these distinguished leaders of the great allied armies saw the faces of each other—the first time that, through their chief martial representatives, France and America shook hands—and the spectacle is described as having been one of the most august and imposing in character.

There were the noble-looking Frenchmen, gayly dressed, and sparkling with jeweled insignia. There was Washington—erect, tall, commanding—in his buff vest, buff breeches buckled at the knee, long-spurred boots, white neckcloth, and blue, buff-lined coat, that shone with a pair of rich, massive epaulettes. . . .

In close proximity . . . was an immense, eager multitude—composed of men, women and children, who had assembled from Hartford and the neighboring towns, to witness the novel and gorgeous spectacle of a meeting in America between the representatives of the two great military families of France and the United States. Everything passed off most happily.

Thursday night the conference was concluded. Friday saw the French officers start on their return to Newport—the Governor's Guards again in martial array—escorting the distinguished guests to the river bank, while thirteen guns renewedly rent the air. The same parade was again produced on the following morning—at which time General Washington and suite shook hands with the hospitable Wadsworth, the worthy Governor Trumbull, and numerous other friends—and, amid volleys of huzzas, started for the headquarters of the army."

General Washington and Rochambeau met in State House Square in front of the old Court House, eighty years later the City Hall of Hartford and now occupied only on special occasions. Here, in the

Photographed through the kindness of Colonel Louis R. Cheney

TABLET NEAR THE ENTRANCE OF THE WADS-WORTH ATHENEUM, HARTFORD, CONNECTICUT, *recording the fact that here stood the house of Colonel Jeremiah Wadsworth, where Washington and Rochambeau met in May, 1781, proceeding to Wethersfield, where the two Generals agreed upon the Yorktown Campaign.*

new building designed by Bulfinch in 1797, Lafayette was welcomed on his visit in 1824, and also the great General Foch in 1922.

The understanding arrived at during this conference is well expressed by de Lauzun's aide-de-camp, Count Dumas, in his memoirs:

"General Washington and General Rochambeau decided on passing the whole winter in passive observation, always holding themselves ready to profit by the most favorable circumstances which might present themselves. The whole of this comparative suspension of hostilities was well employed in putting the American army in good condition for the opening of the campaign; and General Rochambeau, on his side, who was expecting the arrival of the second division, prepared himself to aid our allies with vigor."

The interview, according to Stuart, was continued at the house of Colonel Wadsworth, where the officers retired for the night.

Of the return of the allied officers, Blanchard entered in his diary:

"On the 24th, our military and naval generals arrived. They had had an interview with General Washington, from whom they returned enchanted: an easy and noble bearing, extensive and correct views, the art of making himself beloved, these are what all who saw him observed in him. It is his merit which has defended the liberty of America, and if she enjoys it one day, it is to him alone that she will be indebted for it.

(I wrote this in 1780. The event has shown how right I was; it is to Mr. Washington's courage, to his love for his country and to his prudence that the Americans owe their success. He has never been inconsistent, never discouraged. Amidst success as amidst reverses, he was always calm, always the same; and his personal qualities have done more to keep soldiers in the American army and to procure partisans to the cause of liberty than the decrees of the congress.)"

It was an agreeable surprise to the members attending the conference to learn after adjournment that, through Governor Trumbull's thoughtfulness, the State had arranged to pay the costs, the records of the Council of Safety stating that:

"Agreeable to the orders of his Excellency three hundred forty-five pounds are to be drawn from the treasury for the reception and entertainment of General Washington and the French general and admiral at Hartford."

On the return journey, on the 23d, General Washington was entertained at Litchfield at the hospitable mansion of General Oliver Wolcott, later Governor of the State; at Fishkill he met M. de la Luzerne, the French Minister, and his suite on the way to an interview with General Rochambeau in Newport.

Eight months elapsed, whereupon another conference was decided upon—this time the meeting place being designated as Wethersfield, then Hartford's rival and situated about five miles from Connecticut's present capital on the road to Middletown. This second conference would no doubt have been held in Hartford had it not been for the fact that the Connecticut legislature was then in session; moreover, it is likely that General Washington chose to meet his French colleagues in the quiet village of Wethersfield where they might be free from undue publicity. Washington also had pleasant recollections of his two visits there. Count de Barras, the new Admiral, it will be remembered, had recently arrived in Boston to succeed de Ternay, and within a few days he sent word to Washington that his General and himself would like to discuss the future plans, adding: "I am very impatient to have the honor of making an acquaintance with you, and to assure you that I have nothing so much at heart as to render myself serviceable to the King and to the United States." Washington selected May 22 as the day. On the eve of the departure of the French delegates, the enemy appeared off Block Island and threatened Newport, therefore de Barras was unable to be present, but his country was ably represented by Rochambeau and the Chevalier de Chastellux, the latter taking the place of de Barras. It will be remembered that one of the forts of Newport was built by and also named Chastellux. It was decided that de Barras should remain at Newport, rather than accompany the fleet to Boston, and it was also arranged that de Choisy should have charge of the five hundred French and the American militia to be kept there also. It was also decided to proceed against New York, but later this plan was changed to a Southern campaign in conjunction with Admiral de Grasse, largely through the persuasion of de la Luzerne. Blanchard makes this mention of the Wethersfield interview in his diary:

"M. de Rochambeau set out for Hartford, on the same day, with the Chevalier de Chastellux; a meeting with General Washington had been appointed, to confer about the operations of the campaign. The bad weather returned again. . . .

On the 26th, M. de Rochambeau returned from his interview with General Washington and on the succeeding days made arrangements for a movement of the troops."

Washington left New Windsor on the Hudson on the 18th of the month, his diary referring to his journey reading as follows:

"May 18th (Friday). Set out this day for the interview at Wethersfield with the Count de Rochambeau and Admiral Barras. Reached Morgan's Tavern, 43 miles from Fishkill Landing, after dining at Col. Vanderburg's.

19th (Saturday). Breakfasted at Litchfield, dined at Farmington, and lodged at Wethersfield, at the home of Joseph Webb.

21st (Monday). Count de Rochambeau, with the Chevalier de Chastellux, arrived about noon. . . .

22d (Tuesday). Fixed, with Count de Rochambeau, the plan of the campaign. This day Americans and French dined together at Collyer's Tavern, in Wethersfield.

23d (Wednesday). Count de Rochambeau set out on his return to Newport, while I prepared and forwarded dispatches to the Governors of the four New England states. . . ."

The representatives of the two allied nations met in the Joseph Webb house, which was once part of the chain of houses owned by Wallace Nutting of Framingham, Massachusetts, situated on the main road in Wethersfield. This attractive town has changed but little in all these years, and it does not require as much imagination as is usually the case to look back on those days and see the dignitaries from Hartford and Windsor arriving either in their coaches or on horseback to meet General Washington, who, by the way, is depicted on horseback on the old signboard. The history of this historic house is so well told by Mrs. William H. H. Smith that two paragraphs will bear quoting:

"At night when all had left and the general sat talking it over with the Webbs, sipping their last toddy together, and after they had escorted him to his north front chamber, placing wax candles in silver candlesticks there, and the great man stood by the window and through the young trees and over the lilac bushes, looked across to the new meeting house with graceful spire silvered by the moon, what were his thoughts then? . . .

Again my fancy peoples these rooms with gay uniforms, stiff brocades, powdered hair, shoe-buckles and knee-buckles of brilliants, a high comb or a brooch here and there, set with small diamonds, that company of dazzling youth, brave with high purpose. Here again Dame Abigail and Madam Mehitable came to the front as ladies of the mansion. The Frenchmen and their aides were entertained at these three houses; again Washington had his north front chamber here; again the ladies did the honors, assisted by the young ladies of the neighborhood."

Those who now stop there for tea visit the first-floor room, the walls of which once bore scenes of the war, showing Rochambeau, Lafayette and Washington, and then mount the old stairway to see the rooms occupied by the two famous Generals. As a skeptical wit once announced, he would like to see an old house where Washington or Lafayette had *not* stopped.

Photographed for the State Street Trust Company by William G. Dudley, of Hartford   *Kindness of Hon. Louis R. Cheney*

WEBB HOUSE IN WETHERSFIELD, CONNECTICUT,

where the historic conference between Washington and Rochambeau took place on May 22, 1781.   It was built in 1752, and is now kept as a tea-house and relic of Revolutionary days by the Society of Colonial Dames. Chastellux accompanied Rochambeau, while Generals Knox and Duportail, a Frenchman serving with the Americans, were with Washington.

Colonel Louis R. Cheney, Ex-Mayor of Hartford, has given us such an interesting and vivid description of this important event in our history that we are taking the liberty of quoting it:

"One hundred and forty years ago, in a modest little village on the Connecticut River, a great American general took counsel with an illustrious French general whose nation had pledged itself heart and soul to aid America in her final struggle for freedom.

On the appointed day, in the town of Wethersfield, Connecticut, General George Washington met Count de Rochambeau, in one of the most momentous military conferences in the world's history. The American General wished to strike a final blow and sought the views of Rochambeau to the end that a plan of operation might be perfected; and the combined military strategy of the sagacious, open-minded American leader and the thoroughly trained, keenly intelligent French officer, proved to be the decisive factor in terminating the War and bringing about an American victory.

It is interesting to recall the events and circumstances in connection with the presence of this famous hero of France on humble New England soil; furthermore, it brings us to a deeper realization of the close and cordial relations which existed between France and America in those troublous times. It had been a time to test the souls of men. America found herself bankrupt in funds and credit, handicapped by a weak and inactive Congress, and threatened with the possibility of mutiny in her Army of the North which had long remained unpaid. In dire distress Congress called upon France for help and France promptly and generously answered that call.

On Saturday, May 19th, General Washington, with Generals Knox and Duportail, arrived at Wethersfield, where he was given lodgings at the house of Joseph Webb, an enterprising merchant and a loyal American citizen. The French officers from Newport did not arrive until Monday, the 21st. About noon of that day General Rochambeau, accompanied by General Chastellux and their suites, arrived at Wethersfield. The townspeople must have been strongly impressed with the importance of the advent of Rochambeau and his train, for the French officers were met at Hartford by no less than General Washington and were by him escorted to Wethersfield in company with army officers and a number of his intimate friends. What pride must have filled the hearts of the good citizens of this little hamlet as they welcomed within their own gates the great general of France! They greeted him and his men with a formal salute of cannon; and the gallant Frenchmen accepted with courteous grace this enthusiastic tribute from the sturdy sons of the liberty-loving country they so much admired.

How splendidly inspiring a figure must have been that of Rochambeau, seasoned war veteran of two-score-and-fifteen years, known by his contemporaries to be an upright, religious man and the honest, dependable ally of America! But to the good people of Wethersfield he no doubt appeared— as, in fact, history has since described him—'an affable gentleman, very fine looking, his physiognomy being noble in the highest degree and his manners those of one perfectly accustomed to society.' It is no wonder that the ordinarily peaceful little village bustled with excitement over the arrival of the French contingent and at once busied itself in establishing proper quarters for their comfort. The hostelry chosen for his honor was Stillman's tavern which stood on the site of the present Richard A. Robbins house, and it was here that the allied officers and their retinue dined that evening with some of Wethersfield's most prominent citizens. We may well imagine that, after their journey from Newport, the appetites of the French soldiers were not lagging, and that France paid substantial compliment to the culinary achievements of New England.

The dinner over, the party repaired to the Congregational Church, where a concert was tendered them by the church choir. The church which they attended still stands, with its quaint old burying-ground at the rear; indeed, the building is still in active use as a place of worship. Perhaps the young French gallants may have been forgiven if they stole occasional glances at the many shy, sweet maiden faces in the singers' gallery and in the pews of the church. The musical entertainment may not have appreciably increased their religious fervor, but it at least served to send them back to the tavern with pleasant thoughts of an evening spent in old New England.

The conference between the allied generals was set for the following day, Tuesday, May 22d, at the Joseph Webb house. This house was known in the Revolutionary days as 'Hospitality Hall,' and at this time it is likely that the young and charming wife of Joseph Webb acted as hostess. It may be easily imagined that she rallied to her support many of Wethersfield's fairest damsels, who must have been far from unwilling to assist her in entertaining those gallant officers, who represented the flower of French and American chivalry.

The Webb house, so famous in American history, still stands a proud and silent witness to the words of mighty import which passed between a great American soldier and a great soldier of France on that conference day. Within this dwelling these two high-hearted men and their advisers held grave consultation in the interest of the common cause of liberty; and, although their opinions differed, each displayed respect and tolerance for the views of the other; no hint of petty jealousy marred the dignity of the occasion. With what eagerness must Rochambeau have acquainted Washington with the information contained in the recent despatches,—namely, that the Count de Grasse had set sail from France with a fleet, and that these naval reinforcements, laden with supplies, might soon be expected to arrive! Encouraged by these advices, the American leader must have experienced a deep sense of gratitude to France for assistance sent in this hour of great need.

The conclusion arrived at was a compromise—either to operate against New York or to extend their views southward as circumstances and a naval superiority might permit; and perhaps the most important result of the conference was the securing of entire harmony between the French and American commanders. On the day of the conference it is recorded that Governor Trumbull, of Connecticut, dined with Generals Washington and Rochambeau at Stillman's Tavern, on which memorable occasion it is probable that 'enterprises of great pith and moment' were discussed. During the days of this conference Wethersfield must have been more than ordinarily active; furthermore, the atmosphere lent to the peaceful countryside by the presence of the gaily clad French and American officers, must indeed have been an invigorating one; and when, on the morning of May 23d, the French soldiers left for Newport, it is probable that many a winsome lassie watched their departure with misgivings; and perhaps there might have been a few soldiers in the escort of General Rochambeau who experienced unaccustomed pangs of regret at being so soon obliged to answer the call of duty. General Washington left Wethersfield the next day, May 24th, having remained over to prepare important despatches.

The sons and daughters of New England have cause to feel a peculiar thrill of pride over the

From a photograph taken for the State Street Trust Company by William G. Dudley of Hartford   *Kindness of Hon. Louis R. Cheney*

THE WETHERSFIELD CONGREGATIONAL CHURCH, WETHERSFIELD, CONNECTICUT,

where the French officers attended a concert given by the church choir on the evening of their arrival, the 21st of May, 1781, in this attractive old New England town. The conference took place the following day. General Washington attended Sunday morning service in this same meeting-house the previous day, the 20th. The church is still in use, and is near the old Webb house, where the conference was held. The old burial ground in the rear is very quaint.

fact that their forefathers were privileged to extend hospitality to General Rochambeau, the faithful friend of America; to them indeed must come a keener realization of the service rendered by France to America in those dark days. The children of New England and of France may well remember the tribute paid by Washington to Rochambeau made perpetual on the statue of the French hero in Lafayette Square, Washington:

'We have been contemporaries and fellow labourers in the cause of liberty, and we have lived together as brothers should do in harmonious friendship.' "

While at Wethersfield, Washington wrote to Lafayette; but, as every one knows, the letter was intercepted. Nevertheless, as one writer put it, "the web that was finally used was woven at the Webb house."

The history of this old house is an interesting one. Richard Webb came to Cambridge and joined the Hooker Migration to Hartford in 1636. His son, Joseph, married a Wethersfield woman, and they soon built this historic house, where they resided until his death; the property had belonged previously to Samuel Wolcott, a large owner of the land nearby. It is of interest also to mention that Silas Deane, one of our Commissioners to France, married Webb's widow, residing in the Goodrich house next door, also once the property of Wolcott. A mile away lived Colonel Solomon Welles, whose son Roger was captain under Lafayette, and one of the hundred men, all over six feet tall, who formed his particular command. The Webb house later came into the Welles family, but it is now owned by the Society of Colonial Dames and is shown with great pride by Mrs. Case, the lady in charge. The booklet on the Webb house refers also to the Churchill house at Newington nearby, and recalls the time when, at one of the balls which were occasionally held on the ordination of a minister, one of the young women of this family is said to have danced through two pairs of white satin slippers in one night.

To us there is much romance in the old houses of those days, described so attractively by Mrs. Smith in her pamphlet on the Webb house: "Then, for comfort: the big fireplaces, the toddy closets, the cool cellars for vegetables and fruits stored in plenty for a year, the cool cupboards for mince pies and election cake, always ready for company, the saddle-room and the sparkin' bench, all these are in the building of the house, when the house was the home, and tell their own 'sermons in stone.' "

A FORGOTTEN MONUMENT—"LA CHAPELLE EXPIATOIRE," WHERE D'ESTAING LIES BURIED

IN the "Mémoires Édités de Balzac," the great romancer sets down this astonishing anecdote: In the most terrible days of the Terror, two aged Catholic sisters concealed themselves in a miserable little hiding place in the very heart of Paris. They shared their abode with an old priest who in the disguise of a mendicant succeeded in bringing in enough food to keep the three alive. One day a stranger penetrated into the abode of this wretched trio and asked the old priest if he would celebrate an expiatory Mass for Louis the Sixteenth, who had just paid for the errors of his reign by his death on the scaffold. The old priest was at first terrified, as he thought the demand was a ruse to discover his identity; but when at last the stranger assured him of his good will, he consented to perform the office. There, in the midst of poverty and affliction, an altar was set up and the necessary fittings were improvised. The first Mass was said in the presence of the two aged nuns, the stranger, and the bare walls. When the office was finished, the stranger announced that he had no money with which to pay for the service, but that he would leave a small box which would be found to contain a recompense. Thereupon he disappeared, and when the astonished Father opened the box he found the handkerchief which Louis had in his hands at the very moment when he was beheaded.

"CHAPELLE EXPIATOIRE" AT THE END OF RUE D'ANJOU, PARIS,
*showing the common plot in which 1,200 victims of the French Revolution were buried, including Brissot and Admiral d'Estaing.
Louis XVI and Marie Antoinette were also buried there for a short time.*

EXTERIOR OF "CHAPELLE EXPIATOIRE,"

in which Admiral d'Estaing and 1,200 other victims of the French Revolution lie buried.   The building was erected by the King in 1816 as a resting place for his royal ancestors, who were interred there for a short time, previous to their removal to Saint Denis.

The sacred relic was stained with the blood of the King—all of which information was made known by a note which was enclosed with the handkerchief.   From that day on, the three pious old people were mysteriously supplied with all that they needed for comfort and safety. On January 21 of the following year, the stranger returned and again asked that a Mass be celebrated for the repose of the King's soul.   He steadfastly refused to tell his name, disappearing as mysteriously as he had come.   When the Terror was over, it became known that the stranger was none other than Charles Sanson, the executioner who had operated the guillotine which had cut off the head of the King.   Every year this man came with his whole family, always in heavy mourning, and paid for the celebration of the expiatory Mass. His son continued the penance for years after his father's death.

This strange tale sheds a very fine light on these stirring times.   While a lawless mob was murdering its sovereigns and all the well-born of the land, there were many who shared in the destruction in order to save their own heads, but who had not the slightest heart in their actions.   This foolish mob was not content with beheading the King, but also consigned his remains to an open grave which bore no inscription whatever.   Six months later, when the Queen suffered a like fate, it is said that her body lay on the ground for some weeks before it was accorded an interment, and that when the formalities were fulfilled, a bill was rendered to the state for the coffin of one "citoyenne Capet."

But there was a certain citizen, Descloseaux, who made it his business to see where the fallen monarchs were buried; and as soon as he dared do so, he purchased the place and fenced

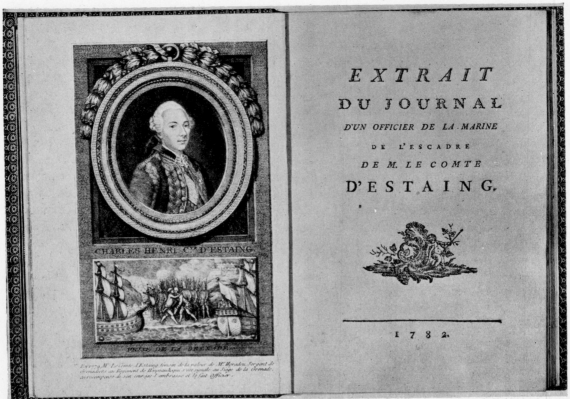

FRONTISPIECE AND TITLE-PAGE FROM A DIARY OF A MARINE OFFICER

serving in the French squadron under the command of d'Estaing "during the American War. Printed in the year 1782." The Admiral himself is shown in the picture, and the scene below represents his capture of Grenada a short time before our War. It is believed that d'Estaing may have written this diary under the "nom de plume" of "an officer of the Squadron."

it in. That property was then a part of the famous old cemetery of the Madeleine, which at that period stood in the general region now occupied in part by the Church of the Madeleine. When Louis XVIII came into power, Descloseaux made known his precious secret and was rewarded most generously. The new King then set about the business of preparing a fitting resting place for his unfortunate royal ancestors, and by an ordinance of January 16, 1816, the construction of the "Chapelle Expiatoire" was decreed.

The building is the work of the famous Fontaine, the architect of Napoleon's staff, who is also the author of the beautiful Arc de Triomphe du Carrousel in the gardens of the Tuileries. The Chapelle was five years in building, and the expense ran into millions of francs. Unhappily, the result was not what might have been expected from so great a genius.

The bones of the unhappy king and queen did not rest long in the splendor of the new Chapelle-cemetery, for it seemed fitting to transport them to St. Denis, where lie the earthly remains of most of the monarchs of France. The Chapelle was never very cordially received, and even after the royal remains had been removed there were numerous agitations to destroy it. The Commune ordered its destruction, but the royal troops entered Paris the day after the order had been given and so it was saved. Strange as it may seem, there are still rumors that it is to be torn down, and there is not a little feeling that it is of no great value either historically or artistically.

SUJET   ALLEGORIQUE.

*Dédié à Monsieur le Comte d'Estaing
général de ses Armées Vice Amiral de*   *Chevalier des Ordres du Roi Lieutenant
France, Né le 24 Novembre 1729.*

*Photographed from an old engraving in the Cabinet des Estampes of the
Bibliothèque Nationale in Paris*   *Kindness of Paul F. Cadman*

**ALLEGORY SAID TO REPRESENT THE ARRIVAL OF THE COUNT D'ESTAING ON HIS FLAGSHIP,
THE "LANGUEDOC," IN AMERICA,**

*at either Boston or Newport. On the shield of the Goddess of War is a picture of Louis XVI. Neptune is seen wielding his
trident as the French Admiral is about to step ashore from his small boat. This picture shows a typical battleship
of the period.*

Whatever the judgment on the art of the monument may be, it certainly has some historic worth that cannot be lightly disregarded; for it is the resting place of more than a thousand of the noblest, both in title and in deed, of those who fell under the Revolutionary knife. Among these was the beautiful Charlotte Corday, who, though a real champion of the cause of liberty, was so impassioned against the excesses of the Terror that she planned and succeeded in the assassination of Marat. For us, however, the ground is both sacred and historic, because it holds the remains of Admiral d'Estaing, whose name is intertwined with the history of our national beginnings. It was he who brought the first French fleet to Newport in 1778. He himself was an ardent supporter of liberty, and perished by the guillotine on the 28th of April, 1794. There is no stone nor plaque to mark his grave. He shares a common plot with the hundreds of others who experienced his fate. The only record of his burial is a document, now in the Archives Nationales, which records the names of those who were buried in the cemetery of the Madeleine: "Affaire de M. d'Estaing, La Tour du Pin, etc.   Vingt Floreal an 11."   His biographers call him Charles Hector, Count d'Estaing, but the certificate of his death reads: Charles Henri, Comte d'Estaing.   He came from Auvergne, as did Lafayette.

The Boston *Gazette*, under date of May 15, 1780, refers to his arrival in France: "Paris, December 17.   We are very impatient here to see the Count d'Estaing, who is expected this evening at Versailles.   It is given out that his Majesty expresses so great a desire to see that general that he has sent a carriage to meet him on the road for dispatch, and for the greater conveniency, as the wounds he received in America are worse than was at first reported, since he has been obliged to make use of crutches."

The Count d'Estaing, it is said, wrote from Brest to M. de Sartine, desiring him to ask permission of the King to fall at his feet and thank his Majesty for the confidence with which he had vouchsafed to honor him.   "At my feet?" replied the Monarch.   "Oh, no.   It is in my arms that I will receive him."

D'Estaing served as president of the French Society of the Cincinnati.

A STORY OF THE ILLUSTRIOUS FRENCH REGIMENTS OF OUR REVOLUTIONARY WAR

NOT a few of the French infantry line regiments of the World War boasted a glorious history which had been centuries in the making, and by no means least among this number was the famous Eighteenth, the lineal descendant of the grand old Royal Auvergne, a regiment that brought glory to Rochambeau and honor to France.

This illustrious unit was first formed under Henry the Fourth in the year 1608, at which time it was called by the name of its commander, the Regiment du Bourg. In 1626 it had the honor of guarding the remarkable dike which Richelieu constructed to complete the blockade of La Rochelle; this was the beginning of a long series of valorous actions all of which are properly recorded by the successive historians of the regiment for the edification of recruits and for the preservation of the *esprit de corps*. Nine years later the name Auvergne was adopted without the descriptive "royal," and this title held good until 1776, when a royal ordinance prescribed that all the existing regiments should be divided into two. Out of the Auvergne, two units were formed, one of which kept the name of the parent organization while the other adopted the denomination "Gâtinais." Both terms indicate part of ancient France, from which no doubt the majority of the personnel was recruited.

The Gâtinais enjoyed the distinction of embarking for the zone of action even before France had formally declared her intention of sending troops to aid the insurgent English colonies. In 1777 the regiment landed at the Island of Santo Domingo and in 1779 it became a part of the forces of Admiral d'Estaing. Its first introduction to American soil, however, was at the unhappy siege of Savannah in September, 1779, where it is told "they fought valiantly and retreated in perfect order when they were outnumbered and beaten." During this attack the rallying call—"Auvergne"—was the shout of every soldier both in advance and in retreat.

After wintering at Martinique, it returned under the command of the Marquis de Saint-Simon, landed at the Chesapeake and became a part of Rochambeau's forces. It was this unit, together with the Regiment des Deux-Ponts, which played the principal rôle, insofar as the French troops were concerned, in the siege of Yorktown. Rochambeau had formerly held a command in the original Auvergne regiment, and it is not surprising that he addressed these brave Gâtinais on the eve of the battle with these words, which have been repeated by almost every historian of Franco-American events:

"My children, if I have need of you this night, I hope that you will not forget that we have served together in the brave regiment of Auvergne, surnamed 'sans tache' (without stain), which name it has merited since the day of its formation. . . ."

In his "Mémoires," Rochambeau tells how they all cried out that if he would give them their old name again, they would willingly fight until the last one was killed. They kept their word and "fought like lions." When their commander recounted the story of their valor to the King, a royal ordinance was at once issued, giving back to the regiment its old name Royal Auvergne. A Boston colonel narrated an incident that took place during the World War. Some of our soldiers were conversing in camp with a group of Frenchmen, and asked to what

CANNON CAPTURED AT YORKTOWN
and presented by General Washington to the Royal Auvergne regiment.

regiment they belonged. "To the old Royal Auvergne, *sans tache*," was the rejoinder. Officially, though, it now carries a new name.

After the capitulation of Yorktown, this regiment was quartered at Gloucester, Virginia. In due time Rochambeau held a solemn review, after which the good news was announced and the title, Royal Auvergne, conferred. Washington presented Rochambeau with three English cannon captured during the siege, one of which is shown here. The generous Commander in turn presented one to the Regiment des Deux-Ponts and one to the Army Museum in the Hôtel des Invalides at Paris. The third was guarded as a precious trophy by Rochambeau himself until unhappily it fell a victim to the Revolution and was melted into cannon more suitable to the needs of the Revolutionists.

In 1791 the French Government decreed that all regiments should abandon their special names and should henceforth be known by numerical designations. To the soldiers of the Royal Auvergne, such an order must have been bitter, indeed; but apparently the old esprit was maintained intact, for not long after this we read this high praise from no other than Bonaparte himself:

"Brave 18ème, je te connais, l'ennemi ne tient pas devant toi"
(Brave 18th, I know you well; the enemy will never hold against you)

and the use of the second person singular probably indicates more affection than familiarity. These words spoken at the battle of Rivoli have since become the motto of the unit.

The Touraine regiment was first formed in 1625, but it did not adopt the name until 1636. This famous body of troops was present at the Siege of La Rochelle, the Defense of Candie and many other famous battles, including that of Minden in 1757, where Lafayette's father was killed. In America it took part in the Battle of Brimstone Hill. The regimental records contain the account of a young soldier, Claude Thion, who was detailed to carry bombs from an ammunition dump to a battery. In carrying out these instructions, a ball tore his right arm away so that it hung only by the tendon; whereupon the brave lad cut the tendon, let his arm fall, and, lifting the bomb to his shoulder, he carried it on to the battery. A certain second lieutenant called Bertrand is responsible for the motto of the regiment; for as he was dying at the battle of Melegnano he uttered the words: "Je meurs pour le drapeau."

The four organizations which we are now going to describe are of particular interest to us, for we have followed them in the previous volume on their long march from Yorktown to Boston, where they embarked for foreign waters.

The Royal Deux-Ponts, which shared the honors with the Royal Auvergne at the Siege of Yorktown, was originally composed of Germans from the Duchy of Deux-Ponts in the Saar Basin. It was in a sense the property of Colonel Deux-Ponts and was successively commanded by members of this famous family. It was first put into the service of the King of France in 1758. The German regulations were preserved and the pay of the soldiers was continued at the same rate that was current among the German troops. This regiment had a fine record for esprit, fighting quality, and for the maintenance of its equipment. It merited great praise for its conduct in America, and this record was continued, calling forth high praise from Maréchal Ney, styled by Napoleon "The Bravest of the Brave." The organization is perpetuated today in the 99th Infantry.

The Soissonnais, of which Vicomte de Noailles, Lafayette's brother-in-law, was second in command, had its beginnings as far back as the year 1598, when it was first formed by a group of very select "gentilshommes." It enjoyed the distinction of embarking with Rochambeau, and also of taking part in the Siege of Yorktown, where it worked in close connection with the Bourbonnais. This was the regiment which wintered in Rhode Island and of which it is said that it was so well disciplined that its soldiers astonished both the Americans and the Indians by their order and by their respect for property. One account goes so far as to declare that, in the summer season, the soldiers did not even touch the fruit which ripened over their very tents. The regimental motto: "Qu'importe—soyons vainqueurs" was adapted from the words of the brave grenadier Castelet, who was mortally wounded in the Battle of Geisberg, and who called to his companions as they passed: "What difference does it make if I die—we have won the battle." The honor of the Soissonnais is ably defended today by the 40th infantry line regiment, which maintained its traditions in the World War.

When the Spaniards were menacing Amiens in 1597, one Philibert de Merestang gathered together some scattered and detached troops from the garrisons of Provence and formed what was so soon to become the famous Bourbonnais, the senior of the French regiments in America. After a long period of activity in Corsica and Brittany, this unit was favored with the privilege of embarking with Rochambeau, and with the Deux-Ponts it shared this enviable reputation even before it left Brest: "aussi solide par sa composition qu'aucun regiment français et dans le meilleur état" (as solid in its make-up as any other French regiment, and in the best of condition). This regiment took Pigeon Hill in the battle of September 30,

FRENCH BATTLE-FLAG

carried by a French regiment in America during the Revolutionary War.

1781, and six days later assisted in opening the way to the final attack on Yorktown. Since the year 1791 and through the World War, the 13th line regiment has carried on the standards of the Bourbonnais. Its motto is "En avant sur les canons."

The Saintonge regiment, of which Rochambeau's son was a colonel, bore a name which means much to America, for it was from the Province of Saintonge that both Samuel Champlain and Sieur de Monts sailed on their explorations, and it was also from there that many of the best Huguenot families came to New England. This unit was formed in 1684 from a part of the more ancient regiment of Navarre, its identity ending in 1791 when it became the 82d. It fought in a great many battles. In America it took part in the capture of Stony Point, where its famous Lieutenant-Colonel de Fleury, on whom we have here included a chapter, won the only medal given to a foreigner during the entire War of Independence. The motto of the Saintonge, "Le premier dans la place," is taken from the words of de Fleury during this attack.

De Lauzun's legion, created by royal decree in 1780, was made up of volunteer adventurers, mostly foreigners, many of whom were young nobles. It might be compared to Roosevelt's "Rough Riders."

Kindness of William Hooper

THE BRITISH SURRENDERING THEIR ARMS TO GENERAL WASHINGTON AFTER THEIR DEFEAT AT YORKTOWN IN VIRGINIA, OCTOBER 1781

To the defenders of American Independence this print is most respectfully inscribed by their fellow citizen, J. F. Renault.

RODERIGUE HORTALEZ ET CIE

TO Pierre Augustin Caron de Beaumarchais, "Watchmaker to the King," sometimes spoken of as the "garçon-major of Franklin," author of the popular comedies, "Le Barbier de Séville" and the "Le Mariage de Figaro," and to that great statesman, Count de Vergennes, Minister of Foreign Affairs, America owes a great debt of gratitude, for they persuaded King Louis to furnish, indirectly, supplies to America during the Revolution. Beaumarchais, witty, satirical, secretive, was also a man of adventure, intrigue, fascination and resourcefulness combined with a boldness that was irresistible. Added to these accomplishments, it is also said that he was a shipbuilder, contractor and secret service agent. As to personal attraction, he has often been likened to Lafayette—in fact, one of our correspondents in the Middle West writes that if he "had only had a chance with the belles of Boston, New York, Philadelphia and Richmond, he might have made the French General look like a wall flower." "Apropos of Lafayette," he continues, "did you ever hear this story? I was stationed near his old château for a few weeks during the War. Many American soldiers visited it. Finally a pile of cracked stone was dumped in the front yard with a polite sign which expressed the hope that the 'soldats americains' would get their souvenirs from there and stop cracking pieces off the château." The other benefactor, Vergennes, who had just come into office, was the earliest friend America had in the French councils, and by degrees he was able to persuade the King to take up our cause.

It is not generally known that in September, 1775, Beaumarchais was sent to England as a secret confidential agent, with no official connection and unknown to the French Ambassador in London, to get in touch with the secret agent of the revolted American colonists and to report as to their strength. He sent very strong and optimistic reports as to the probability of American success, which greatly influenced Vergennes. Early in the year 1775, he secured the King's assent to furnish a million livres to the colonies, and to appoint Beaumarchais as the secret agent through whom the aid was to be given. The latter answered the suggestion, declaring that "if your Majesty has not at hand a more clever man to employ in the matter, I undertake and answer for its execution without anyone being compromised, persuaded that my zeal will supply my want of talent better than the talent of another man could replace my zeal. The Americans are as well placed as possible; army, fleet, provisions, courage, everything is excellent;

Photographed by Paul Lemare through the kindness of James H. Hyde

From an old French print in the Bibliothèque d'Histoire et de Géographie de la Ville de Paris

BEAUMARCHAIS'S RESIDENCE IN BOULEVARD ST. ANTOINE, PARIS,

bought by him in 1787. Here he lived for fifteen years. The building was demolished in 1826. The street is now renamed Boulevard Beaumarchais.

ANOTHER VIEW OF THE "HÔTEL" OF BEAU-
MARCHAIS IN BOULEVARD ST. ANTOINE,
NOW BOULEVARD BEAUMARCHAIS, PARIS

The gardens were the wonder of the day.

but without powder and engineers, how can they conquer or how even can they defend themselves? Are we willing to let them perish rather than loan them one or two millions? Are we afraid of losing the money?" His enthusiasm for the "Bostoniens" knew no bounds.

With the approval of Vergennes, Beaumarchais lost no time in organizing the firm of Roderigue Hortalez et Cie, in June, 1776, and on October 9 leased through Louis Letellier, the King's architect and controller of his estate at Versailles, large offices in a building at No. 47 Rue Vieille-du-Temple. Here in former days was the private residence of Lord de Rieux, a Maréchal of France. The building, now standing, was erected in 1638 by Denis Amelot and his son, the Vicomte de Bisseuil, and is known today as the Hôtel de Bisseuil. Many have been its owners. An investigation shows that its present owner is M. Brenot, who purchased the property a few years ago, and who has recently renovated the building. It is through his kindness and the help of James H. Hyde, and with the permission of Frederic Contet, that we have been able to procure the pictures showing the "hôtel" as it used to look during the days of its occupancy by Roderigue Hortalez et Cie. It is classed by the government as one of the historic monuments of Paris, but it seldom has been described or pictured. A modern view on another page shows the building as it is today. M. Brenot owns the original lease executed by Beaumarchais. At one time the building was occupied by the Embassy of the Netherlands, which has given to it also the name of Hôtel de Hollande. It was here that Beaumarchais wrote his "Mariage de Figaro."

The instructions given to Beaumarchais at the time of organizing this firm were, "You will found your house, and at your own risk and perils you will provision the Americans with arms and munitions and objects of equipment and whatever is necessary to support the war. You shall not demand money of the Americans, because they have none, but you shall ask returns in commodities of their soil, the sale of which we will facilitate in our country." Tobacco, rice, and wheat were to be shipped from America. In writing to Arthur Lee, he mentions "the difficulties I have found in my negotiations with the Minister have determined me to form a company which will enable the munitions and powder to be transmitted sooner to your friend on condition of his returning tobacco to Cape Francis." Of course, the *friend* meant Congress.

By means of this fictitious firm, France was able to ship to the struggling thirteen States, clothing for 20,000 soldiers, 30,000 muskets, 100 tons of gunpowder, 200 brass cannon—some of which it is said bore the King's monogram—24 mortars, together with the necessary shot and shells; also medicine, and surgical instruments, disbursing through its office over 21,000,000 livres. At the same time Beaumarchais wrote to Congress under date of August 18, 1776, "The respectful esteem that I bear toward that brave people who so well defend their liberty

COUNT DE VERGENNES

Minister of Foreign Affairs from 1776 to 1783, and the earliest friend America had in the French councils.   He was able
to persuade his King to allow Beaumarchais under an assumed name to ship war supplies and ammunition to
America, enabling this country to carry on the war until the French armies and fleets later appeared on the scene.
Vergennes signed the Treaty of Versailles.   He lived in Quai Malaquais, but died at Versailles.

TICKET OF ADMISSION TO BEAUMARCHAIS'S
BEAUTIFUL GROUNDS IN PARIS,
signed by himself, in the year 1790.

under your conduct has induced me to form a plan concurring in this great work, by establishing an extensive commercial house solely for the purpose of serving you in Europe, there to supply you with necessaries of every sort, to furnish you expeditiously and certainly with all articles, clothes, linens, powder, ammunition, muskets, cannon or even gold for the honorable war in which you are engaged." There was at that time no factory in America where muskets or cannon could be made in any quantity, and it was also well-nigh impossible to obtain gunpowder. In fact, an article in Mr. Ford's *Dearborn Independent* and one in the *American Historical Review* written by O. W. Stephenson of the University of Michigan, stated that ninety per cent of the gunpowder used by America was furnished by France—an incredible fact, but nevertheless the truth. Mr. Stephenson, an authority on this subject, states also that nine-tenths of the guns and ammunition used by the American army, up to the time of Burgoyne's surrender, came from France through Beaumarchais or his firm. The translator of Chastellux's travels commends this capable and energetic Frenchman upon the large sums of French money brought into this country by the French fleets and armies, adding that the money of our allies in circulation here in 1792 was thirty-five millions of livres, or nearly a million and a half sterling.

With much skill and perseverance, this capable and energetic Frenchman had this ammunition and equipment withdrawn from the French arsenals in small lots and collected together at Havre and Nantes. The Colonies did not provide the promised vessels; therefore he was obliged to fit them out himself, which proved a great financial strain on the firm's resources. At one time he equipped ten merchantmen, one of which he named "Fier Roderigue"—causing Silas Deane to address Congress, "I should have never completed what I have but for the generous, the indefatigable and spirited exertions of Monsieur Beaumarchais, to whom the United States are on every account greatly indebted; more so than to any other person on this side of the water." One of his vessels he named for the "Count de Vergennes," and it is of interest to recall that L'Enfant, who planned our Capitol, first came to America on her. Some of these first ships put in at Portsmouth, New Hampshire, and it is said that the people of the city were so jubilant to see such a quantity of supplies and ammunition that they assembled on the shore and cheered vociferously.

When Beaumarchais was in great difficulties financially, he unselfishly wrote, "Through all these annoyances, the news from America overwhelms me with joy. Brave, brave people, their warlike conduct justifies my esteem and the noble enthusiasm felt for them in France!"

PIERRE AUGUSTIN

CARON DE BEAUMARCHAIS,

Né à Paris, le 24 Janvier 1732,

Mort dans la même ville le 19 Mai 1799.

PIERRE AUGUSTIN CARON DE BEAUMARCHAIS,

a benefactor of the American people, who under the assumed name of Roderigue Hortalez et Cie, with the connivance of the King and Minister of Foreign Affairs Vergennes, was able to ship money and war supplies to the thirteen Colonies to enable them to prosecute the war.

Face de l'hostel de Bvveüil vieille rue du temple du dessein du S.r Cottart

I. Marot fecit

HÔTEL AMELOT DE BISSEUIL, ALSO KNOWN AS THE HÔTEL DE HOLLANDE, 47 RUE VIEILLE-DU-TEMPLE, PARIS,
where Beaumarchais established his firm of Roderigue Hortalez et Cie in 1776, which supplied the American army with volunteers, money, ammunition,
and other war supplies, enabling the Colonies to prosecute the war until France became an actual ally of this country. This building was
also occupied at one time by the legation of the Netherlands. It has been classed by the government as an historic monument.

He naturally expected that Congress would return thanks, at least, even if the tobacco was slow in coming. There was, however, no answer to his letters. During the year 1777 he sent over to America cargoes valued at over 5,000,000 francs without receiving even an acknowledgment. He finally wrote in despair: "My money and my credit are gone. Relying too greatly on returns so often promised, I have exhausted my own funds and those of my friends. . . ." His next move was to despatch to this country his trusted friend and agent in America, Theveneau de Francy, but still no results followed. One of the volunteer officers in the French army, some of whom were actually assisted financially by him in getting to America, in speaking of Beaumarchais, is reported to have said, "Tell him that his fame pays the interest of his debt, and that I have no doubt of its payment in this way at usurious rates. . . ." If this important aid had not been given early during the war, before the Treaty of Alliance of 1778, the American army probably could not have held on for the arrival of the French fleet and armies.

Still another difficulty soon arose—as to whether certain supplies sent by Beaumarchais

From an old French print in the Cabinet des Estampes, Bibliothèque Nationale, Paris

Kindness of James H. Hyde, M. Brenot, the present owner of the building, and Frederic Contet, editor of the "Vieux Hôtels de Paris"

FRONT DOOR OF HÔTEL AMELOT DE BISSEUIL, OR HÔTEL DE HOLLANDE, NO. 47 RUE VIEILLE–DU–TEMPLE, PARIS

The building served as the offices for Beaumarchais's firm. It has recently been purchased by M. Brenot, who has renovated the building.

were on his own account, or from the French Government. Arthur Lee stated that they were presents from the King and that no payment was expected, whereas the other commissioners differed, reporting to this country that we were expected to remit for them.

In 1786, it was learned that there was a discrepancy of a million livres between the amount credited the United States as a gift prior to the treaty of 1778, and the amount as stated in the contract of 1782 between Franklin and Vergennes. The latter explained that the "lost million," as it has been termed, had been advanced on June 10, 1776. That this sum was actually used in purchasing supplies for America has never been questioned, for papers were produced showing the endorsement of the King and Vergennes; but this Government has always tried to relieve itself from the responsibility of payment on the assumption that the supplies were intended as free gifts from the King. The total amount of these presents, including 2,000,000 livres interest on the 1778 loan, reached a total of 11,000,000 livres, or approximately $1,800,000. To this day America has never offered to repay this amount, nor has France ever demanded a settlement. The loans, including the sum obtained by France from Holland, amounted to 35,000,000 livres, or over $6,352,500. This debt, with interest, was paid about thirty years afterwards, but the Beaumarchais "lost million" was in dispute long after his death in 1799. Just before dying he wrote from his garret in Hamburg, where he was seeking a refuge from the troubles at home, "On leaving this world, I have to ask you to give what you owe

STATUE OF BEAUMARCHAIS, IN PARIS,
NEAR THE PLACE DE LA BASTILLE,

*at the intersection of the historic Rue St. Antoine and
the Rue des Tournelles, where still exist many
of the handsome buildings of his time. Americans
should have assisted in erecting this memorial
to this versatile and energetic Frenchman, who helped
to a large degree in getting our Independence.*

me to my daughter as a dowry. . . . Adopt her after my death as a worthy child of the country! Her mother and my widow, equally unfortunate, will conduct her to you. Regard her as the daughter of a citizen . . . Americans, . . . be charitable to your friend, to one whose accumulated services have been recompensed in no other way! . . ."

Several times either the Attorney-General or the Committee on Foreign Affairs, headed by Edward Everett, recommended its payment. In 1835 the claim, which, with interest, had then reached 4,689,241 francs, was adjusted by a payment of only 810,000 francs.

It behooves this country, in adjusting France's World War debt to us, first of all to learn the facts—to take into consideration the gifts of $1,800,000 and the waived interest of 300,000 or so dollars and the Beaumarchais compromised claim—large sums of money in those days. Many of our high officials have stated that "our debts to France have been all paid," forgetting all the gifts, the interest on these gifts, and the interest of $300,000 waived owing to the inability of our Government to pay it at that time. Hon. A. Piatt Andrew, one of Massachusetts' Representatives in Washington, is using his best endeavors to make this situation clear to the people of America, and his first Resolution states that the cost of the war to France was estimated at over $240,000,000.

Paris commemorated her versatile citizen, Beaumarchais, by changing the name of one of her streets from Boulevard St. Antoine to Boulevard Beaumarchais. The French have also erected a statue to him near the site of his house, and America should have contributed to this worthy memorial.

The only consideration shown by the Council to the president of the College was the vote that "as the house of the Rev'd Mr. Manning is situated so near said Edifice that it may be disagreeable to him to reside therein so long as the College may be improved as an Hospital, if he should incline to remove the Deputy Quarter-Master General is directed to provide a suitable house for him and cause the vegetables growing in the gardens of Mr. Manning to be appraised by three indifferent persons that compensation may be made for the damage done the garden."

Colonel de Corny asked for a house for himself and family and was authorized by the Assembly to occupy that of Major Nathanael Greene in Woodstock, Connecticut, "now occupied by Captain Abimelech Riggs with a very small family who may be accommodated in some other house." As explained by Howard W. Preston in his "Rochambeau and the French Troops in Providence," the house used by the French Commissary was on the north side of Westminster Street, east of Exchange Street and the Industrial Trust Building.

The French made some alterations in the hospital building and caused necessarily some damage, amounting in all to several thousand dollars, which was not settled until fourteen years later.

Photographed through the courtesy of the late John R. Hess

TABLET ON UNIVERSITY HALL, BROWN UNIVERSITY, PROVIDENCE, RHODE ISLAND,

commemorating its occupation by the patriot forces and their French allies. The building was used as a hospital by the French, and those who died here or at other places in Providence were buried in the North Burying Ground of the city.

It is said that the French, while walking back and forth between the hospital and the camp grounds, made use of a path which was called at that time "Camp Lane," now known as Rochambeau Avenue. From "Les Combattants Français de la Guerre Américaine," published in Paris under the direction of the French Minister of Foreign Affairs, we know the names of at least eighteen French soldiers who lost their lives in Providence, and it is safe to assume that nearly all died either in camp or in this improvised hospital in University Hall. These unfortunate men were buried near the south entrance of the North Burying Ground, then the only public cemetery in the town. A French Delegation was planning to come to America during the latter part of 1881, on the occasion of the Yorktown Centennial, and doubtless this anticipated event gave to Rev. Frederic Denison the idea of erecting a lasting memorial over these graves. Accordingly, he made a careful search and succeeded in unearthing some of the remains, including a complete skeleton, which was found beyond doubt to be that of a Frenchman. The authorities of the town laid out the grounds, and through appeals in the *Providence Journal* funds were quickly raised to erect the impressive memorial to be seen there today. The base was laid at the time this French Delegation visited the city, each officer then placing a bouquet of flowers on the stone—the whole forming a cross. On the eastern side appear the words, "La Gratitude de Rhode Island"; while on the

Photographed through the courtesy of the late John R. Hess

MEMORIAL IN THE NORTH BURYING GROUND
IN PROVIDENCE, RHODE ISLAND,

*to eighteen or so French soldiers who died in camp or in the
hospital in University Hall, of Brown University, in
Providence, during the Revolutionary War. On the reverse side
are the words, "Our Allies during the Revolution."
Appeals for this monument were made through the "Providence
Journal."*

reverse side are the words: "Our Allies in the Revolution." On the south end is cut a Revolutionary cartridge-box, and the date 1782. On the top appear three fleurs-de-lis. On the other end is this inscription:

TRIBUTE OF THE PEOPLE. | DECORATED BY THE | FRENCH DELEGATION, | NOVEMBER 1, 1881. | DEDICATED BY THE | CITIZENS OF PROVIDENCE | JULY 4, 1882.

The monument was dedicated with appropriate ceremonies, which included a parade. Those present were the French Consul General and other guests of that nation. There were also present the Gardes Lafayette of New York, a celebrated organization now merged with the 8th Regiment, but still allowed to carry its former standard inscribed with the names of the battles in which Lafayette partici-

pated. The French Colony in Providence showed much interest in the dedication, contributing French flags and mottoes for the occasion. At the north end of the memorial was a century plant, indicating that a hundred years had gone by since the burials. At the dedication, a salute of twenty-one guns was fired in honor of the French; and among the orations was one by Rev. Mr. Denison, who referred especially to the losses suffered by France off the Capes and at Yorktown compared to those of this country—the former losing five hundred and three men and the latter only one hundred. General Foch also visited this monument. The

Americans and the French decorate the monument every Fourth of July.

Near this part of the burial ground is the grave of General Alfred Nattie Duffié, who, as the inscription says, was "born in Paris, May 1, 1835—Lieutenant in the French Army—Colonel in the First Rhode Island Cavalry—General in the United States Army 1861–1865."

The French saw much of Providence, and in their diaries made some interesting records. Commissary Claude Blanchard often went there and refers to the city:

"M. de Capellis and I left Boston on the 30th [July 1780] and slept at Providence, which is distant 45 miles, that is to say, about fifteen leagues. The road is pleasant. We find also some pretty handsome villages, and, as it was Sunday, we continually met people who were going to the temple or returning from it, most of them in light carriages, drawn by a single horse. There are few inhabitants

Photographed through the courtesy of the late John R. Hess

MARÉCHAL FOCH AT THE MEMORIAL IN THE
NORTH BURYING GROUND, PROVIDENCE, RHODE
ISLAND,

*erected to the memory of the French soldiers who died while the
French army was in the town. This monument was
visited also by the French Delegation that came to Yorktown in
1881 to attend the centennial there. It was dedicated
by the people of Providence on July 4 of the following year.*

in this part of the country who do not own one; for, without being rich, they are in easy circumstances. They cultivate the earth themselves, with the help of some negroes; but these estates belong to them and they are owners. We also met some provincial soldiers, who, in obedience to the orders that the Boston Committee had sent to them, were repairing in crowds to Newport, where, in less than three days, there would have been more than four thousand of them, if there had not been a countermand, upon the information which we received that we would not be attacked.

. . . On Thursday the 17th [August], I went to Providence with M. Demars. I have already spoken of this city which I prefer to Newport; it seems more lively, more addicted to commerce, more supplies are to be found there. We there established a very considerable hospital in a very handsome house, formerly occupied as a college [now Brown University].

. . . On the 18th, after having attended to this establishment, I paid some visits in the city, first to Mr. Varnum, he had been made the commander-in-chief of the militia of the country and had been styled general. I then went to Mr. Hancock's whom I have already mentioned; he has come to Providence on account of business; I was very well received by them.

TABLET ON GRAVE OF COLONEL ISRAEL ANGELL IN THE NORTH BURYING GROUND, PROVIDENCE, RHODE ISLAND

He took part in the Revolution and showed great gallantry, receiving the approbation of General Washington. On this tablet appear the words, "Friend of Washington, Lafayette and Rochambeau." In recognition of his military services and his great bravery, both Washington and Lafayette presented him with gold medals. His grave is next to the memorial to the French soldiers who died in Providence and who were buried there.

. . . On the 19th, General Varnum took me two miles from the city to a sort of **garden** where different persons had met and were playing nine-pins; they made us drink punch and tea. The place was pleasant and rural, and this little jaunt gave me pleasure. I was beginning to speak some English words and was able to converse. Besides, General Varnum spoke Latin. On the 20th, I dined at the house of the said general with his wife and his sister-in-law; after dinner some young ladies came who seemed well disposed to converse and to become acquainted with us. They were very handsomely dressed. . . ."

On the 12th of September he again visited the capital of Rhode Island, and with Coste, the chief physician, went to the hospital, where they found three hundred and forty sick; and with the two hundred ill in Newport, Blanchard estimated that almost one-tenth of the entire army was unfit for service. A few days later he was invited to a turtle party, as he called it, describing the event in this way:

"This same day, the 15th, I was invited to a party in the country to which I went. It was a sort of picnic given by a score of men to a company of ladies. The purpose of this party was to eat a turtle, weighing three or four hundred pounds, which an American vessel had just brought from one of our islands. This meat did not seem to me to be very palatable; it is true that it was badly cooked. There were some quite handsome women; before dinner they kept themselves in a different room from the men, they also placed themselves at table all on the same side, and the men, on the other. They danced after dinner to the music of some instruments of Lauzun's legion, which had been brought there expressly. Neither the men nor the women dance well; all stretch out and lengthen their arms in a way far from agreeable. I found myself at table very near a captain of an American frigate, whom I had seen at Nantes. I perceived today whilst trying to converse with the ladies, that I still was very little accustomed to the English language. During dinner we drank different healths, as is usual, we to those of the Americans, and they to the health of the King of France. This extended to every-

Photographed through the kindness of the late John R. Hess   *From an old print owned by the Rhode Island Historical Society*

ROGER WILLIAMS INN, PROVIDENCE, RHODE ISLAND,

as it looked when George Washington and Lafayette stayed there.   It was also known at one time as the "Golden Ball Inn,"
and is now called the "Mansion House."   A modern view appears in Volume I on page 23.

body; for on passing through an anteroom, where some negro servants were drinking, I heard them drinking together the health of the King of France."

In November, Commissary Blanchard was again in Providence, and made a number of entries:

"From the 2d to the 6th, I remained at Providence, in cold weather; but the sun shone and I did not cease to ride on horseback and go to see my laborers in the wood. I also had much to do for Lauzun's legion, which was to proceed to Connecticut to take up its winter quarters, and which passed through Providence. All these details, elsewhere very easy, nevertheless met with many difficulties. . . .

On the 9th, much snow fell and it was very cold, as was the next day. Lauzun's legion arrived at Providence today; it found everything that it needed. The Duke de Lauzun gave a ball, at which I was present for a moment.

On the 11th, the legion remained, the cold continued, but it was fine weather and the sun shone. I dined with M. de Lauzun.

On the 12th, the legion departed.

On the 16th M. Beaudouin, a lieutenant-colonel of Lauzun's legion, passed through Providence to go to and embark at Boston and return to France. I gave him some letters. I go regularly every day to the forest where they are busy about the wood.

On the 24th, it was still pretty fine and I mounted my horse according to my usual practice. I dined at Providence with Dr. Bowen, a physician and a respectable old man. He said grace before sitting down to table; he seemed beloved and respected by his numerous family and had the style and manners of a patriarch. I also dined frequently at the house of Mr. Bowker, a merchant, born in England, but for a long time settled in America. They do not eat soups and do not serve up ragouts at these dinners; but boiled and roast and much vegetables. . . . They drink nothing but cider and Madeira wine with water. The dessert is composed of preserved quinces or pickled sorrel. The Americans eat the latter with the meat. They do not take coffee immediately after dinner, but it is served three of four hours afterwards with tea; this coffee is weak, and four or five cups are not equal to one of ours; so that they take many of them. The tea, on the contrary, is very strong. This use of tea and coffee is universal in America. The people who live in the country, tilling the ground and driving their oxen, take it as well as the inhabitants of the cities. Breakfast is an important affair with them. Besides tea and coffee, they put on table roasted meats with butter, pies and ham; nevertheless they sup, and in the afternoon, they again take tea. Thus the Americans are almost always at the table; and as they have little to occupy them, as they go out little in winter and spend whole days alongside of their fires and wives, without reading and without doing anything, going so often to table is a relief and a preventive of "ennui." Yet they are not great eaters. They are very choice in cups and vases for holding tea and coffee, in glasses, decanters and other matters of this kind, and in habitual use. They make use of wall-papers which serve for tapestry; they have them very handsome. In many of the houses there are carpets also, even upon their stairs. In general, the houses are very pleasant and kept with extreme neatness, with the mechanic and the countryman as well as with the merchant and the general. Their education is very nearly the same; so that a mechanic is often called to their assemblies where there is no distinction, no separate order. I have already mentioned that the inhabitants of the entire country are proprietors. They till the earth and drive their oxen themselves. This way of living and this sweet equality have charms for thinking beings. These manners suit me pretty well. Burning a great quantity of wood is one of their luxuries, it is common. One-half of the districts which I have traversed are wooded, almost altogether with oaks, among which there are some very handsome ones. Yet wood is very dear owing to the difficulty of transporting it. It costs us for a league about 15 livres a cord."

Towards the last of November he made a visit to Mrs. Nathanael Greene, wife of the General, at their house just off the main road in Coventry, Rhode Island, not far from the French Camp at Waterman's Tavern, which he describes most interestingly:

"I took advantage of it (clear weather) to go to Greenwich, a small town upon the coast, five leagues from Providence. Thence I proceeded to Coventry, two leagues from Greenwich. General Greene's residence is there. He is a farmer whose merit has raised him to the rank of general. He was then with the army and possessed the confidence of General Washington; he has even been commander-in-chief of a body of troops in the south; one of his brothers, an inhabitant of the country, had furnished the wagons for transporting the wood which I had caused to be cut, and he drove them himself; such are the manners of this part of America! My object was to pay a visit to the wife of General Greene, whom I happened to see at Newport and Providence. I was accompanied by M. Haake, a captain in the regiment of Royal Deux Ponts, and the chaplain of the hospital. Mrs. Greene received us very kindly. She is amiable, genteel and rather pretty. As there was no bread in her house, some was hastily made; it was of meal and water mixed together, which was then toasted at the fire; small slices of it were served up to us. It is not much for a Frenchman. As for the Americans, they eat very little bread. Besides, the dinner was long; we remained to sleep there. Mrs. Greene's house is situated upon a barren piece of land; this site could have been chosen only on account of the iron-works situated in the neighborhood.* There is not a single fruit-tree, not even a cabbage. Another country-house is pretty near, inhabited by two ladies, who compose all the society that Mrs. Greene has; in the evening she invited them to her house, and we danced; I was in boots and rather tired; besides, the English dances are complicated, so that I acquitted myself badly. But these ladies were complaisant. . . ."

GENERAL NATHANAEL GREENE'S HOME IN COVENTRY, RHODE ISLAND,

where Claude Blanchard, commissary of the French army, and M. Haake, Captain of the Royal Deux-Ponts regiment and Chaplain of the Hospital, were entertained by Mrs. Greene, towards the end of November, 1780. Blanchard gives an interesting account of his visit in his valuable diary. The Greene "mansion" is only a few miles from Waterman's Tavern, where the French army camped on its march to Yorktown and also on its return journey. This house was built by the General himself, but he was able to occupy it only a short time before he was called to take command of his troops. It is now the property of the Nathanael Greene Homestead Association.

This old house is preserved by the Nathanael Greene Homestead Association. General Greene purchased it just before the war, but was soon called away to join Washington's army in Cambridge, Massachusetts.

Some days later the French Commissary was again in Providence, where he witnessed a reunion of Freemasons, which he thus describes:

*There is still a manufacturing plant nearby.

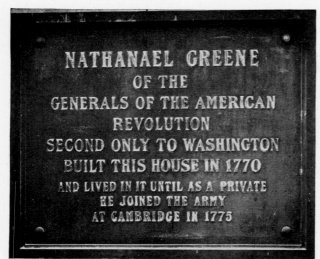

Photographed through the courtesy of the late John R. Hess

TABLET ON THE NATHANAEL GREENE HOUSE IN
COVENTRY, RHODE ISLAND,

*not far from the French camp at Waterman's Tavern.   Commissary
Claude Blanchard, accompanied by a captain in the Royal
Deux-Ponts regiment, visited Mrs. Greene at this house in November,
1780, where they were hospitably entertained.   This tablet
gives a brief description of his career.*

" . . . It was Saint John's day, a great festival for the free-masons. There was a meeting of them at Providence; it was announced in the public papers, for societies of this sort are authorized. I met in the streets of Providence a company of these free-masons, going two by two, holding each other's hands, all dressed with their aprons and preceded by two men who carried long staves. He who brought up the rear and who was probably the master had two brethren alongside of him and all three wore ribbons around their necks like ecclesiastics who have the blue ribbon.

On the 28th, the Count de Vioménil and the Viscount Mesme came to lodge at Providence, and set out the next morning for Boston. Our army remained inactive, they take advantage of it to travel and become acquainted with the country. . . ."

Rochambeau's aide, de Closen, mentions particularly the College hospital.

"In the evening we arrived in Providence, a journey of about 30 miles. This town has about 2500 inhabitants and is partly situated on the river which bears its name, which empties into Newport Bay. The houses and the streets indicate the amiable and pleasant humour of its inhabitants. It is very commercial. The finest building is the college which is very large and exceedingly well built. It is situated on a hill or elevation behind the town, from which one has a very fine view. On it the Military hospital has been erected, even while we were still in Newport, owing to the life-giving air that it has as well as for the facility it offers for assembling all its employees. At the base or foot of this mountain the two rivers, Patuxet and Patuxen, unite. The country between Providence and Bristol is very beautiful, one fancies oneself in Eden. All the roads were bordered with locust trees which were in full bloom and the perfume, although delicious, was almost too strong. The Military camp was at the North Western quarter of the town which had been occupied by Lauzun's Infantry till their departure. The staff hospital as well as that which Lauzun's troops had occupied were well supplied with sufficient provisions."

De Ségur makes a short mention of Providence, which he says

"must be a large city, and might already, at that time, have been considered a pretty little town. It then only contained three thousand inhabitants; but all were in easy circumstances which they owed to assiduous labor and active industry. It is situated in the midst of a valley watered by the river Narraganset, which is tolerably wide and navigable. The name of Narraganset recalls to my mind, that, previously to reaching Providence, I had passed through a village or rather an irregular assemblage of miserable huts bearing that name. It contained the last remnants of the savage tribe of the Narragansets who, during several centuries, had enjoyed the undisturbed possession of this province. . . ."

The Marquis de Chastellux was also well pleased with Providence, for he writes in his Memoirs:

"The 12th I set out at half past eight for Providence, where I arrived at noon. I alighted at the College, that is to say, at our Hospital, which I examined, and dined with Mr. Blanchard, Commissary of war. At half past four I went to Colonel Bowen's, where I had lodged in my first journey; I drank tea there with several ladies, one of whom, rather handsome, was called Miss Angel. I was then conducted to Mrs. Varnum's, where I again found company, and from thence to Governor Bowen's, who gave me a bed. . . .

The Town of Providence is built on the bank of a river only six miles long. . . . It has only one street, which is very long; the suburb, which is considerable, is on the other side of the river. This town is handsome, the houses are not spacious, but well-built, and properly arranged within. . . . It may contain two thousand five hundred inhabitants. Its situation is very advantageous for commerce; which accordingly is very considerable in times of peace. Merchantships may load and unload their cargoes in the town itself, and ships of war cannot approach the harbour. Their commerce is the same with that of Rhode Island and Boston; they export slaves, and salt provisions, and bring back salt, and a great deal of molasses, sugar, and other articles from the West Indies; they fit out vessels also for the cod and whale fishery. The latter is carried on successfully between Cape Cod and Long Island; but they go often as far as Baffin's Straits, and Falkland Islands. The inhabitants of Providence, like those of

Photographed through the kindness of the late John R. Hess

BEAUTIFUL RESIDENCE OF GOVERNOR WILLIAM GREENE,

brother of the General, at Warwick, Rhode Island, where Lafayette, Rochambeau, General Nathanael Greene and General Sullivan consulted with the Governor of the State and Council during the Revolution. The date on the chimney is 1680.

Newport, also carry on the Guinea trade; they buy slaves there and carry them to the West Indies, where they take bills of exchange on Old England, for which they receive woolens, stuffs, and other merchandise. . . .''

Stone, in "Our French Allies," has an interesting chapter on the life in Providence while the French were there, referring to the balls and parties, to the beauties of those days— the Misses Bowen, Miss Checkley and Miss Waity Arnold, the latter having had the honor to dance with Lafayette. Stone also mentions the charms of Miss Sally Church, who so captivated an officer of the Bourbonnais, de Silly, that he sent her this message through his friend Dr. Drowne: "If you had given me your heart, I would not have returned it." The Doctor replied, "I received your generous epistle the 14th instant, and delivered with pleasure the enclosed inscription to the amiable Miss Church. She received it with one of those smiles which would make the blood thrill in a hermit's veins. . . ." Another attractive Providence girl, Miss Bathsheba Bowler, married one of the French officers quartered in the town, M. Lanfrey Delisle, who took her to France, where she became very popular. Captain Pierre Dubosque married Sally Arnold and lived in his bride's city, where he died.

Photographed through the courtesy of the late John R. Hess

JOSEPH RUSSELL HOUSE, NORTH MAIN STREET, PROVIDENCE, RHODE ISLAND,

where Chevalier de Chastellux, Maréchal-de-Camp and author of his "Mémoires," had his headquarters while in Providence. This building has been raised and stores added underneath. We are indebted to Mr. Howard W. Preston for the facts collected in regard to this old house, one of the three in Providence, used by French officers, that remain standing today.

SWORD AND SCABBARD PRESENTED BY GENERAL
ROCHAMBEAU TO GENERAL NATHAN MILLER,
A RHODE ISLAND SOLDIER OF THE REVOLUTION

*General Miller was a resident of Warren, Rhode Island, and was
of French ancestry. These two officers had such regard
for each other that they exchanged swords. This weapon is now
owned by George L. Cooke of Providence, a descendant
of General Miller.*

Count Dumas refers to an experience in connection with Providence:

"I had left at Providence, in the house of Dr. Bowen, and especially entrusted to his amiable daughters, a small box containing various papers and notes which I had made in the course of our two campaigns. This box, which I had supposed to be lost, has been carefully preserved by Mrs. Ward, the youngest of those ladies, the only survivor of her family, and who has done me the honor to remember me. After a lapse of forty years, having met at New York with General Lafayette during his triumphal progress, Mrs. Ward was so good as to inquire after me, and requested the General to convey this box to me, with an affecting testimony of our former friendship."

Count de Ségur wrote:

"I do not recollect to have seen anywhere else an assemblage, in which a greater degree of mirth prevailed without confusion, in which there was a greater number of pretty women and married people living happily together, a greater proportion of beauty free from coquetry, a more complete mixture of persons of all classes, whose conduct and manners presented an equal degree of decorum, which obliterated all appearance of unpleasant contrast or distinctions."

Rochambeau made his first visit to Providence during the latter part of August, staying with Deputy Governor Jabez Bowen in Market Square in the "grande rue près le pont." While there, he presented to his host a spoon which has been a treasured relic in the family ever since. He also gave a sword to his friend General Nathan Miller, of Warren, and this valuable gift has been handed down to a descendant. An illustration appears above. The French General was also in Providence for a short time on a number of other occasions.

As in Newport, the leading officers of the French army were lodged with the most important families of the town, and this list is also preserved in Fraunces' Tavern in New York. These locations are very clearly defined by Mr. Preston in his book, already referred to. Only three of these buildings, however, are now in existence, and even these have been considerably altered. The one that served as the headquarters for Baron de Vioménil and his brother and two of his aides, Brison and d'Angely, is known as the Joseph

JOSEPH BROWN HOUSE, 78 SOUTH MAIN STREET,
PROVIDENCE, RHODE ISLAND,

*where Baron de Vioménil, Colonel of the Bourbonnais, had his
quarters while the French army was in camp in that
city, as well as the Chevalier de Vioménil; his two aides, Brison
and d'Angely, were also quartered here. As pointed
out by Howard W. Preston in his "Rochambeau and the French
Troops in Providence in 1780–81–82," the entrance to
this building was on the second story, with a double flight of stairs.*

Brown house, at 78 South Main Street, the former home of the Providence National Bank. Mr. Preston explains that "the entrance was then in the second story with a long flight of steps, up which, it is said, one of the French officers, in a moment of exhilaration, rode his horse and into the hall; when unable to force the animal back down the stairs, he was obliged to ride through the house and return down the hillside to the street." Chevalier de Chastellux was quartered in the Joseph Russell house on North Main Street. The building has been raised, and stores added on the lower floor. The third of the old "mansions" still preserved is that of Nicholas Brown, 27–31 South Main Street, where were lodged three of Rochambeau's aides—de Fersen, de Vauban and de

Photographed through the courtesy of the late John R. Hess

FORMER CITY HALL, MARKET SQUARE, PROVIDENCE, RHODE ISLAND

At the request of Major Dumas, the upper part and a portion of the lower floor were allotted to the French army for storage purposes. Rochambeau's headquarters were also in Market Square, just at the left of City Hall, in Governor Bowen's house. The City Hall is now used by the Chamber of Commerce.

Damas. All three of these buildings are shown in illustrations. There is still one other, the Brown house, near Butler Hospital, which is still standing and which is said to be the second oldest brick house in Providence. It was visited by some of the French officers, and, according to Stone, a splendid ball was given there. Another building used by the French was the Market House, which the Town voted to lend to the army in which to store the baggage. The upper lofts were granted for this purpose under certain conditions.

One of the war brides was a Pawtucket girl who married a French Canadian, Lieutenant Pierre Douville, whose remains now lie in the Swan Point Cemetery of the city. His grave is marked by a triangular pyramidal monument bearing this inscription:

PIERRE DOUVILLE

was born in Canada, a subject of the King of France. He settled in Providence as a merchant, and served as a Lieutenant in the American Navy during the War of Independence; after which he was recalled by his King, and appointed to the command of the French ship-of-the-line *L'Impétueux*, which he defended in the desperate battle between the French and English fleets off Ushant, on the first of June, A.D. 1794, until his last spar was shot away, and until he had received eighteen wounds, of which he died; thus closing an unspotted life which had been bravely and consistently spent in the service of his adopted and of his native country.

He served with D'Estaing and de Ternay. There is a portrait of him in Brown University.

Photographed through the courtesy of the late John R. Hess

NICHOLAS BROWN HOUSE, 27–31 SOUTH MAIN STREET, PROVIDENCE, RHODE ISLAND,

where three of Rochambeau's aides-de-camp, de Fersen, de Vauban and de Damas were lodged while in Providence with the army. The Trust Company is again indebted to Mr. Preston for the facts he has unearthed regarding this and the Joseph Russell house.

Photographed through the courtesy of the late John R. Hess

HEADSTONE OF CAPTAIN JOHN GEORGE
CURIEN IN MINERAL SPRING CEME-
TERY, PAWTUCKET, RHODE ISLAND

*This French officer left the army while in camp on
North Main Street in Providence, when the
main division proceeded to Boston. While in camp
he met a woman whom he married, the couple
spending the rest of their lives in Pawtucket. The words
on the gravestone appear in the text.*

Mineral Spring Cemetery in Pawtucket has a monument to the memory of Captain John George Curien, who died in 1824, and who, as the tombstone indicates:

> . . . crossed the raging ocean,
> This country for to save;
> 'Twas France that gave him birth,
> And America a grave.

He was in the service of Louis XVI and was well along in life when the French troops encamped near North Main Street in North Providence. Many people visited the camp, and among them was a lady with whom the Captain fell in love and married. They settled in Pawtucket, where he died at the advanced age of ninety-one.

Bristol, on the east shore of Narraganset Bay, half-way between Newport and Providence, has a special interest for us for the reason that, after the retreat from Rhode Island, in September of 1778, General Sullivan stationed Lafayette there. The latter realized that this duty would be a difficult one, for he wrote to General Washington:

"I am now intrusted by General Sullivan with the care of Warren, Bristol, and the eastern shore. I am to defend a country with very few troops, who are not able to defend more than a single point. I cannot answer that the enemy won't go and do what they please, for I am not able to prevent them, only with a part of their army, and yet this part must land not far from me. But I answer, that if they come with equal or not very superior forces to those I may collect, we shall flog them pretty well; at least I hope so."

Lafayette's headquarters while at Bristol were in the Joseph Reynolds house, situated not far north of the town itself, on the east side of the main road leading to Warren, the chief highway in Revolutionary times. This old house, shown in a picture, was built in the year 1698, and at the time of the Revolution was still owned by the same family. The bedroom of the French General was supposed to have been one flight up in the northwest end of the second floor. There is little change in the house from Revolutionary days. A colonel in the World War is often a visitor to Bristol, and on one of his pilgrimages to this old Rhode Island town he gleaned this information:

"There is a story current in the family that word was sent to Bristol that Lafayette and his staff would spend the night there, and the General himself was assigned to the Reynolds House. The Mrs. Reynolds of that day immediately began to put the house in order and was especially solicitous to have the room reserved for Lafayette made immaculate. She was called out during the day, and upon her return found a number of French officers in the house, they having arrived earlier than expected. On going to Lafayette's room Mrs. Reynolds was much distressed to find a young man sitting at the desk writing. She welcomed him but told him she was sorry to have to ask him to take some other room, as that one was reserved for the Marquis, whereupon he informed her that he was himself the Marquis notwithstanding his youthful appearance."

Another version is that a young French officer arrived at the Reynolds home and asked for something to eat, whereupon the negro steward, Cato, conducted him to the table which had been prepared for the commander. The officer delayed over his meal so long that Mrs. Reynolds, believing that the General himself would soon arrive, requested her visitor to leave so as to prepare the table. To her great surprise, she was informed that the Frenchman was none other than Lafayette himself.

The State has placed a tablet on the Reynolds house inscribed with these words: "This house built about the year 1698 by Joseph Reynolds was occupied by Lafayette as his headquarters September 1778 during the War of American Independence."

Another interesting incident connecting Bristol with the French took place on Poppasquash Point at the ancient Herreshoff homestead, known as the De Wolfe or Byefield or Vassall house, which was

Photographed through the courtesy of the late John R. Hess

JOSEPH REYNOLDS HOUSE, BRISTOL, RHODE ISLAND,

used by Lafayette as his headquarters when requested by General Sullivan to take up his station in Bristol during the latter part of September, 1778. He is supposed to have used the bedroom in the northwest corner of the second story and to have had his office in the southwest end of the lower floor. This house is situated on the east side of the main road leading to Warren. On the right of the door can be seen the tablet affixed by the State.

used as a hospital for French soldiers either during the Revolution or at the time of the French-Indian Wars. Du Bourg refers to it as a magnificent hospital. We believe that it served this purpose during Revolutionary days, for Claude Blanchard mentions a hospital several times in his diary. "On the 13th (July)" he writes, "I was at Poppasquash on the mainland, twenty leagues from Newport, to examine an establishment which M. de Corny had arranged for our sick. I stopped at Bristol, a village not far from Poppasquash, and looked for an inn where I might dine; . . . I was with Mr. Demars, the steward of the hospitals, and Mr. Corte, the first Physician." . . . "We sent some of the sick to Poppasquash." . . . He again visited this place, where there were 280 sick. "Poppasquash," he adds, "forms a kind of landscape surrounded by trees." He refers to the affable character and good looks of the people of Bristol, and declares that the oxen and cows were at least as handsome as those of Poitou.

Poppasquash, situated between Narraganset Bay and Bristol Harbor, according to our informant, is a corruption from Papoose Squaw, and there is a legend to

Kindness of Willard B. Luther

TABLET ON THE JOSEPH REYNOLDS HOUSE, BRISTOL, RHODE ISLAND,

commemorating the occupancy of the building by Lafayette while stationed at Bristol in September, 1778, during the struggle for American Independence.

Kindness of Willard B. Luther and the late John R. Hess

THE NATHANIEL BYEFIELD OR VASSALL HOUSE, POPPASQUASH POINT, BRISTOL, RHODE ISLAND,

which served as a hospital for French soldiers during the Revolution. Claude Blanchard, a Commissary of the French army, in his diary mentions visiting a hospital there. One authority believes that it was used for French prisoners at the time of the French-Indian War of 1755 and 1756. This building, only recently burned, was also owned by the well-known Herreshoff family. Barrack Meadow, where some of the French soldiers are supposed to have been buried, is nearby.

the effect that during the Indian Wars a squaw with her papoose fled across the harbour in a canoe and hid on that point from pursuing settlers. For many years this house occupied by the French has been owned by the well-known Herreshoff family. It was burned in January, 1925.

Some of the photographs used were taken by the late N. G. Herreshoff, Jr., a son of the famous yacht designer, and much of the information came from either Lewis or Miss Julia Herreshoff. Lewis Herreshoff wrote us just before his death: "There is a spot close to the recently built house of my brother Charles where tradition has it that French soldiers were buried, and in my early youth I avoided these places in our sports; one spot in particular I had great fear of, it had an elder bush on it. In one room there are marks on the floor where a three-legged pot just taken from the fire had burned spots." In the wall an old French sword was discovered. The location of the burial place mentioned above is now known as Barrack Meadow, but no graves have ever been identified. Here were the barracks—now no longer— in which, it is said, the French prisoners were kept during the French and Indian Wars during the years 1755 and 1756. It is said that in one of the old documents in the town clerk's office there is a record of a rental from the state in which the tenant claims a rebate on the ground that the reservation for the French deprived him of the use of part of the land.

General Lafayette changed his location to the nearby town of Warren for the sake of better security, advising Washington on the 24th of September, "I have removed my station from Bristol and am in a safer place behind Warren." This old shipping port at the beginning of the war was in a flourishing condition, but suffered very severely during the struggle. An interesting incident was the transfer of the records of Newport County to Warren, also for greater safety. The regiment of Colonel Israel Angell was in camp in the fields on the eastern slope of Windmill Hill in the northerly part of the town near the Kickemuit River, and here southeast of a ledge of rocks on the summit of the hill Lafayette had his marquee. A post in the ground used to mark this spot, but it no longer exists; there are still, however, some earthworks on the east side of Belcher's Cove said to have been thrown up under the direction of the Marquis himself.

Photographed through the kindness of Willard B. Luther

BARRACK MEADOW, POPPASQUASH POINT, BRISTOL, RHODE ISLAND

Tradition tells us that in this field, the property of Charles Herreshoff, some French soldiers were buried; but the location of the graves has never been learned. The barracks used probably during the French and Indian Wars were also erected here, but were later removed.

Virginia Baker gives us a glimpse of these days: "The gallant French officer was very popular with the townspeople, his frank and engaging manner winning all hearts. Tradition states that he was extremely partial to the old-fashioned 'Rhode Island johnny-cakes' baked on a board at the hostelry of Ebenezer Cole, famous throughout the colonies for its good cheer; and that he and an American officer once engaged in a 'johnny-cake match,' which he easily won, outstripping or rather outeating his competitor by two or three cakes of more than ordinary size.

"In October (after the arrival of Rochambeau), a detachment of French troops was quartered in Warren and remained there during the winter. These troops occupied during a portion of their stay the old camping place at Windmill Hill. They are said to have been admirably disciplined, and were very friendly with the neighboring farmers, whose wives supplied them with brown bread, for which they displayed as great partiality as Lafayette evinced for Landlord Cole's Rhode Island johnny-cakes." Cole's Hotel used to be one of Warren's landmarks.

Miss Baker also narrates an amusing incident that is supposed to have taken place in Warren during the war: "As the retreating column filed slowly along Main Street, a party of ladies who were watching it from the windows of what is now the Fessenden Hotel espied, lagging far behind his comrades, a diminutive individual encumbered with a large drum, and very much the worse for the numerous drams of West India rum with which he had regaled himself. The ladies determined to make him prisoner. One of them, placing herself at the head of the party, snatched a brass candlestick from a table near by, and, followed by her companions, ran into the street. Pointing the candlestick at her victim, she commanded him to halt. Pale with terror, the little man staggered back exclaiming, 'Don't fire, ladies! Don't fire! I surrender.' The ladies surrounded him and triumphantly conducted him into the house, where they locked him securely in a closet. He expressed great pleasure at being captured, saying that he was exhausted with the weight of his heavy drum."

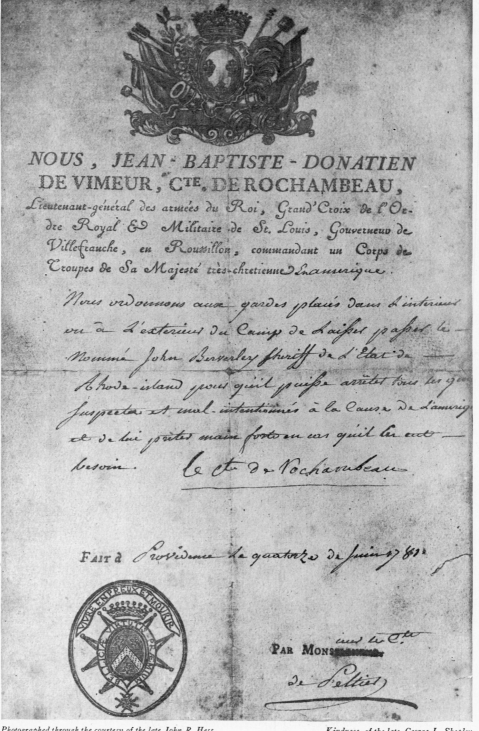

Photographed through the courtesy of the late John R. Hess   *Kindness of the late George L. Shepley*

PASS ISSUED BY GENERAL ROCHAMBEAU TO JOHN BEVERLEY, SHERIFF OF RHODE ISLAND,

authorizing him "to arrest all suspects and persons antagonistic to the American cause, and to use force if necessary." The date is the 14th of June, 1781. This picture is taken from a very rare original now in the library of the late Colonel George L. Shepley of Providence.

One of the town records states that upon the request of the French Commissary, General de Corny, a committee was formed to confer with him relative to the repairing of the ferries between Providence and Newport.

Lafayette remained at Bristol for some weeks and then set out for Philadelphia with the idea of returning to France to help the American cause.

THE "SALLY" OF WISCASSET

WISCASSET, Maine, was once one of the most important commercial ports east of Boston, and at times there were so many foreign vessels in the harbour that some of the residents jocosely remarked that one could walk across their decks from the Wiscasset shore to Davis Island. Many of these ships called there for cargoes of timber, which made the port well known in Europe, particularly in England and France. From there, too, were shipped the masts for the "Constitution." It was quite natural that numbers of settlers should have been attracted there from Massachusetts. A book written by Nat Wilder, Jr., entitled "A Royal Tragedy," describes a rather mythical character, to which he gives the name of Nathaniel Cloud, as one of the early pioneers of Wiscasset, where he carried on the trade of shipbuilding. This interesting though visionary story goes on to describe how one day a stranger walked in and introduced himself as Mr. Pry, whereupon one of those present is said to have exclaimed: "Why, it's the Marquis"; for, by this name, according to Wilder, he was known to the people of the town. Bennette Claude de St. Pry is supposed to have come to Wiscasset from Lyons, France, in the year 1789, establishing salt works on the Sheepscott River at a place then called Jeremy Squam Island in Wiscasset Bay. Many of the inhabitants, according to the story, were confident that he was an official of the French Government and that his real business was to study events in America, watching carefully the results of our Revolution. This book then describes Pry's house, with its French ornaments and decorations, and its Gobelin tapestries; and soon, of course, a romance is introduced. This Frenchman proceeds to fall in love with Sally, the daughter of Captain Cloud. The real name of the captain of the "Sally" was Clough. Curiously enough, the "Marquis" suddenly disappears, no one knows where.

Wilder proceeds beyond the limits of the historian by recording Colonel James Swan and General Henry Jackson of Boston as owners of an interest in Pry's salt works, and by further stating that when Pry left Wiscasset the two New Englanders then became agents for his successor, a Captain Decker.

Colonel Swan, some months later, sent his son to Maine to attend to some of the firm's business there, and on his visit he called at the Clough homestead, where he was well known and where he was hospitably welcomed. He had a second object in view in making this journey, for he wanted again to see Sally Clough. After supper he and Captain Clough discussed business and finally shipping. Their conversation is described in "A Royal Tragedy" in these words: "Captain Clough," said Swan, "if you will build the vessel which you planned about the time of the Indian outbreak, and will load her with good spar timber and tobacco, my father will guarantee a quick sale at Havre at good prices. . . ."

"It's a great opportunity," replied Captain Clough, "and I don't propose to let it slip. . . ."

"Have you drawn your plans, Captain?" asked Frank Swan, surprised at the news that the keel would be laid soon.

"Plans? Bless you, my boy, we don't want any plans for a schooner; we just build 'em. Mathematical fiddle-sticks! Drawings! Nothing of the kind. It's done by rule of thumb, my boy. We build as we go. If the sheer of her stern doesn't look right, why, we just change it till the eye is satisfied. Mathematics would make her too precise and stiff. She would probably be cranky and perverse like. Sort of inanimate as it were."

"You don't claim that a ship has life, do you, Captain?" asked Swan with a smile.

"Sure," replied the Captain. "Some boats sail themselves, are quick in stays, easy to steer, and mount the waves like a duck. Others stick their nose under every wave that comes along. They won't come about, and you can't keep them within two points of the course. Stubborn, you know, just like a farm critter."

"Maine turns out the best farmers and the best sailors," remarked Frank.

"Yes," said Captain Clough, "and Maine sailors make good farmers after they make their last port."

The vessel was built forthwith, and the Captain's daughter christened her "Sally"— named for herself. In another week or so, as the tale goes, this little Maine ship, the property of Swan, was loaded with lumber, sailing on a June day in 1793 for France with the Captain's daughter and Frank Swan as passengers. In the Custom House is the record of the first register of the "Sally," but there is no record that the daughter ever sailed in her. On the thirty-second day of the voyage, land was sighted and the story again introduces Claude St. Pry, who appears on board the French frigate "La Belle Poule" to examine the "Sally's" papers. The American vessel was, thereupon, ordered to Havre, and a prize crew placed on board. The Captain brought the case of the seizure before Gouverneur Morris in Paris, but there did not appear to be much hope of a prompt settlement; for it was learned that the fall of the Bastille had just taken place and that Americans were being advised to leave the country.

"We will find one friend among the French, anyhow," Captain Clough is supposed to have said to his daughter.

"And who is that?" asked Sally.

"Lafayette," replied the Captain. "He returned to France as soon as our war of the Revolution was over."

"Yes," interrupted Frank Swan, "and he entered the French army. He is a general now. He had been a warm friend of the King and Queen. When it was suspected that the King would try to flee the country, Lafayette was ordered to the frontier to meet the Prussians and Austrians. This was in June, last year. The King and Queen were living in the Tuileries, and when they tried to escape, Lafayette was in camp far from Paris. It was there that he first heard the news that the royal family had fled to Varennes. They were captured there by a mere accident. A man in the crowd which gathered about their carriage at the inn, where the party stopped, recognized the King from his likeness on a piece of money in common circulation."

"Contrary to the general belief, the consular agent tells me that General Lafayette had nothing to do with the escape. In fact King Louis looked upon him as his jailor, because Lafayette had previously been in charge of the dragoons at the Tuileries, and made his rounds every night to make sure that the royal family were in their apartments. . . ."

The reader of "A Royal Tragedy" soon hears of Sally Clough and Frank Swan in Paris, where they are endeavoring to procure the release of the "Sally." Both are pictured as being imprisoned, but not before they had witnessed the death of the Queen. The family has established the fact that the Captain was actually in Paris at that time.

In the meanwhile, this Wiscasset ship and her Captain were at Havre, an object of much interest to the people of the town. Presently the Chevalier de Rougeville is supposed to

MARIE ANTOINETTE HOUSE, AT NORTH EDGECOMB, NEAR WISCASSET, MAINE,
which was supposed to have been renovated to receive the King and Queen at the beginning of the French Revolution. Some articles of furniture were doubtless brought over from France to make the royal pair comfortable, and placed in this old house, which dates back to 1791. It was formerly located on Jeremy Squam Island at Westport nearby. Only one article of furniture can be definitely traced—the sideboard shown in another illustration.

have arrived at that port to consult secretly the Captain, the conversation being described in these words:

"I have come on a very important mission," said de Rougeville, "and one that will interest you as much as it will my principals, because if you do what is asked of you, I can promise you that your vessel will be released immediately. The only condition is that you take a small party to America on board your schooner.

"The flight of the parties to whom I refer must be made in absolute secrecy. It will be necessary for you to sail from Havre for some port in England or America and remain off this harbour until you can pick up a small boat with these passengers aboard. It may be possible to load certain baggage and freight in the harbour before you sail, but even that is dangerous. Are you willing to undertake it?"

"How about my cargo?" he asked abruptly.

"The government will take it, and pay your own price," said the Chevalier promptly.

"It's a bargain," replied the Captain. "When do you want the vessel, and how will I get my instructions?"

After many weeks of delay and anxiety the official announcement arrived to the effect that the Maine vessel was released by the King's order and that the cargo of tobacco and lumber would be purchased at once.

There were many plots to rescue the royal family after that fateful day at Versailles in June of 1792, and it was also quite natural that the French officers, who had served in the Revolutionary War and who were friendly to the King and Queen, should wish to serve them and should turn to the New World as a place of refuge for them. It is a well-known fact that

Vicomte de Noailles, brother-in-law of Lafayette, came to Philadelphia in 1792 to arrange for a refuge for thousands of his countrymen at a place in Pennsylvania called Frenchtown, and it is also claimed by those interested in tracing this Wiscasset tradition that there was a definite plot to bring Louis XVI, Marie Antoinette and the Dauphin to this Maine seaport, General Knox to act as consignee. Rochefoucauld visited the Pennsylvania refuge, also Louis Philippe and probably Talleyrand. The former in his diary mentions that there was a King's house and a Queen's house there and that many refugees had come over from France to make up a colony of considerable size. We also learn that the Quakers nearby used to drive out to Frenchtown to partake of the excellent meals prepared by the French cooks at the inns in the town and to trade at the French shops, which offered new articles just received from France.

To return to our story, the Chevalier de Rougeville was supposed to have been sent to interview Captain Clough to arrange for the details of the plot, M. Le Ray de Chaumont being called into their secret councils. The Chevalier was to take charge of the royal family, and in the meantime the other two are supposed to have arranged to send on the "Sally" certain pieces of furniture, tapestries, ornaments and garments to be used by the King and the Queen on their arrival in New England. The King's fate on January 21, 1793, changed the plans of rescue, but there was still hope of saving the Queen and her son. It was arranged by de Chaumont that some one was to be substituted for the Dauphin, who was to be taken by the river route to Havre. The Queen was to be sent to Honfleur and from there by boat to the Maine schooner, which was to lie off the cape near the mouth of the Seine, thus avoiding Havre. Gouverneur Morris in his diary records that Rochefoucauld and Lafayette knew of a plot to rescue the Queen; and an entry, near the end of July, 1792, mentions some funds sent to him by the King "for distribution among those who were concerned in executing the project for removing the King from Paris." Morris paid over a balance to the King's daughter. He was also asked to act as custodian of the King's papers, but he declined to serve in this capacity.

It is believed that some one gained access to the prison and handed to the Queen some flowers in which was concealed a letter explaining the method of rescue.

"I cannot go," she said. "Leave me, I implore you, and save yourselves. . . . My husband has gone before me, and I long to join him in the world beyond."

"Most Gracious and Respected Queen," began the Chevalier, "your children are safe and you . . ." but Marie Antoinette interrupted him.

"I am no longer queen. I say to you, one and all, I prefer death by the guillotine, as my poor husband died. . . ."

Uttering these words, Marie Antoinette is supposed to have reeled, and would have fallen had not the Chevalier supported her. The rescuers were surprised by this unexpected dénouement and the great crowd in the corridor which had assembled there for the purpose of creating a disturbance could not understand why the plot did not materialize. The "Sally," therefore, had to sail without her royal passengers. Some persons assert that Talleyrand came to America on this voyage, but this was not the case. He is also supposed to have visited the Marie Antoinette house when he made his journey through Maine and Massachusetts—which is far more probable. On the twenty-eighth day out, the coast of Maine was sighted, and on the following day Monhegan was passed. There is a tradition that the interest was very great when the French furniture and beautiful tapestries were landed on the wharf at Wiscasset, and many a silent tear may have been shed by the onlookers, bringing to mind the sufferings

MARIE ANTOINETTE SIDEBOARD,

supposed to have been brought over in the ship "Sally" of Wiscasset, Maine. It was used in the Marie Antoinette house at Edgecomb, near Wiscasset, so called for the reason that it was said to have been prepared for the occupancy of the Queen, who was to have been brought to Maine on this ship.

of the Queen and her terrible fate. It is claimed by some writers that these French relics of the Revolutionary days were placed in an old residence near Wiscasset, still known as the Marie Antoinette house, and that they proved a great attraction for visitors. This colonial house was built in 1791 on the north point of Jeremy Squam Island, now called Westport, by Captain Joseph Decker. Many years later, in 1838, Captain Gardner Gove, a merchant of Edgecomb, ferried it over the Sheepscott River and had it dragged to its present location on the mainland at North Edgecomb, near Wiscasset, by means of a long string of oxen. A daughter had been born to the Cloughs and they named her Antoinette, a name that has been continued in the family to this day.

There are legends of this Marie Antoinette furniture in the neighborhood of Wiscasset, but the only article that can definitely be traced is an inlaid mahogany sideboard, shown in an illustration, which was bought by the Swans. It then became the property of Colonel Swan's son, who married Caroline the daughter of General Knox, and the coveted piece of furniture was taken to the Knox home, called for the French town, "Montpellier," in Thomaston, Maine, where it remained for many years. It is now owned by Hon. Percival P. Baxter, formerly governor of Maine, and son of the late Hon. James P. Baxter of Portland. The urn was lost for some time, but was finally discovered in Chelsea, Massachusetts, and replaced in its original position. This relic is still known as the Marie Antoinette sideboard. General Knox furnished his house with other articles brought by Swan from France.

Among the articles stored in the Wiscasset house were two Sèvres vases, which are said to have been presented by Frank Swan to his family physician for saving the life of his wife during a serious sickness. They are now in the Metropolitan Museum in New York; on one is a scene depicting Louis XVI receiving word of the birth of the Dauphin.

The Swan residence in Dorchester, now demolished, was also known as the Marie Antoinette house, as it was fitted out with some of the same kind of furniture and ornaments that once had been in the Edgecomb dwelling. In fact, Swan brought from France so many articles that Francis S. Drake, the writer, declared that "between the guillotine which took off their heads, and Swan, who took off their trunks, there was little left for the poor Frenchmen." The visit of Lafayette to the Swan family in the year 1824 revived the story of this plot.

Another French settlement in the State of Maine was made by a Madame La Val, who built a mansion "elegant as a Paris salon" as someone described it, at Lamoine near Mt. Desert Island, where she brought some émigrés in the year 1791. She named her place "Fountain La Val," and she doubtless would have remained there many years longer had she not been persuaded six years later to desert her novel settlement and her friends to become the wife of the governor of Demerara.

THE DISCOVERY IN PARIS OF THE REMAINS OF
ADMIRAL JOHN PAUL JONES

"Tels hommes rarement se peuvent présenter,
Et quand le Ciel les donne, il faut en profiter."

(These are the words of Molière on an engraving of John Paul Jones done by Jean-Michel Moreau, le Jeune, dated Paris, 1780, and given to the Bostonian Society by Benjamin F. Stevens in 1889. This print is supposed to be the best portrait of the Admiral, as well as one of the earliest, and was drawn in Paris from life. Moreau was one of the best of the French engravers.)

NO. 19 (formerly No. 42) rue de Tournon, in Paris, presents much the same appearance today as it did one hundred and thirty-five years ago; but in the 1790's this street was one of the better ones of the city, and No. 42 was no mean dwelling. It was in this house, on the 18th of July, 1792, that Admiral John Paul Jones, at the early age of forty-five, made his will, referring to himself as being

"In a parlor in the first story above the floor, lighted by two windows opening on the said street of Tournon, sitting in an armchair, sick of body but sound in mind, memory and understanding."

This house was at the time owned by Madame d'Arbergne, who had kept the inn at L'Orient, a naval station in Brittany, where the Admiral had first taken lodgings some years before, when he was refitting the "Ranger." When he settled down in Paris in the year 1783, he purchased this house for her in order to give her a start in business. Aimée de Télison, a daughter of Louis XV, proved herself a devoted friend up to the time of the Admiral's death. We read of her supplying a sailor's hammock in the garden adjoining his apartment, where the invalid might spend more peacefully his last days. He had purchased a small house in Rue Vivienne for her after his return from England, a year or so before his death; and thus we see, as others have expressed it, that as the French Revolution progressed, this daughter of a Bourbon king was entirely dependent upon the son of a Scotch gardener.

A few hours after making his will, in the words of the letter of Monsieur Marie Jean-Baptiste Benoist Beaupoil, a major in the French army and an aide-de-camp to Lafayette during our Revolutionary War, written to one of the sisters of the Admiral, "he paid the debt we all owe to Nature." He was found lying on the edge of his bed, and in his clenched hand was the little watch given to him by Marie Adelaide d'Orléans (Duchesse de Chartres) with her miniature on the dial, the same watch he had used when timing his battles.

The French Assembly at once passed a unanimous resolution honoring his memory, and voted that "twelve of its members should assist at the funeral of a man who had so well served the cause of liberty . . ."; while some of the Assembly even went so far as to propose that he should be buried in the Pantheon among France's illustrious dead. In fact, France claimed him as her own.

When John Paul Jones returned to Paris in May, 1790, after a visit to England, where he was received with great distinction, it was noticed that his lungs were not strong, and he was induced, chiefly owing to the insistence of his great friend Aimée de Télison, to have a consultation of physicians. Among them was Dr. Gourgeaud, who had been fleet surgeon on the Marquis de Vaudreuil's flagship, "La Triomphante," and who was then serving as Medical Director of the French Navy. The Admiral left Boston after the siege of Yorktown with the French fleet on this same ship, and it was only natural that he should call in the friend and surgeon whom he had known so well.

HOUSE AT 19 RUE DE TOURNON (FORMERLY NUMBER 42), PARIS,
where Admiral John Paul Jones lived for some time and where he died on July 18, 1792.   He is said to have died on the third floor in one of the front rooms.   The building at the head of the street is the Senate.

Several years later, in 1792, Admiral Jones returned to Paris from The Hague, where he had been making a business visit, and he appeared to be much worse.   His last appearance in public of which there is any definite account was on Wednesday, July 11, of the same year, just a week before his death, when he attended a session of the Assembly.   On that occasion he was honored with the privilege of the floor during the debate concerning the universal armament of France by sea and land.   He did not dare make a speech for fear of coughing; and when the session ended, which was somewhat late in the evening, he went to a supper given by Barère, Cambon and others, at the Café Timon, at that time one of the rendezvous of the Central Jacobin Club.   It is interesting to know that this supper was planned by his intimate friends for the purpose of formally introducing him to the colleagues of the Central Jacobin Group as "the coming Admiral of France."   In fact, they toasted him with this title, to which he finally replied in part: "Gentlemen, pardon me, but let me say that this is no time for jest or raillery, no matter how well meant or how gentle.   You all know my sentiments.   I do not approve, I cannot in conscience approve, all that you have done, are doing, and, alas, intend yet to do.   But I feel that I ought to take advantage of this—perhaps my last—opportunity to define clearly my attitude.   Whatever you do now, France does.   If you kill my good friend the King, France kills him. . . ."   This was probably the best extemporaneous speech that he ever made, and he delivered it in excellent French, being able to converse as freely in this language as in English. At this interesting dinner he appeared to be fairly well, and coughed so little that no one realized his end was near. It was nearly three o'clock in the morning before the meeting broke up, whereupon the Admiral, with several companions, walked to his house in Rue de Tournon, about one-third of a mile distant. Six days later the end came.

For some astonishing and wholly unaccountable reason, Gouverneur Morris, who was then the United States Minister to France, did not claim the body, nor did the United States, and it therefore happened that the remains of John Paul Jones, "Protestant heretic," were buried in the tiny cemetery for foreign Protestants which was near the great hospital of Saint Louis, far outside the inner fortifications of the city. In less than four years this burial ground was officially closed; revolution, riot, and catastrophe passed over it, and slowly but steadily the restless city crept out beyond its narrow walls and built over the silent, unprotesting graves. One hundred and thirteen years passed, during which time all trace of the patriot's tomb was obliterated.

In December, 1904, General Horace Porter, then United States Ambassador to France, addressed a letter to M. Justin-Germain Casimir de Selves, Prefect of the Seine, expressing his chagrin that the body of John Paul Jones had rested for more than a century in an unknown grave, and he further explained that it was the desire of his Government and the American people to find the remains and

Photographed from a French print   *Kindness of Paul F. Cadman*
in the collection of the State Street
Trust Company

ADMIRAL JOHN PAUL JONES AS HE APPEARED IN 1779, AT THE TIME OF HIS VICTORIOUS SEA FIGHTS OFF THE COAST OF FRANCE

A friend of his wrote after one of his victories: "The famous Paul Jones is awaited with impatience. The Queen has said in the last few days, that she wished to attach a waving plume to his hat. This was thought charming, and at once orders were given to the Court Milliner, Mlle. Bertin, for hats 'à la Paul Jones.'" Mlle. Bertin was the Queen's milliner and had her shop in Rue de Richelieu. Various new coiffures were invented, some being called "à la Boston," "à la Philadelphie," and "à la Belle Poule," the latter with complicated rigging and batteries attached.

confer upon them the honor due to so great an officer. M. de Selves was at this time the president of an organization known as "La Commission du Vieux Paris," whose sole function was to carry on researches in connection with the history of Paris, its members being chosen entirely from savants and experts. It was from the minutes of this organization that most of the data for this article have been obtained. General Porter laid before the Prefect the results of five years' study on the problem, a study in which he had been admirably aided by certain members of his diplomatic staff, who had consulted all the documents extant relative to the famous Admiral. Certain of these papers deserve special consideration, since they contributed positively to the success of the search.

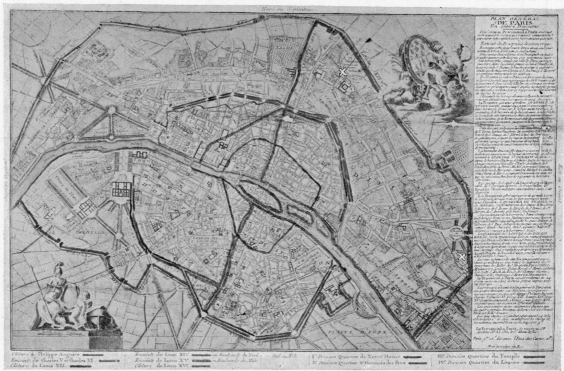

Photographed for the State Street Trust Company by Giraudon, Paris   Kindness of Paul F. Cadman

OLD MAP SHOWING THE CEMETERY FOR FOREIGN PROTESTANTS WHERE JOHN PAUL JONES
WAS BURIED ON JULY 20, 1792

The Picpus Cemetery, where Lafayette and his wife were buried, is also shown.   The map is interesting because it shows how the various fortifications have been creeping outwards as the city has been growing.   Both cemeteries have been marked with crosses.

The original certificate of burial, unfortunately, was destroyed when the annex to the Hôtel de Ville was burned during the Commune of 1871; but happily, Charles Read, an experienced archæologist, had made in the year 1859 a copy of the register in which this certificate was entered.   The copy reads as follows:

"Today the 20th of July 1792 in the IV year Liberty at eight o'clock in the evening, in conformance with the decree of the National Assembly of yesterday, in the presence of the delegation of the said Assembly, Bravet, Caubon, Rouyer, Brival, Deydier, Gay Vernon, the Bishop of the Department of the Haute-Vienne, Chabot, Vicar of the Department of the Loir-et-Cher, Carlier Petit, Le Josnes, Robouame and a delegation from the Protestant synod of Paris composed of MM. Maron, pastor, Perreaux, Bernard, Marquis Monguin and Empaytaz, elders, was buried in the cemetery for Foreign Protestants, John Paul Jones, born in England and a citizen of the United States of America, formerly an officer in the navy of the said States, age forty-five, died on the eighteenth of this month at his residence situated at number forty-two rue Tournon, of 'hydropisie de la poitrine,' in the faith of the Protestant religion.   The said burial took place in our presence by Pierre François Simonneau, Commissioner of the King for this section and Commissioner of Police for the section of Ponceau, in the presence of M. Samuel Blackden, Colonel of Dragoons in the service of the State of North Carolina and citizens of the United States of America; J. C. Mountflorence, former major in the service of the United States; Marie J-B Benoist Beaupoil, former officer in the French Army, residing at number seven passage des petits Pères, and Louis Nicolas Villeminot, commanding officer of the detachment of grenadiers of the gendarmerie which escorted the delegation of the National Assembly, and others who signed here with us."

The document perhaps next in importance was a letter written by a distinguished officer of the American Revolution, Colonel Samuel Blackden, mentioned in the above burial certificate and otherwise spoken of as a "rich planter from North Carolina" to Mrs. Janette Taylor of Dumfries, Scotland, the eldest sister of the Admiral:

"Great Tichfield Street,
LONDON, Aug. 9th.

Madam,—I had the honor of receiving your letter of the 3d instant, and shall answer you most readily. Your brother, Admiral Jones, was not in good health for about a year, but had not been so unwell as to keep house. For two months past he began to lose his appetite, to grow yellow, and show signs of the jaundice; for this he took medicine, and seemed to grow better; but about ten days before his death his legs began to swell, which increased upwards, so that two days before his death he could not button his waist-coat, and had great difficulty of breathing.

I visited him every day, and, beginning to be apprehensive of his danger, desired him to settle his affairs; but this he put off till the afternoon of his death, when he was prevailed upon to send for a 'notaire' and made his will. Mr. Beaupoil and myself witnessed it at about eight o'clock in the evening, and left him sitting in a chair. A few minutes after we retired he walked into his chamber, and laid himself upon his face, on the bed-side, with his feet on the floor; after the Queen's physician arrived, they went into the room and found him in that position, and upon taking him up, they found he had expired.

His disorder terminated in dropsy of the breast. His body was put into a leaden coffin on the twentieth, that in case the United States, whom he has so essentially served, and with so much honor to himself, should claim his remains, they might be more easily removed. This is all, Madam, that I can say concerning his illness and death.

I most sincerely condole with you, Madam, upon the loss of my dear and respectable friend, for whom I entertained the greatest affection and as proof of it, you may command the utmost exertion of my feeble abilities, which shall be rendered with cheerfulness.

I have the honor to be, Madam, Your most obedient humble servant,

S. BLACKDEN."

The burial certificate offered positive proof that the body of John Paul Jones had been buried in the Cemetery for Foreign Protestants, Colonel Blackden's letter corroborating the nature of

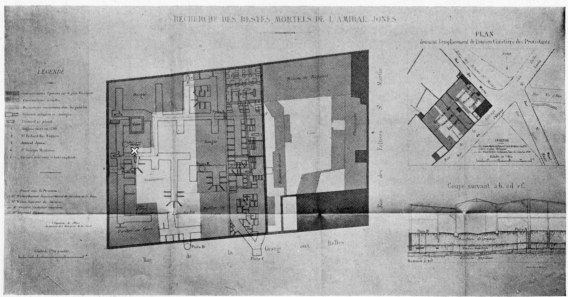

Photographed for the State Street Trust Company by Giraudon, Paris,
from a plan in the Bibliothèque de la Ville de Paris

Kindness of Paul F. Cadman

CIMETIÈRE DES PROTESTANTS, PARIS,
showing the exact spot at the left of the picture where the body of Admiral John Paul Jones was found one hundred and thirteen years after his interment.

Photographed from a sketch by Dr. Jules Sottas
Kindness of Dr. Jules Sottas and Paul F. Cadman

SKETCH OF L'ORIENT AS IT LOOKED IN JOHN PAUL JONES'S DAY

The artist presented the original to the Trust Company's representative when he found that he was interested.   L'Orient and Quiberon Bay were two of the Admiral's bases for operations while in France.   From this port he sailed in the "Bonhomme Richard" in June, 1779, and a few months later he again left this harbour in the same vessel, which was soon to make the well-known capture of the "Serapis."

the malady already mentioned in the burial certificate, and also explaining the fact that the remains had been interred in a lead casket.   Whereupon it was part of General Porter's task to establish the exact cemetery in which the body was buried, and then to locate the site of that cemetery in the Paris of 1905.   A man of smaller faith and less imagination would have concluded that the lead of the casket had been made into Revolutionary bullets and that the venerable bones had been transported to the sublime confusion of the catacombs; there was evidence, however, that neither of these indignities had happened.   Had there not been ample proof that the body had been buried in a lead casket, the search would, of course, have been futile.   M. Simonneau, the Frenchman mentioned in the burial certificate as the King's Commissioner and also Commissioner of the Police, was a warm friend of the Admiral, and he was naturally indignant at the failure of the United States to make proper provision for the funeral of so loyal a son.   He, therefore, paid the entire funeral expense himself, a sum of four hundred and sixty-two francs, which was considerable for those times.   John Paul Jones left an estate of more than thirty thousand dollars, but it is probable that he had little ready cash at the time of his death.   Happily, M. Simonneau's timely assistance not only made possible a respectable funeral, but also assured the success of the tardy efforts of the United States to recognize properly her first Admiral.

From the personages mentioned in the burial certificate, one may judge that the funeral was performed with proper ceremony; furthermore, there is another document that gave evidence of this fact and provided General Porter with still another valuable clue.   The funeral oration was pronounced by a Monsieur Paul Henri Marron, who was pastor of the Protestant Church at Paris, known as the Church of Saint Louis, and was of a verbose and flowery vein, containing much subtle political propaganda. General Porter succeeded in finding the "minutes" of this parish, probably in the parish register, but unfortunately the four pages containing the records connected with the burial had been torn out. Then followed a search through all the libraries, archives and bookshops of France; and by the rarest good fortune, the few missing pages were fortunately found in the library of the Protestant Historical Society, offering positive proof that the interment had been made in the little Protestant cemetery of Saint Louis. Even with this information, General Porter followed up two rumors to the effect that John Paul Jones was buried in the famous old cemetery of Père-Lachaise or in the little cemetery of Picpus, where rest the remains of Lafayette; but both of these reports proved to be without foundation. An old plan of the cemetery, dated 1773, was then found, also some records showing that the burial ground had been officially closed in the year 1793, but that a few burials had been afterwards permitted. Soon after this latter date, the location had been sold by the Government to a contractor, who immediately began thereon the construction of some second-class buildings. The site is now perhaps one of the most dismal sections of Paris, being located in the angle of the two streets now called Rue de la Grange-aux-Belles and Rue des Écluses Saint-Martin in the northeastern quarter of Paris. Until recently, this district was known as "Le Combat,"

Deux Puits de Recherches devant l'Immeuble rue Grange-aux-Belles N° 41

Photographed for the State Street Trust Company by Giraudon, Paris,   *Kindness of Paul F. Cadman*
from a picture in the Bibliothèque de la Ville de Paris

RUE DE LA GRANGE–AUX–BELLES, SHOWING HOUSE NO. 41,
near the place where the Admiral's remains were unearthed. The cemetery is now covered by five houses.

MINIATURE OF JOHN PAUL JONES, PAINTED
BY HIS GREAT FRIEND THE COUNTESS DE
LA VANDAHL IN 1780

This interesting relic was presented by a niece of the Admiral,
Janette Taylor of Dumfries, Scotland, to Alexander
B. Pinkham, U. S. N., who on a visit to Arbigland, Scotland,
in 1831 noticed the dilapidated condition of the
house in which Jones was born and had it renovated at his
own expense. The miniature was finally given by
him to the United States Naval Academy.

not because of any noble battle, but merely because cock-fights, dog-fights and even bull-fights were staged there. The modern "Metro" station which marks the general area is also called at the present time "Le Combat." It is interesting also to record that in the attempt to locate the exact burial place, it was discovered that the Rue Vicq d'Azir was in the immediate vicinity, this being likewise the name of the Queen's physician who had been in constant attendance on the Admiral during his last days. There is a slight possibility that this street had been so named for the good Doctor on account of his services to John Paul Jones. No bit of evidence, however minute, was passed over in this interesting search.

Finally, the site of the old cemetery was determined with a fair degree of precision, but even at this stage of the proceedings the difficulties seemed almost insurmountable and the possibilities of success exceedingly uncertain. Imagine standing in front of a block of comparatively modern buildings and knowing that somewhere, perhaps twenty-five to fifty feet under one of them, was the object of your search. Unfortunately, news of the plan leaked out, and immediately wild rumors were circulated as to the fabulous sums that the rich United States Government would pay for the rights of exploration,—rumors which were so persistent that General Porter was obliged to forego any attempt at negotiation for a period of two years. During this time President Roosevelt became very much interested in the matter, and in 1905 he sent a message to Congress urging the appropriation of thirty-five thousand dollars, the amount estimated to be required for the completion of the work. The undertaking seemed, however, so fantastic that no action was taken by our Government, and General Porter, who, by the way, only recently died, was obliged to obtain the necessary funds from private sources.

In February of the same year, the necessary options had been secured and the guarantees provided. In response to General Porter's request, the Prefect of the Seine appointed Monsieur Paul Weiss, an expert mining engineer, to assist in the excavations. In his excellent report on the task, rendered to the Commission du Vieux Paris, M. Weiss pays a fine tribute to the patient efforts of the American Ambassador and Major Bailly-Blanchard. His report also enumerates a few of the difficulties overcome. More than twenty-five metres of shafting were sunk, some two hundred and fifty metres of galleries dug, and more than one hundred and seventy-eight metres of soundings were made. Moreover, the buildings occupying the ground were built on flimsy and shallow foundations, which necessitated much re-enforcing before the work could proceed. In addition to all these difficulties, a great amount of water was encountered, which made it necessary to keep pumps in constant operation. Finally, the level of the burials was reached, and it was discovered that there had never been any systematic attempt to plan the cemetery, and many of the bodies had apparently been buried in the ground without coffins. Had the Admiral's remains been interred even in a casket of stout wood, identification would have been impossible. It is a weird and fascinating story—that of the digging and delving among the bones of a long-forgotten cemetery with the persistent hope of finding one particular body in a state of preservation that would render identification possible. One can imagine the excitement when the first lead casket was

Photographed for the State Street Trust Company by Giraudon, Paris, from a picture in the Bibliothèque de la Ville de Paris   *Kindness of Paul F. Cadman*

THE INTERIOR OF THE EXCAVATIONS, SHOWING GENERAL PORTER, M. BLANCHARD AND M. WEISS AT WORK

One of the coffins has just been unearthed. That containing the Admiral was the third found.

discovered and the consequent disappointment when the name-plate revealed it to be that of an unknown Englishman; and again a second metal coffin was found, only to prove to be that of Sir Richard Hay.

On March thirty-first, 1905, a third lead casket was unearthed, which bore no external identification whatever. Unless there were means of proof inside, perhaps this, too, would have to be discarded. An inventory of the personal effects of the Admiral at the time of his death enumerated seven uniforms and twelve decorations; there was a chance that he had been buried in the uniform of a naval officer and that some of the insignia might still be preserved. It was known, though, that the custom at the time of his death was to bury the dead in a simple funeral shroud. At all events, if the remains were found, the life measurements were known and there at least would be some evidence. The casket was first opened in the presence of General Porter, Mr. Bailly-Blanchard, M. Géninet, Monsieur Weiss and several workmen. The body was discovered to be particularly well preserved, owing to the fact that the casket had been filled with alcohol. A comparison of the skull of the corpse with a medal of the Admiral showed the same general characteristics—the high forehead and prominent cheek-bones, the contour of the eyebrows, and the general appearance of the hair gave ample evidence that the success of the search was assured. Nevertheless, it was necessary to procure every available proof.

In the report of the "Commission du Vieux Paris," the detailed testimony of the experts is given. On the night of April 8th, the body was taken to the Medical Department of the University of Paris, where four experts, Drs. J. Capitan, V. Cornil, George Hervé and G. Papillault, made a long and studied investigation. They established positively that the subject had died of the same disease which had taken John Paul Jones; also that death had occurred at approximately the same age as that at which the Admiral died, and that the body measurements were practically identical.

Perhaps the most interesting chapter in this investigation was the use of two busts of John Paul Jones, attributed to Jean Antoine Houdon. Jones was a Mason, and belonged to the Lodge in Paris called "La Loge des Neuf Sœurs," one of the most famous in the world.

THE BODY OF ADMIRAL JONES,
lying in state in the Chapel of the American Church of the Holy Trinity in Paris, before being transported to Annapolis.

At a meeting on May 1, 1780, which he attended, the Lodge ordered a bust executed by this well-known sculptor. Twenty casts were made in 1804, one being presented to General Washington, another to Lafayette, another to Annapolis, several becoming the property of persons in New York and New England. The original of one of these is in the Museum at Philadelphia, there being a replica of it in the Trocadéro in Paris. It presents the Admiral in full naval regalia, and is an exceedingly careful and detailed study of the face, showing all the energy and fire of the great sea-fighter. There is another statue, a "terre cuite" (or "baked clay"), which belonged to the Marquis de Biron and represents rather the gallant gentleman than the vigorous fighter. It is known that Houdon worked a great deal from life, and it was discovered that practically all of the measurements of the face and head of the corpse were identical with those of the Philadelphia bust.

"It is possible," said Dr. Papillault's report to the Commission, "to admit the extraordinary coincidence—such as a subject buried in the same place, having a high social position, the same height, the same age, the same colored hair, and having the facial characteristics mentioned above—the same proportions. If the number compared were millions it could happen, but the number is very small. Finally, there is the evidence that the deceased died of the same malady which Paul Jones had."

The closing paragraph of M. Weiss's report reflects the generous spirit in which the French Government assisted throughout the entire undertaking:

"The discovery of the remains of Admiral Jones is then scientifically established, and we are happy to have contributed to bringing back to the light of day the celebrated man-of-the-sea who covered himself with so much glory at the moment when the arms of ancient France and the young American Republic of the United States were fighting in close union."

The patient and persistent search of more than six years was amply rewarded by the accumulation of such positive proof.

FRENCH ARTILLERY CAISSON,
bearing the coffin of John Paul Jones, moving along the Champs Élysées, Paris, July 6, 1905.

FRENCH DRUM CORPS AND AMERICAN SAILORS
drawn up along a street in Paris during the memorial ceremonies for John Paul Jones.

General Porter now turned gladly to the happier task of arranging for fitting ceremonies attending the transportation of the body to America. The remains were placed in the original lead casket and sealed in one of handsome oak. The casket was then draped in the American flag and covered with flowers, and was left for several days at the medical school, where it was the constant object of sincere and reverent homage. It was then transferred to the chapel of the American Church of the Holy Trinity in the Avenue de l'Alma, now Avenue George V, where it lay in state while the Ambassador was awaiting his instructions from Washington. On Friday morning, July 1, 1905, a squadron of American warships, under the command of Rear Admiral Charles D. Sigsbee, arrived in Cherbourg to "claim America's illustrious dead." This was the beginning of the commemoration ceremonies which continued until July 8th, when a French torpedo boat, the "Zouave," flying the "Stars and Stripes" at the masthead, bore the casket to the "U. S. S. Brooklyn" for the voyage to the United States.

Those who witnessed the interesting and impressive ceremonies in Paris held on the Admiral's birthday, July 6, 1905, could scarcely have believed that the body of the hero to whom they were offering homage had lain for one hundred and thirteen years in a forgotten grave. The ceremony has often been compared to the celebration held at the time Napoleon's ashes were brought back from St. Helena. The Tricolor of France and the American Flag decorated the gun-carriage on which the casket rested when it was taken to the Invalides. It was a solemn and beautiful tribute not only to a man, but to an American whose

Photographed by Giraudon, Paris, from a copy in the Bibliothèque Nationale, Paris   *Kindness of Paul F. Cadman*

COMMEMORATIVE MEDAL PREPARED BY CONGRESS
at the time of transferring the body of John Paul Jones to America.

deeds of valor had called from a French man-of-war "the first salute ever given to the American Flag by a foreign power." In the American Church of the Holy Trinity, if the uniforms and decorations offered a brilliant setting, they were entirely overshadowed by the imposing dignity of the oaken casket shrouded in the American Flag and Naval Ensign, banked by palms and funeral sheaves. During the services in Paris, Lieutenant-Commander Harry George, U.S.N., in a speech said he hoped that some famous Frenchman would die in America and afford the United States an opportunity to return the honors shown to the Americans while they were in Paris!

When the two regiments of French infantry and the two batteries of French artillery marched in solemn procession down the Champs Élysées from the Church to the Invalides, together with the six companies of Bluejackets and the two companies of Marines, the uppermost thoughts were of the old alliance, the glorious friendship of the 70's. No one who saw or marched that day could foresee two regiments of Marines in the Bois de Belleau or the marching hundreds of thousands who would one day seal that alliance for all time.

In the Esplanade des Invalides, a tribune had been raised and here the casket was placed, surrounded by the ambassadors and ministers of nearly every country in the world, while the French and American troops marched and countermarched before it, saluting as they passed.

From Pont Alexandre III across the Seine, the body was dispatched in a special train to Cherbourg, where the tributes were continued. On entering the harbour, with the French flag flying, the "Brooklyn" fired a salute, and, curiously enough, the thick fog that hung along the coast immediately began to roll away as if driven off by the cannon. While on shore, the American sailors visited the graves of some of their fellow countrymen, who had been killed on June 19, 1864, in the fight off Cherbourg between the United States "Kearsarge" and the Confederate cruiser "Alabama." The French, with their usual thoughtfulness, so characteristic of them, had decorated the graves. The Fourth of July was celebrated with a torchlight procession, concert, luncheon, garden party, reception by the Mayor, boat races and a Venetian fête. On this same day, a joint cable was sent to President Roosevelt. It was indeed a proud day for General Porter.

The American fleet left Cherbourg amid the cheers of those who had gathered there to witness the impressive ceremonies, whereupon the "Brooklyn" and sister ships sailed for America on what has often been called the "last cruise" of John Paul Jones. The fleet was

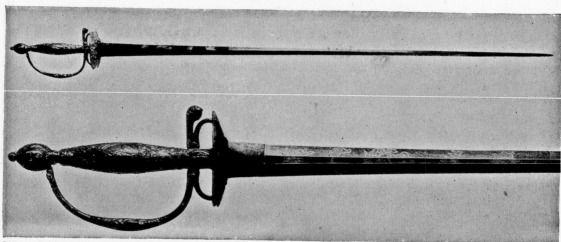

GOLD SWORD PRESENTED BY LOUIS XVI TO JOHN PAUL JONES

With it was bestowed the Royal Order of Military Merit with the title of "Chevalier," a decoration never before bestowed by France upon a citizen of a foreign country. With the sword came a letter from the King expressing the great confidence he had "in the use he would make of it for his glory and that of the United States." The sword is now owned by the Dale family in Philadelphia, and was loaned by the owner and placed on the Admiral's coffin when, many years later, he was buried at Annapolis.

met off Thomas Point near Annapolis by the French man-of-war "Jurien de la Gravière," and on July 24th the body was brought ashore and deposited in a temporary brick vault on the grounds of the Naval Academy, French sailors assisting as pallbearers. Commemorative ceremonies took place on April 24, 1906, on the anniversary of the capture of the "Drake" by the "Ranger," which was a most impressive occasion, officials of France, America and other countries taking part. The body was deposited in a niche in Bancroft Hall, and later, on January 26, 1913, was placed in the crypt under the Naval Academy Chapel.

On the casket was the gold-hilted sword given by Louis XVI and made by La Veuve Guilmino of Versailles; upon it appear the words:

VINDICATOR MARIS LUDOVICUS XVI REMUNERATOR STRENUO VICTOR

the translation of which is: "Louis XVI, rewarder of the valiant, asserter of the freedom of the sea." The figure of the sun and three fleurs-de-lis appear on the sword, also the motto "Vive le Roi." This interesting relic was loaned by the Dale family of Philadelphia for the occasion. There have been many misunderstandings in regard to its history, but it appears conclusive that Jones gave the sword to Gouverneur Morris, his executor. A few months after the Admiral's death, his sister, Mrs. Mary Taylor of Dumfries, Scotland, took charge of most of his effects, including this weapon, and had it given to his friend Robert Morris, who, in turn, presented it for life to Commodore John Barry, Senior Officer of the American Navy at that time, to be handed down by him to each Senior Officer in turn. It is believed that Barry, however, misunderstood these directions and bequeathed it to Captain Richard Dale, and it has remained in the possession of a member of his family ever since.

On the day of the final services at Annapolis, President Roosevelt sent a telegram to the President of France. On this occasion, Ambassador Jusserand mentioned in his excellent address that "it is for France a souvenir to be proud of, to remember that the earliest of those ships meant to carry the thirteen stripes and the 'thirteen stars in a blue field, representing a new constellation' as reads the resolution of Congress passed in 1777, was the 'Alliance,' an appropriate name, built exactly on the model of the French frigate 'La Terpsichore,' the plan of which had been given to Jones by the Duke de Chartres out of sympathy for America." Jusserand also pointed out that the greatest and most heroic part of the Admiral's career was spent in France, which was another motherland to him. Several days later, on April 26, 1906, the French who were present at the funeral services attended also the laying of the corner stone of the monument in the campus of St. John's College at Annapolis to the memory of the French sailors and soldiers who had died in America during the Revolutionary War. General Porter, who was commended by Congress for his untiring interest in discovering the remains, in his address said that "John Paul Jones bore the standard of his country for the first time to France; he returned with it draped upon his bier."

MAL LUI VEUT MAL LUI TOURNE DIT LE BON HOMME RICHARD

Sujet Mémorable des Révolutions de l'Univers

Photographed from an old print in the Cabinet des Estampes in the Bibliothèque Nationale   *Kindness of Paul F. Cadman*

ALLEGORY REPRESENTING THE DESTRUCTION OF THE ENEMY'S COMMERCE

THE SOCIETY OF THE CINCINNATI

ROCHAMBEAU when on his deathbed requested that the Eagle of the Order of the Cincinnati, together with the Grand Cross of the Legion of Honor, be placed on his bed, as these were the two of all his many decorations that he valued the most. The Society was formed in America at two meetings held on May 10 and 13, 1783, at the cantonment of the army on the Hudson, by the officers of the American army. One of the objects of the Society was to "render permanent the cordial affection subsisting among the officers of our army" who had taken part in the war.

To General Knox belongs the title of founder of the Cincinnati, for it appears from an entry in Jefferson's diary that in a conversation with Adams as early as 1776 the American General expressed a "wish for some ribbon to wear in his hat or in his button-hole, to be transmitted to his descendants as a badge and a proof that he fought in defence of their liberties." The original copy of the "Proposals" to organize such a society is in Knox's handwriting and is now among the papers left in the care of the New England Historic Genealogical Society of Boston, by his grandson, Admiral Henry Knox Thatcher, who was at one time president of the Massachusetts Society of the Cincinnati. It is entitled "Rough draft of a society to be formed by the American officers and to be called the Cincinnati," and is dated "West Point, 15 April, 1783." A facsimile of this interesting document, the existence of which was long unknown, is given in the memorial volume of that Society published in 1873. The name, according to the record of the meeting, was chosen on account of the "high veneration for the character of that illustrious Roman, Lucius Quinctius Cincinnatus." The Society was therefore named for this Roman citizen, who was called from the plough to be Dictator, who "left all to save the Republic," and having accomplished this task returned to his former modest rank. On the insignia appears as the principal figure Cincinnatus being presented with a sword and other military insignia by three Senators; on a field in the background is shown his wife standing at the door of their cottage, and near it are a plough and other implements of husbandry. On the reverse is the sun rising, a city with open gates, and vessels entering the port. Fame appears in the act of crowning Cincinnatus with a wreath.

One of the purposes of the organization is thus expressed in the Institution: "To perpetuate, therefore, as well the remembrance of this vast event, as the mutual friendships which have been formed under the pressure of common danger, and, in many instances, cemented by the blood of the parties, the officers of the American Army do hereby, in the most solemn manner, associate, constitute and combine themselves into one SOCIETY OF FRIENDS, to endure as long as they shall endure, or any of their eldest male posterity, and, in failure thereof, the collateral branches who may be judged worthy of becoming its supporters and members." André de Maricourt also expresses in the magazine of "France—États-Unis" one of the objects of its formation by saying that it "sealed in a solemn manner, and in an hereditary way, the friendship of two peoples."

One of the first acts of the meeting of May 10, 1783, was to extend membership to certain grades of French officers, declaring that, the "Society deeply impressed with a sense of the generous assistance this country has received from France, and desirous of perpetuating the friendships which have been formed, and so happily subsisted, between the officers of the

THE DIPLOMA OF THE ORDER OF THE CINCINNATI

belonging to Chevalier de Raimondis, now in the hands of a family in Draguignan, Department of Var, France. Raimondis lost his arm in a sea fight on the way to Boston, and was given a sword by citizens of this city. These diplomas were from a plate engraved by the French bank-note engraver, Le Veau, and were all signed by George Washington as President and by Henry Knox as Secretary.

Allied Forces, in the prosecution of the war, direct that the President-General transmit, as soon as may be, to each of the characters hereafter named, a medal containing the Order of the Society, viz.: His Excellency the Chevalier de la Luzerne, Minister Plenipotentiary, His Excellency the Sieur Gerard, late Minister Plenipotentiary, Their Excellencies the Count d'Estaing, the Count de Grasse, the Count de Barras, the Chevalier des Touches, Admirals and Commanders in the Navy, His Excellency the Count de Rochambeau, Commander-in-Chief, and the Generals and Colonels of his army, and acquaint them, that the Society does itself the honor to consider them members.''

In June, at another meeting, Major-General Steuben informed the Convention that he had transmitted to the Chevalier de la Luzerne, the French Minister, a copy of the Institution of the Society and the votes passed, and that the representative of France had replied "declaring his acceptance of the same and expressing the grateful sense he entertains of the honor conferred on himself, and the other gentlemen of the French Nation, by this act of the Convention.''

It was voted, ''That the letter of the Chevalier de la Luzerne be recorded in the proceedings of this day, and deposited in the archives of the Society, as a testimony of the high sense this Convention entertains of the honor done to the Society, by his becoming a member thereof.''

The first paragraph of this letter follows:

"PHILADELPHIA, 3d June, 1783.

Sir: I have received with much gratitude, the Institution of the honorable Order that the officers of the American Army have founded. If courage, patience, and all the virtues that this brave army have so often displayed in the course of this War could ever be forgotten, this Memorial alone should recall them."

As the French army had left this country before it was decided to organize the Cincinnati, General Washington, who was elected first President General on October 29, 1783, and held the office until his death, wrote Rochambeau this letter, at the same time sending a copy of the Institution:

"The officers of the American Army in order to perpetuate those friendships which have been formed during a time of common danger and distress, and for other purposes mentioned in the Institution, did, before their separation, associate themselves into a Society of Friends under the name of the 'Cincinnati', and having honored me with the office of their President General, it becomes a pleasing duty to acquaint you that the Society have done themselves the honor to consider you and the Generals and Colonels of the Army you commanded in America as Members.

Major L'Enfant, who will have the honor to deliver this letter to you, will execute the Order of the Society in France, amongst which he is directed to present you with one of the first Orders that are made, and likewise with Orders for the other gentlemen of your army, which I take the liberty to request you would present to them in the name of the Society. As soon as the diploma is made out, I will have the honor to transmit it to you."

The latter transmitted the contents through the Minister of War to King Louis XVI, who promptly on December 18th signified his approval, and the French Order of the Cincinnati was organized on July 4, 1784. Up to that time the King had not allowed his officers to wear any foreign decorations; he immediately, however, made an exception in favor of the insignia of the Society of the Cincinnati. So eagerly was membership in this Order sought that it soon became one of the most coveted in Europe.

Soon after the formation of the Cincinnati, prominent men and newspapers violently assailed it, but the hostility soon subsided. The same antagonism existed also in France for a time. The new building where one of the early meetings in this country was held had just been struck by lightning, and someone said it was an "event ominous of the storm brewing from another quarter against the Cincinnati." Even the clear-sighted Franklin wrote against it in 1784: "Others object to the bald eagle as looking too much like a turkey. . . . I wish it had not been chosen as the representative of our country; he is a bird of bad moral character; he does not get his living honestly. . . . He is therefore by no means a proper emblem for the brave and honest Cincinnati of America, who have driven all the 'king birds' from our country." John Adams also strongly opposed the Order. Later, however, Franklin became an honorary member and Adams accepted an invitation to address the Society.

One of the particularly interesting facts in connection with the Cincinnati is that the medal of the Society (shown on page 174) was designed by Major L'Enfant, who laid out the Capitol of this country. The Society, after reading L'Enfant's letter, voted "that the bald eagle, carrying the emblems on its breast, be established as the Order of the Society, and that the ideas of Major L'Enfant respecting it and the manner of its being worn by the members, . . . be adopted. . . . Also, that silver medals, not exceeding the size of a Spanish milled dollar, with the emblems, as designed by Major L'Enfant, and certified by the President, be given to each and every member of the Society, together with a diploma on parchment, whereon shall be impressed the exact figures of the order and the medal, as above mentioned. . . ." The designer recommended that the execution of the medal be done in Paris, and a number of the eagles were executed and transmitted to General Washington, it being resolved that "the thanks of this Convention be transmitted, by the President, to Major L'Enfant, for his care and ingenuity in preparing the aforementioned designs, and that he be acquainted that they

Kindness of Frederick S. Whitwell

ORDER OF THE CINCINNATI

cheerfully embrace his offer of assistance, and request a continuance of his attention in carrying the designs into execution, for which purpose the President is desired to correspond with him." If the silver medals were executed, none appear to have come to this country, and no specimens are known to exist.

Steuben wrote in connection with this Frenchman's journey: "You have sent L'Enfant to France to procure some gold Eagles; but you have forgotten to give him some coppers for his tavern expenses. Mr. R. Morris, General Greene, and myself have made a credit of six hundred dollars, without which the ambassador of the Order would have made his entrée into the Philadelphia Jail."

General Washington on May 15, 1784, first pinned the insignia of the Cincinnati on his coat and frequently wore it thereafter. During the same year Count d'Estaing, the ranking naval officer in France and first President of the French branch, sent to General Washington the Eagle of the Order of the Cincinnati set in emeralds and diamonds, as a gift of the French naval officers who were members. After Washington's death this present was handed down for some years to the succeeding Presidents, until it was given to the General Society. It was then voted that it be "considered appurtenant to the office of President General" and it is still worn by the President General at official meetings of the Society.

A letter written by a French officer in 1784 to Washington explains the important position held by the Society in France:

"The order of the Cincinnati has had here a great success up to now. The King has permitted the French officers who are members to wear the ribbon. Everyone wishes to have it, and those who have not served in America for the necessary period of time are being forced to make use of their commissions and their discharges in such a way as to be able to obtain the honor of wearing it. I assure you that this has created and is now creating more interest here than one would believe. The officers of the French Army are very flattered to receive this honorable distinction and the Count Rochambeau makes much of it. Marquis Lafayette, who has the duty of passing upon the French officers who have served in America, receives every day requests of this kind, coming from persons who ought really to know that they have no occasion to be admitted."

It is of special interest to learn that Lafayette passed upon the foreign candidates before the King finally signified his approval. The first meeting of the officers of the French army was held on January 7, 1788, in the "Hôtel" of General Rochambeau, No. 40 Rue du Cherche-Midi, where the General was living when he received word from his King to take command of the army about to be sent to America. The French officers holding commissions from our Congress held their meetings in Lafayette's house. The Order was most successful in France.

We find that Lafayette wrote to Knox from Paris, under date of January 8, 1784:

"Our association meets with great success. On Thursday next a sufficient number of Eagles will be made to answer immediate purposes. I intend inviting all the American officers to my house, and to conduct them in a body, with our regimentals, to the General of the French Army, to whom we will present the marks of the association. You will receive many applications relative to an addition to the brotherhood. But as nothing will be decided before the assembly in May, I have time to send you my observations."

From Paris Colonel Gouvion wrote to Knox, in March, 1784:

"The Order succeeds extremely well in this country, but the news we have from America give me some uneasiness. The American gentlemen who are in Paris, and not members of the Society, are much against it; chiefly, Mr. Jay, who went the other day so far as to say that if it did take well in the States he would not care whether the Revolution had succeeded or not."

The first French list prepared by the general-in-chief comprised seven general officers, eight brigadiers, and eighteen colonels. It is said that just after the war they made a subscription of sixty thousand francs, in aid of the impoverished officers of the American army, but Washington, in the name of his associates, courteously declined to accept the gift. Some of the descendants of the original

Kindness of Frederick S. Whitwell

ORDER OF THE CINCINNATI

Given to its first president, George Washington, by the French naval members of the Society. It is more elaborate than the usual Order, and is set in diamonds.

members started a movement to reorganize the Society which had been dormant just before the coup d'état of Louis Napoleon, but it was checked by that tragic affair.

The Revolutionists believed the Society was really called Saint Cincinnatus, and so its existence in France soon ended. The last members were elected in the year 1792. Steps were taken in 1887 to revive the French Society by the Marquis de Rochambeau, Comte d'Ollone, Vicomte de Noailles and other Frenchmen; the association formed by them never actually dissolved, but, after the death of the two former men, remained in a state of inaction. An American committee in 1922 visited France, and, with the help of the Duc de Broglie, reorganized the Society, and it was formally recognized by the general body in America in 1923. It is active and well thought of today. Among the French members whose names are well known on this side of the Atlantic owing to the fact that their ancestors participated in our Revolution, are, besides the Duc de Broglie, Marquis de Chambrun, a relative of Lafayette, Baron de Montesquieu, Vicomte d'Aboville, Éthis de Corny, Comte de Guichen, Comte Louis de Ségur, Marquis de Rochambeau, and Vicomte de Noailles.

The Institution provided that State societies should be organized in the thirteen original States, and this was accomplished. In Virginia, New Hampshire, Connecticut, Rhode Island, Delaware and Georgia, however, the State societies for different reasons gradually discontinued their meetings and became dormant, but since 1849 they have all been reorganized upon the old basis and have been recognized by the General Society. The total roll is now about eleven hundred. Membership is confined to descendants of Revolutionary officers in the oldest male line, or failing that in collateral branches. The original member must have served three years in the Continental line, or have been in service at the close of the war, or have been a descendant of one who died in service. In some States, provision is made that the descendant of an officer who had the right to join, but did not, may now join upon payment of an admission fee; or that a person who has a clear right may waive his right and the societies may elect for life the member next in line. Honorary members may also be elected, for life only.

The General Society has held its meetings regularly since its organization—always in one of the thirteen original States—and will meet in Boston for its next Triennial in June, 1929. There are many persons who are not familiar with the Cincinnati, and a story is told of one of its meetings held in Richmond, Virginia. One of the residents of the city expressed a curiosity to know why the organization did not meet in its "home town." At some of these earlier meetings the members wore cocked hats, knee breeches, and powdered hair.

The first meeting of the members of the Massachusetts Society, of which Hon. Winslow Warren is now the president, was held at the cantonment of the Massachusetts line near Newburgh, on the Hudson, on June 9, 1783, Brigadier-General Paterson presiding. General Benjamin Lincoln was chosen president and General Henry Knox secretary. There were three hundred and forty original members. The first meeting in Boston was held on February 18, 1784, and the first annual meeting of the Society was held July 4 of the same year, at the "Bunch of Grapes" tavern which stood on the site of the building where the State Street Trust Company now has its offices. Meetings continued to be held there for five years, after which Concert Hall, on the corner of Court and Hanover Streets, was used regularly until 1822 and occasionally until 1846. Dr. Joseph Prescott was the last surviving original member. Former presidents have been Benjamin Lincoln, John Brooks, Robert Gould Shaw, James W. Sever, Henry Knox Thatcher, and Samuel C. Cobb. At the annual meeting in 1789 the members adjourned from the "Bunch of Grapes" tavern to the Old Brick Meeting House to hear an oration by Dr. Samuel Whitwell. On September 14, 1789, the members of the Massachusetts Society dined on board the "Leopard," a French ship of seventy-four guns, of which Marquis de la Galissonière, a member of the French Order of the Cincinnati, was captain. On September 24 the Society gave the French soldiers a brilliant entertainment in Concert Hall, where a picture of King Louis XVI graced the occasion. On October 27, President Washington was waited on by the Society. He was then on a visit to Boston, accompanied by Viscount de Pontèves, Marquis de Traversay, and Chevalier de Braye, of the French Society.

In 1824, upon Lafayette's arrival in Boston, the Society visited him at Governor Eustis's in Roxbury and then joined the procession which received him on his entrance into the city. He was escorted by the Boston regiment to the mall on Tremont Street, where the school children were drawn up to receive him. On August 26, the Society proceeded in a body to his headquarters, where General Brooks delivered an address. On July 4, 1834, resolutions were adopted, relative to the "decease of Lafayette, the consistent and uniform friend of civil liberty, for whose public and private virtues, for whose heroic deeds and generous sacrifices for the welfare of mankind, his memory will be cherished in our hearts with sentiments of the highest respect." A copy of the resolutions, together with a letter of condolence, was forwarded by the Society to the bereaved family. Many years later, on November 21, 1881, descendants of Lafayette, Rochambeau and de Noailles were welcomed in Boston by the Cincinnati.

JEAN ANTOINE HOUDON—SCULPTOR OF MANY AMERICANS

WHEN Louis Aimable, who was the Grand Master of all French Masons in 1894, wrote his history of the famous Lodge of the Nine Sisters, more properly, the Lodge of the Nine Muses, he quoted from the correspondence of Grimm and Diderot as follows:

"This portrait (Houdon's bust of John Paul Jones) is a new chef d'œuvre worthy of the chisel which seems destined to consecrate to immortality all the great men of every sort. . . ."

This prediction came near being literally true insofar as it applied to the great men who were contemporary with the eminent sculptor, Jean Antoine Houdon. America has a peculiar share in the glory of this genius, for his "consecration" was bestowed, through his art, on Washington, Lafayette, Franklin, Jefferson, John Paul Jones and Robert Fulton. Perhaps his bust of Joel Barton, American minister to France, saved that worthy gentleman from the shadowy obscurity which is the lot of ministers who do not achieve celebrity.

Houdon was born at Versailles on March 20, 1741, which town has a statue to his memory. While he was still a child, his parents moved to Paris, where his father had secured a post as "concièrge," or janitor, of the newly founded École des Élèves Protégés. This school had been established to give a better preparation to the art students who were candidates for the Royal Scholarships at Rome. Perhaps destiny led the humble parent to that lowly employ, otherwise the son of the janitor might never have put his foot inside an art academy. Who can tell when genius enters the human soul! One writer suggests that the art and beauty of Versailles may have been Houdon's first inspiration; but, as he was a very small boy when he left the royal suburb, it is more probable that he first felt his calling while watching students

HOUDON AND HIS WIFE

From the Bibliothèque Mazarine   *Kindness of Paul F. Cadman*

BUST OF FRANKLIN BY JEAN JACQUES
CAFFIERI

*This artist claimed that this work entitled him to be selected
as the sculptor of George Washington and he was
much disappointed not to be chosen.*

at this royal school. Hart and Biddle in their admirable work on Houdon tell how he used to steal into the classrooms and gather bits of clay with which he imitated the work of the students.

His genius at modeling early attracted the notice of some of the professors at the school, notably Pigalle, and once the start was made, his career unfolded with astonishing rapidity. At fifteen he was a medalist, and at twenty he was a candidate for the Prix de Rome, which he won with distinction. For three years after his appointment he tarried in Paris, working always at his art; then he spent nearly four years at Rome, where he achieved a reputation by securing commissions for works in competition with many Italian sculptors. After his return to Paris his rise was phenomenal, and his great success with the bust and statue of Voltaire established his fame beyond all question.

In the Salon of 1777, Jean Jacques Caffieri, a sculptor of no mean ability, exposed a bust of Franklin (shown in an illustration) which called forth very favorable criticism. Franklin, called by Carlyle the "Father of all Yankees," had only just arrived in Paris, and the popular interest in the Quaker Philosopher was at its height. One year later, in the Salon of 1778, Houdon's bust of Franklin was shown and, in the words of Monsieur André Michel, this work "dismissed Caffieri from the field." The latter took his defeat, however, with very bad grace, and left no stone unturned to outdo his famous rival. Houdon's bust of Franklin was his first contribution to American history, and the execution of the work was the beginning of enduring friendship between the artist and the statesman.

The John Paul Jones bust was entered in the Salon of 1781, where it provoked only the highest praise and added more laurels to the already famous artist. It was not until three years later that Houdon took up permanent residence in the hearts of the American people. On June 22, 1784, the General Assembly of Virginia decided to erect a monument to Washington. The first plan was for an equestrian statue, but the State funds were very low and the burden of the war debt was very heavy. Franklin and Jefferson were then in Paris, and they were appointed a committee to find a first-rate sculptor, not necessarily in France, but in "any State of Europe." Charles Wilson Peale, the celebrated Philadelphia painter, was commissioned to paint a portrait of Washington, which was duly executed and sent to Jefferson to serve as a model for the intended statue. Happily, the Paris committee did not have to scour Europe, for the greatest living sculptor was then not only at their door but was quite a member of the family. This was Houdon, of whom a critic of the time justly said:

". . . the modern Phidias whose magic chisel prints at his will on the marble, now the graces of the beauty, now the expression, the force and the vigor of genius. . . ."

The news of Houdon's appointment to such an important mission was too much for Caffieri. That disgruntled gentleman started a correspondence with Franklin in which he put forth all his claims to the task, including the fact that he had gratuitously wrought the bust of Franklin himself and was therefore entitled to his assistance in securing a work for which ample remuneration was offered. Then followed a lot of correspondence between William Temple Franklin and Caffieri which ended in a very brusque letter from young Franklin, and a very dejected reply from the defeated artist. This closed Caffieri's part in the "sculpturing of America," and it is rather unfortunate that this cloud should rest on the fame of a man who possessed not a little talent and whose bust of Franklin is a very creditable piece.

Photographed for the State Street Trust Company by Giraudon, Paris   *Kindness of Paul F. Cadman*

HOUDON'S BUST OF JOHN PAUL JONES,
which helped to identify the remains of America's famous Admiral, described in a previous chapter.

Houdon was overjoyed at the prospect of making a statue of the great American General; but, although he did not depreciate the portrait which Peale had sent to be his model, he at once expressed his wish to see his subject with his own eyes. Accordingly, Jefferson opened a correspondence with Governor Harrison and urged that his request be granted. The good Governor was not averse to doing all in his power to erect a proper memorial to Virginia's greatest citizen, but as an administrator he was alarmed at the additional expense, and he was especially troubled by the fact that an expensive portrait had been provided against the very emergency in question. However, Jefferson's opinion had much weight, and negotiations for the voyage were begun. Houdon was to have one thousand guineas for his work and all his travelling expenses for himself and two aides, who, he insisted, should accompany him. Such terms would have been acceptable had it not been for the fact that the artist also required a very generous life insurance in favor of his family in case he should die during the voyage. This final item, approximately ten thousand francs, was too much for the State financiers of Virginia, and, had it not been that Jefferson personally agreed to underwrite this insurance, the negotiations would probably have fallen through altogether. Happily for us, they were successfully concluded; and so it was that when Franklin arrived at Havre after that difficult journey from Paris, he was delighted to find his good friend Houdon already on board the ship which was to take the first ambassador for the last time from his beloved France.

HOUDON'S BUST OF GEORGE WASHINGTON
NOW IN THE LOUVRE, PARIS

It was made at Mount Vernon and kept by the sculptor
until his death, whereupon it went to the Louvre.
The final cast is now in the State Capitol of Richmond,
Virginia.   The mask made at Washington's home
is now owned by J. P. Morgan.

It is interesting to note how anxious Jefferson was that Houdon should be well received. He seems to have considered the visit not only as one of art and business, but rather as a mission from France to America. Lafayette was also much interested in this undertaking, for he sent a letter by Houdon to General Washington in which he said: "Nothing but the love of glory and his respect for you could induce him to cross the seas, as his business here far exceeds his leisure, and his numerous and gratified friends make him very happy at home." It is also delightful to read of the simple cordiality with which the distinguished Frenchman was received at Mount Vernon and how he set to work almost at once to make the precious model which was to him the sole reason for his voyage. Washington makes these entries in his diary under date of Sunday, October 2, 1785: "After we were in bed (about eleven o'clock in the evening), Mr. Houdon sent from Paris by Dr. Franklin and Mr. Jefferson to take my Bust, in behalf of the State of Virginia, with three young men assistants, introduced by a Mr. Perin, a French gentleman of Alexandria, arrived here by water from the latter place." (Wednesday, October 19.) "Mr. Houdon, having finished his business which brought him hither, went up on Monday (17th), with his people, work and implements, in my barge, to Alexandria, to take a passage in the Stage for Philadelphia the next morning." Houdon's stay at Mount Vernon was a red-letter time in his life, and it is certain that he "guarded a bon souvenir" of the event, for he speaks of it frequently throughout the remainder of his life. In the "Life of Houdon" written by Hart and Biddle, his passage to this country is amusingly told: "We knew that he was disappointed by the non-arrival at Havre of his tools and materials . . . half-dozen shirts for four persons! He must have passed through several Sundays without a clean one. . . . To which Temple Franklin replied: 'Our belongings have reached here after a voyage of three months. Yes! M. Houdon has suffered much. During his passage we took up a subscription of Shirts and Stockings in his favor, and on arrival here he was obliged to make purchases for himself and for his workmen.' "

The expense account which was a part of the contract is a most astonishing document. Happily, it is preserved in the archives of the State of Virginia. A facsimile is produced in the work by Messrs. Hart and Biddle.

When at last the models were ready, Houdon set out at once for France to begin his work in marble, but the difficulty arose almost immediately of deciding whether or not the statue should be wrought to represent Washington in ancient or in modern costume. Washington was consulted, and expressed his opinion with delightful modesty to the effect that, after all, he was not versed in things artistic and that it would be better for others to decide. After much discussion, modern military uniform was accepted.

Both Jefferson and Houdon entertained high hopes that the original plan for an equestrian statue might still be adopted, but public economies stood in the way. It is possible that Houdon did make a small equestrian model, but if he did so, its whereabouts remains unknown.

As to the final result, perhaps the best answer is contained in the words of a Frenchman whose long residence in America and whose intimate knowledge of history make him a worthy critic. Monsieur Jusserand says:

"Whoever would see Washington face to face, live in his atmosphere, and draw the moral benefit of being in the great man's presence, has only to go to Richmond. To those who know how to listen, the statue knows how to speak."

This bust of Washington was shipped from Havre to Richmond, and was placed in the rotunda at the Capitol, where it still

Photographed for the State   *Kindness of Paul F. Cadman*
Street Trust Company
by Giraudon, Paris

HOUDON'S BUST OF BENJAMIN FRANKLIN,
in Houdon Hall in the Louvre. A cast is in the Boston Athenæum.

rests. The State of Virginia was very pleased with Houdon's work, but it was many years later (in 1910) that it was decided to present a duplicate to France, and this is now in "Independence of America Hall" at Versailles. The mask of Washington's face, cast by Houdon, is now one of the many valuable possessions of J. P. Morgan. The preliminary bust made at Mount Vernon was carefully preserved by the sculptor until his death, and is now in the Louvre. Another copy is in the Museum of Fine Arts in Boston. His bust of Franklin is in the same hall, which is named for Houdon. Other casts of Franklin are in the American Academy of Arts and Sciences of Boston, given by the sculptor to Thomas Jefferson; a marble cast is in the Metropolitan Museum of Art in New York, while another is owned in Philadelphia.

Houdon contributed to the Salon of 1781 a number of his works, including the much admired bust of John Paul Jones, which came into such prominence in identifying the remains of the Admiral mentioned in another chapter. A copy was given by Jones to Jefferson, which found its way into the Boston Athenæum, only to disappear mysteriously some years later. Two copies by Houdon belong to the National Academy of Design in New York and to Charles H. Taylor, of the Boston *Globe*, who has placed it on exhibition with the Marine Museum of Boston in the Old State House.

JEAN ANTOINE HOUDON IN HIS STUDIO IN PARIS IN THE FAUBOURG SAINT–HONORÉ

Franklin and Jefferson selected him to make a bust of George Washington. This famous sculptor of a number of important Americans spent fifteen days at Mount Vernon in the autumn of 1785. A replica of this statue was presented by Virginia to France, and it is now at Versailles.

There is still another of Houdon's busts of interest to us. The State of Virginia, in appreciation of Lafayette, had one made of the French General for the State Library in the Capitol, and at the same time presented a second copy to the City of Paris, which was unfortunately destroyed during the Revolution. Lafayette was so pleased that he wrote to Washington: "A new instance of the goodness of the State of Virginia has been given me, by the placing of my bust at the Hôtel de Ville of this city. The situation of the other bust will be the more pleasing to me as, while it places me within the capitol of the State, I shall be eternally by the side of, and paying an everlasting homage to, the statue of my beloved general." At one time the bust of Lafayette was opposite that of the American General. One of Houdon's busts of Lafayette is also at Versailles in the United States Hall. There are several busts of Jefferson by Houdon in this country, one in the New York Historical Society and another in the American Philosophical Society of Philadelphia.

Perhaps it may be of interest to add an incident in Houdon's life as told by Hart and Biddle: "He began now also nightly to frequent the performances at the Théâtre-Français . . . On the day of its reopening Houdon came as usual, but a new ticket-taker had been engaged since his last visit.

" 'Sir, sir, your ticket!'

" 'I don't need any,' and the venerable figure continued to advance.

" 'But, sir, no one enters without a ticket.'

" 'I have my entrance, sir.'   (Growing warm.)

" 'But how do you call yourself?'

" 'How I call myself!'   (Voice growing louder.)   'How I call myself!'   Then, pointing to the statue in the peristyle, 'I'm the father of Voltaire!'   And he passed in triumphantly without further reply.   The amusing part is that the next evening, as Houdon passed in, the ticket-taker turned to his assistant and instructed him to inscribe on the register of entries for the evening, 'M. Voltaire, le père.'   It is easy to imagine the hilarious reception of this at the Théâtre, and for some time after our old habitué passed under this cognomen entirely."

Houdon's studios were in the Faubourg Saint-Honoré, and later he moved opposite the Chapel of Saint Nicholas, near Rue de Balzac.   Paris has named a street for him, and Versailles, Dijon, Tours, and Montpellier all treasure some of his works.

The following vignette from a map of Boston, published in Paris in 1776, is supposed to be the earliest representation of the emblematic pine tree.   The Provincial Congress of Massachusetts in April, 1776, ordered the naval flag to be a green pine tree upon a white ground, with an inscription "Appeal to Heaven" on the reverse side.   The "London Chronicle" gave this same description of a flag captured on an American cruiser.

End of Volume II